The Partial Rapture "Theory" EXPLAINED

Escaping the Coming Storm

Rev. J. W. (Bro. Chip) White, Jr.

PRESS

Copyright © 2008 by Rev. J. W. (Bro. Chip) White, Jr.

The Partial Rapture "Theory" Explained
Escaping the Coming Storm
by Rev. J. W. (Bro. Chip) White, Jr.

Printed in the United States of America

ISBN 978-1-60477-684-3

Unless otherwise indicated, Bible quotations are taken from:
    The King James Version, (Cambridge: Cambridge) 1769.
    Nelson Electronic Bible
    Nelson Electronic Library

www.xulonpress.com

ACKNOWLEDGMENTS

S pecial Thanks goes to :
My Mother. The late Arnell Louise (Walton) White. Her passing occurred January 1981.

Her love and instruction were unparalleled, bar none. It was through her influence I learned the practice of self control and the importance of moderation.

My Father, the late James William White Sr. He witnessed the initiation of this project, but has since been separated from us to join our mother in the presence of the Lord. His passing occurred December 18, 2006 (The same day his final grandchild, my youngest son Joshua James, was born). Yea, that was one tough day. He was my best friend. His support in a thousand in one ways and his help in ten times as many applications were irreplaceable by any standard.

Darlene ,,,, (White) Alford : My sister. With the absence of our mother, she has been a unique strength in my life. She heads up my sibling support group (the late Dale W.), Scott W, & Kenny White. Brothers.

Randy Hill & Phillip Love my two second best friends in the physical. Without whom this manuscript could not, and would not have been written.

The late Rev. Floyd Augustus Walton Sr. of which who's influence was second to no one. He was the pastor of several Baptist churches throughout south Texas, most prominently North Beach Baptist Church, Corpus Christi, Texas. His love for the Lord, his family and ministry was with out doubt, unwavering.

Lt. Dennis Martin. Texas Law enforcement officer extraordinaire. My two time partner and back up, once under, twice over. He quite inadvertently supplied me with one of the most important concepts used in my Bible study. When faced with the undeniable facts of the situation, well, "There it is".

My children who are my pride. Nikki, James III, Katie, Hannah, Joshua James, Kimberly, & Amy.

My grandchildren who are my joy. Shyann, Justin, Tenna, and Aidyn James (AJ).

It is for both these groups that this manuscript goes to print. Our descendants, the Church's future.

Greetings

This manuscript is written primarily to the Church. The Church consists of each and every individual who has accepted Jesus Christ as their savior. That acceptance includes the understanding without question that he is first and foremost the only direct spiritual offspring of God (only begotten of the Father) and second, literally the physical offspring of the virgin Mary (God manifested to us in the flesh) with all the implications which that knowledge entails as described and taught by the scriptures as best we can understand those teachings. If the doctrine of your denomination does not subscribe to these two criteria in its core, it is in error.

The scripture says he will return one day for those who have been waiting for his reappearance. This is the subject that will be addressed in this study. The return of Jesus Christ in most evangelical circles is referred to as The Rapture, in others it is called The Second Coming. And I might add, there is no one single denomination that constitutes the Church, as difficult as that is for some to accept.

If by chance you are reading this book, and you have not accepted Jesus as your Savior, I pray I have written to the Church well enough for you to recognize the need to do so. The experience of the Rapture is reserved by the Father, for the Son, through the Spirit for the express purpose of the Son (Jesus Christ) acquiring possession of his espoused (engaged) Bride that he has purchased with his own blood.

All believers who are prepared for the arrival of their Lord and Savior Jesus Christ in this generation, as well as the dead in Christ are included in the Bride of Christ.

The unprepared, in any respect, will be left behind to endure The Great Tribulation Period that Jesus described to his disciples as documented in Matthew 24, Mark 13, and Luke 21 and is known as the Olivet Discourse. The Great Tribulation is also the main subject of the book of Revelation, in which John (who was present at the Olivet Discourse), describes in great detail.

If you have not accepted Jesus as your savior, you are not a child of God. You are the physical descendent of Adam, but your spiritual father is Satan (The originator of disobedience and the father of lies).

To become a child of God you must admit your sin, (disobedience through unbelief) turn to the God of the Holy Bible and ask the Father for forgiveness in the name of Jesus his Son, and ask him to have the Holy Spirit take up residence in your heart and life.

You will then be baptized by the Holy Spirit into the body of Christ, which is the Church. Your physical body becomes the temple of the living God in which the Holy Spirit will now dwell.

Through this procedure you will be reborn in the spiritual (soul and spirit) and through the blood of Christ which was shed for all of mankind on the cross, and through the process of divine adoption you become a child of God. Through Jesus, we literally become blood kin to the Creator.

Although this sounds quite complicated, the actual sinners prayer is very simple.

Lord, I am a sinner. Forgive me of my unbelief. I now accept that Jesus died on the cross for my sin, that I may receive everlasting life and fellowship with you through the Holy Spirit. I believe in the blood of Jesus to wash away my sin, and ask the Holy Spirit of God to come into my heart and life. Lead me into a new life in service to you.

If you have not prayed this prayer or one like it, or can not bring yourself to do so now before reading this book, you are an outsider looking in. But, as an outsider, I pray I have written to the Church well enough for you to realize the need to accept Jesus Christ into your life as Lord and Savior. Today is the day of salvation, more so than any other point in human history. **For the time is truly at hand.**

Coming about

I accepted Jesus Christ as my savior at the tender age of seven. That was 1966 North Beach Baptist Church (now, Harbor View Chapel), Corpus Christi, Texas. The Rev. Floyd Augustus Walton Sr. was the pastor, who also happened to be my mothers' father (the current pastor of Harbor View Chapel is Rev. Rusty Maddox).

My immediate family moved to northeast Texas two years later where I grew up in two churches sequentially, both of which were Southern Baptist. Antioch Baptist at the corner of Hwy 2791 & Hwy 96, and Piney Grove Baptist on Hwy 77. Each was ministered to, by what could be considered inside the denomination as, the finest and God fearing men that a church could ever hope to supply itself with.

Bro. Green of Antioch was much like my grandfather (Paw Paw). Each had a love for all people with a burning desire to bring them to a knowledge of salvation by grace through faith in Jesus Christ. Bro. John Withem of Piney Grove was gifted by God with the ability to minister to the members of his church in whatever capacity called upon.

Through these three men of God I was brought to the knowledge of all the basic teachings of the Baptist "faith". All of which were accepted at that time without any question of their accuracy (which, in its foundations is essentially correct). After maturing into an adult and beginning my own personal studies however, with the exception of the afore mentioned foundation which is in agreement with the scripture, Baptist doctrine itself has long since ceased to have an influence on my personal beliefs.

My current understanding of God - his existence, his being, his plan and by extension, Jesus' life, death, resurrection, ascension and return, are shaped exclusively by God's Word and presence alone. Understanding the teachings dealing with his return became an obsession for me as a teenager, and continued into my adult life and ministry. The return of Jesus Christ is the singular most incredible event that will be experienced first hand by the Church and has been the passion of my Bible study since the age of fifteen. It is the exclusive subject of this manuscript and the reason for its documentation and publication.

Thirty-three years after my initial interest in the return of Jesus Christ, which lead to the beginning of my genuine study of the subject, I for the "second time" put pencil to paper for the purpose of documenting the information that has been presented to me from the pages of the Word of God.

The following information is the briefest description of the evidence currently at hand, explaining to the best of my ability the teachings concerning the return of our Lord Jesus Christ. The Church was expected by God to have been looking forward to this event for almost two thousand years. The life that she leads however, suggests she has failed in that endeavor.

In truth, she who is espoused (the Church) should be happily anticipating the return of her Bridegroom, and therefore, comforting one another with those very words. Instead, we have been doing little more than attacking one another inside doctrinal disagreements based on misinterpretations of

God's Word. Of which, according to The Word itself, needs no assistance from us in regards to the process of interpretation.

As an elderly black brother once made comment to me concerning God's Word, " Why don't we just let it say what it say"? I'll second that. "Let the word speak for itself "!

Let me make it clear, I do not claim to have all the answers nor do I have a full understanding of every teaching of God's Word. No one does. No one ever has, and no one ever will in this life. But, the material presented in this manuscript is essentially what I have come to believe as the truth, based on the studies that have been done through the investigations that were prompted by those studies. I do not need to be reminded that my opposition believes these conclusions to be incorrect. This is all too obvious. That is the nature of disagreement and the very concept of opposing views.

From the Church's perspective, the conclusions presented in this work are my opinion. I am aware of that. But from my perspective, the accumulation of information supplied by the scripture, and the conclusions to which they have led have proven themselves to me to be the truth. Therefore for the purpose of disclosure of these teachings, they will be presented as such. Again, I do not need to be reminded of the obvious.

That being said, for years I had questioned a set number of doctrines contained inside many denominations including my own. I was forced to discount the great bulk of them due to clear contradictions with the scripture. These conflicts are contained directly inside many of the teachings that each denomination within its structure present to the Church as truths.

However, when I stand before Christ at the judgment seat to give account **(and without exception, every last one of us will)**, I have enough to answer for already than to be guilty also of ignorantly leading others astray. At the very least, I will always put forth my best effort to insure I have done the genuine prayerful study necessary to minimize lack of understanding thereby maximizing the ability to teach and ultimately preach what I honestly believe to be the truth.

Concerning the lost of the unbelieving world, I continue to pray for every member of the human race to come to a knowledge of Jesus Christ as their Savior, as is the call of the convicting Spirit of God to the whole of his creation.

But, the majority of the membership of the Church is in severe need of a wake up call, "lest the Lord find them sleeping" upon his return. I sincerely believe this manuscript "not" to be that alarm, but in just fashion, if it initiates a field of interest and a course of study that can act toward that goal, my calling will have been fulfilled and complete.

I was discussing all of these ideas with a friend of mine just prior to beginning this final draft. One comment he made while shaking his head concerning a teaching I was attempting to explain, in hopes of him understanding was, "You can't take one verse out of the Bible and build an entire doctrine on or around it".

I answered, "That's not what I'm trying to do. No one understands better than I that every teaching extracted from the scripture must agree with the whole of God's Word, but, what about all of the little intricate details of the scripture that clearly appear, are obviously connected to the subject matter but are not regularly taught"?

I replayed that conversation for a loved one two weeks later (the day I began work on this manuscript). I remember the concern and thoughtfulness in his eyes when he smiled and made a very simple but profound comment himself. "No, you can't build an entire belief or doctrine from any individual verse of God's Word. **But you can believe that one verse**. Then let The Word teach you how that one verse agrees with the rest of the scripture".

Praise the Lord for God fearing parents!
Thanks Dad! I love you. (And I miss you).

The intricate details found in the Word of God that are not regularly taught by mainstream Christianity intrigued me as they were brought to my attention by the Lord during the course of my regular Bible reading. Their manifestation inside the text led me to the study of them. Dad realized the importance of them himself as I shared much of my research with him, although he admitted portions of it was beyond his comprehension. With every new discovery the plan of God became increasingly more fascinating in its depth. There will be a few of these references included in this manuscript which will point to such details found in the Word of God, but they will be limited and scattered.

This publication is dealing specifically with The Rapture of the Bride of Christ and whereas many of the deep subjects taught by God's Word are related to that event, not all are connected directly to it. By that token, many of these topics will not appear here due to time restraints and direct relevance.

However, all of these subjects are just as captivating, and in some cases, because they are largely unknown to the Church as a result of a neglect of their study, upon their disclosure many of them can appear a bit mysterious. Due to the tendency of these principles to be absent inside the teachings of conventional denominational doctrines, they have been viewed at times by the membership of the Church even esoteric in nature. But, through the same ignorance, so are the teachings of the Rapture as a whole.

I have had multiple conversations with numerous individuals over the controversial nature of these teachings. A common argument that has continually arisen is, "What makes you so sure your right"? My response to that question is two fold and both are very simple in their structure.

1 I am not right. The Word of God is. My only "desire" (prayer) is to be in agreement with it.

2 There are hundreds of Christian denominations in existence today. Each with its own diverse beliefs due to their individual interpretations of the scripture. Obviously all of us are not correct, and just as obvious only a few, or in truth only one, can be even close. But, each one believes their understanding of the scripture to be reasonably accurate. Some even consider their beliefs, and therefore their teachings and doctrines to be on some level of absolute.

From the perspective of this scenario, I am no different from any other believer, teacher or preacher in any legitimate Christian denomination you would choose to example. I have as much initiative as anyone to express what I believe to be the truth. You may disagree with those teachings at your own leisure, as I am fully aware the majority of the Christian world is sure to follow suit.

My "ace in the whole" as it were, is that I am entering into this project with the knowledge taught to me by these teachings that the doctrine itself implies it will not be accepted by the majority of the Christian world. According to the teachings of the Conditional Rapture, there is no record contained in the scripture of a mass "awakening" by the Church just prior to the Great Tribulation Period, even though there is a clear cry from the Spirit for her to do so. Although this publication acts as a warning to the Church, the teachings themselves fail to record that she will heed that warning.

So, the most critical question remains. Why do I publish in the face of certain rejection and guaranteed ridicule? That is the simplest of all questions to answer, and in fact each believer should already be familiar with the concept.

I refuse to do anything less than to respond as best I understand to the direction of God in my life no matter what the results. It and I are in his hands. There is no failure when one is following God's will regardless of the outcome in the physical. Although the consequences of my actions concerning this subject and work will not hardly approach the conclusions met by Paul in regards to his calling and ministry, he said it best. For me to live is Christ. For me to die is only gain.

In essence, I have already obtained my goal. God had sent me to deliver a message. With the publication of this manuscript, I have done that. The reader may do with that information as you wish. I live only to do his will.

Grace and peace be multiplied unto you all.

Chapter One

Grace and Peace

The very beginning of the Churches misconception of the traditional Pre-Tribulation Rapture is directly related to its misunderstanding of the New Covenant itself. When opponents of the Conditional Rapture discount the concept outright, more often than not their argument is built on the basis that its teachings violate the "covenant of grace". They contend that if any Christian is omitted from the Rapture, it would be the equivalent of that individual losing their salvation.

Most Pre-Tribulationists believe in eternal security of the believer, also known as once saved always saved, and the concept of a Rapture that is conditional in any way conflicts with their established doctrinal beliefs of salvation. Those beliefs are almost universally derived from and through the denomination of which they are associated.

Although I am opposed to the term "once saved always saved", due to the suggestion one can live whatever lifestyle one wishes after salvation (there are consequences to such actions), I do believe in eternal security of the believer. When the scripture is taken as literal at every occasion applicable, there is no doubt the Bible teaches everlasting refuge for the entire family of God. Fortunately the Lord gave me a term that better fits what the scripture teaches is the truth. Once a child of God, always a child of God.

We will reexamine many of the points made in this chapter in greater detail in the appropriate chapters to come, but in reality that is what salvation is. Becoming a child of God through the blood sacrifice of his Son, Jesus Christ. Upon acceptance of Jesus' sacrifice on the cross we are immersed (baptized into his death) into the Spirit of God (the person of God that tasted death for every man). Upon the completion of the baptism of the Spirit (which is instantaneous) we emerge reborn a new creature and retain within ourselves the presence of the Holy Spirit of God. Through the rebirth experience we literally become blood kin to the creator. (That is an awesome concept).

Through the procedure described he effectively "saves" us from everlasting damnation in hell. Damnation is in reality perpetual separation from the presence of God throughout eternity "future" which, with the inclusion of hell itself, was originally prepared for the devil and his angels. The curse of damnation will include the individual punishments each unbeliever has reserved for his or her own self through their behavior during their lifetime in the physical inside their unbelief. Their actions in this life do not necessitate their attendance, merely punishment. Attendance is dictated by unbelief alone. A person does nothing to reserve themselves a place in hell, a person accepts the free gift of salvation to escape everlasting damnation in hell.

Mark 3:29
29. But he that shall blaspheme against the Holy Ghost **hath never forgiveness, but is in danger of** eternal damnation:

Blaspheme against the Holy Ghost, is the rejection of the Holy Spirit's urging toward repentance from unbelief by any individual under the conviction of that presence. The Holy Spirit can, and regularly does, convict unbelievers of their unbelief repetitively. For many, they are confronted by the Spirit and faced with the reality of its convicting nature multiple times throughout their life. This call to repentance can be initiated by loved ones who intervene through prayer to the Father for the salvation of the unbeliever.

Mark 3:29 mentions the unbeliever is in danger of eternal damnation. They are in danger continually throughout their physical life during their rejection of the call to repentance. If they never yield during their time in this life, at the point of physical death they are guilty of blaspheme against the Holy Ghost and their sin of unbelief goes un-forgiven. They are then doomed to everlasting damnation and separated from the Holy God of creation (in the Spiritual) throughout everlasting. There will be no second chance.

The illustration and comparison of the rebirth experience can be seen in Jesus' discussion of that process with Nicodemus. In that lesson Jesus likens the spiritual birth to the physical birth. Nicodemus was understandably confused when Jesus told him that a person must be born again.

He was, of course, speaking of a believers rebirth through the Spirit of God which was to be initiated with his physical death on the cross (in its representation of his spiritual death/ separation from the Father) and subsequent resurrection from the grave. But by comparing the salvation experience to the birth process, Jesus places the condition of permanency on the final state.

Once an individual is physically conceived there is no process that can reverse or change who the biological parents of the offspring are. (And make no mistake, conception is the continuation of the pre-existence of life given by God. Any willful interruption of that process constitutes a deliberate extermination of the continuation of life).

By the same token, once a person is reborn through the Spirit of God, they become a child of God never again to be anything else. Our relationship to God is not in question, he is our heavenly Father. Our fellowship, however is quite a different matter. It is the fellowship with our Heavenly Father (or in most cases the lack of fellowship) that we will be investigating.

Since the scripture teaches there are conditions to be met in order to take part in the Rapture of the Bride of Christ, the doctrine can not be in conflict with "grace". We understand from the scripture, that it is by grace we are saved.

Ephesians 2:4-10
   4 But God, who is rich in mercy, for his great love wherewith he loved us,
   5 Even when we were dead in sins, <u>hath quickened us together with Christ,</u> **(by grace ye are saved;)**
   6 And hath raised *us* up together, and made *us* sit together in heavenly *places* in Christ Jesus:
   7 <u>That in the ages to come he might shew</u> the exceeding riches of <u>his grace in *his* kindness toward us through Christ Jesus</u>.
   8 **For by grace are ye saved through faith**; and that not of yourselves: *it is* the gift of God:
   9 Not of works, lest any man should boast.
   10 For we are his workmanship, created in Christ Jesus unto good works, which God hath before ordained that we should walk in them.

Verse four declares God's love for his creation. That love evokes the grace of God that benefits us initially through the availability of salvation, and then through fellowship with God inside salvation. Verse five points out even when we were dead (separated from God) in sin (the disobedience of unbelief) he had "quickened" us (given us life) together through Jesus Christ. This was done through his foreknowledge at the beginning of creation. Since the physical was spoken into existence by him in a "moment" before time complete from beginning to end. Through the very nature of the process of creation itself, he knows the end from the beginning. We are preordained through our choice in him at the point of creation itself. This is confirmed in verse six in that we have already been raised up together and are made to sit in heavenly places.

Since we are informed by God's Word it is by grace (the grace of God) we are saved, we know salvation is obtained by way of grace. But what is grace. If we are saved by grace, and we just determined we are, then grace and salvation can not be the same thing, although it is obvious they are akin to one another under the New Covenant.

In reality, grace is the good favor of God. We, as the children of the living God are charged by him to stay (or continue) in his grace (or good favor).

Luke 2:40
40 And the child grew, and waxed strong in spirit, filled with wisdom: and **the grace of God was upon him**.

The child being spoken of in this passage is Jesus himself. He waxed (was empowered, increased with vigor, was strengthened, was made strong) in the Spirit of God. Through the Spirit he was filled with wisdom, and the grace (good favor) of God was upon him. Jesus was in good favor with the Father (was, is and ever will be, perpetually) by continually being obedient to the will of God in all things. But the grace of God being upon him had nothing whatsoever to do with salvation. Jesus being God manifested in the flesh, was in no need of salvation himself (no matter who has told you otherwise). Therefore, although grace (the good favor of God) is a necessary part of salvation, (there would be no salvation without God's good favor) it is not salvation in and of itself.

Genesis 6:8
8 But Noah **found grace** in the eyes of the LORD.

Noah found grace in the eyes of the Lord which lead he and his family to salvation in the physical in the form of escaping the global flood that God used to destroy the disobedient society (rebellious in race) of that day. The story of Noah and the Ark is a good example in the physical of what is true in the spiritual. God's grace was not salvation in and of itself but through the grace of God, Noah was warned aforetime, was obedient to God in his orders to construct the Ark, and eight souls plus every "kind" of animal type that was alive at that time was saved.

Grace can not save alone, but obedience to the will of God in accordance with his good favor (grace) with which he loved us to the point of his own death (separation) does. The scripture uses many such illustrations from the physical world to draw attention to its counterpart in the spiritual. We will be looking at several during the course of our study.

Ezra 9:7-8
7 Since the days of our fathers *have* we *been* in a great trespass unto this day; and for our iniquities have we, our kings, *and* our priests, been delivered into the hand of the kings of the lands, to the sword, to captivity, and to a spoil, and to confusion of face, as *it is* this day.
8 And now for a little space **grace hath been** *shewed* **from the LORD our God**, to leave us a remnant to escape, and to give us a nail in his holy place, that our God may lighten our eyes, and give us a little reviving in our bondage.

The aforementioned passage states that Israel had been in trespasses against the Lord and for those iniquities they had been delivered into the hand of enemy kings which in turn led to slaughter for some, and bondage for others. But God had given a little relief in that he had shown them a certain amount of grace (good favor) so to leave them a remnant by which the nation would escape (survive). Again the scripture gives us an example in the physical of what is true in the spiritual.

We looked at this next verse already at the beginning of this short chapter, and every moderately informed Christian is familiar with the jest of its teachings from the surface text. But, it is important to continually remind each other that we should never overlook anything is God's Word.

Always pay attention to the details. That is where the meat, referred to by Paul, is to be found. Be vigilant in your study while investigating and examining the scripture, continually relying on the Spirit for discloser of the truth contained in God's Word. In essence, we need to continually listen for, and when detected be attentive to, that still small voice of God.

Ephesians 2:8-10
> 8 For **by grace are ye saved through faith**; and that not of yourselves: *it is* **the gift of God**:
> 9 Not of works, lest any man should boast.
> 10 For we are his workmanship, created in Christ Jesus unto good works, which God hath before ordained that we should walk in them.

The gift of God is salvation, and we are saved by God's grace through faith in his promise to do. And he will. Always. This is confirmed again (salvation by grace through faith) in our next passage.

Romans 5:15

15 But not as the offence, so also *is* **the free gift**. For if
through the offence of one many be dead, much more
the grace of God, and **the gift by grace**, *which is* by
one man, Jesus Christ, hath abounded unto many.

The free gift of God is salvation. Through disobedience
Adam caused death (separation from God, or the state of
being lost) to pass onto all his descendants. The reconciliation of mankind to God is salvation through his Son, Jesus
Christ. The gift of salvation is obtained by way of grace.

2ndCorinthians 5:18-19

18 And all things *are* of God, **who hath reconciled us
to himself by Jesus Christ**, and hath given to us the
ministry of reconciliation;

19 **To wit, that God was in Christ, reconciling the
world unto himself**, not imputing their trespasses
unto them; and hath committed unto us the word of
reconciliation.

Hebrews 2:15-18

15 <u>And deliver them who through fear of death were all
their lifetime subject to bondage</u>.

16 For verily he took not on *him the nature of* angels;
but he took on *him* the seed of Abraham.

17 Wherefore in all things it behoved him to be made
like unto *his* brethren, that he might be a merciful
and faithful high priest in things *pertaining* to God,
to make reconciliation for the sins of the people.

18 For in that he himself hath suffered being tempted,
he is able to succour them that are tempted.

It would be accurate, although a little unorthodox, to
state God has granted us salvation out of the "goodness" (or

grace) of his own heart. This leads us to Luke's record of the acts of Paul and of the writings of Paul themselves.

Acts 13:14-16
14 But when they departed from Perga, they came to Antioch in Pisidia, and went into the synagogue on the sabbath day, and sat down.
15 And after the reading of the law and the prophets the rulers of the synagogue sent unto them, saying, *Ye* men *and* brethren, if ye have any word of exhortation for the people, say on.
16 Then Paul stood up, and beckoning with *his* hand said, Men of Israel, and ye that fear God, give audience.

Paul goes on to refresh his listeners memories with a history lesson concerning the promise from God of the coming messiah through the blood line of the people of Israel. He makes mention of John the Baptist and confirms he fulfilled his course and mission concerning the message of the arrival of God manifested in the flesh. Then he shares with his audience the amazing gospel message (good news) of the Son of God's sacrifice for the world, and the wonderful love of God for his creation (man) and his will for all peoples to accept the gift of salvation in Jesus Christ. Upon the conclusion of the lesson to his fellow Judeo brethren,

Acts 13:42-44
42 And when the Jews were gone out of the synagogue, the Gentiles besought that these words might be preached to them the next sabbath.
43 Now when the congregation was broken up, many of the Jews and religious proselytes followed Paul and Barnabas: who, speaking to them, **persuaded them to continue in the grace of God.**

44 And the next sabbath day came almost the whole city together to hear the word of God.

Many of the Jews and the religious proselytes (Gentiles converted to Judaism) believed and received the message of Paul, and were persuaded to follow he and Barnabas. That message was spread throughout the community, and the next Sabbath day nearly the entire city turned out to hear the message of the Gospel. It is quite a simple matter to see why this was so.

The Jews and religious proselytes who had heard the gospel and accepted the salvation message were told by Paul and Barnabas to "continue in the grace of God". One can not continue in something they have never been in possession of. That is exactly what they had spent that week doing. Continuing in the grace (or good favor) of God will center you not only inside God's will for your life, but inside the Spirit of God itself. The presence of God in our life not only gives one confidence and assurance, but will empower us to be bold toward the witness of the truth that is in him (and in us). This they undoubtedly did, and spent the week spreading the good news they were now privy to.

Our final point of interest to be made concerning the relationship between grace and salvation in accordance with the writings of Paul is concerning the many letters he wrote to the various churches and individuals throughout his ministry. Much of this work is what comprises almost half of The New Testament itself. (Yes, almost half. Many scholars believe, and most Christians are under the impression that Paul is responsible for the book of Hebrews. He is not. I am unaware of the identity of the writer, but according to the scripture it was not Paul).

1ˢᵗCorinthians 1:1-3

1 Paul, called *to be* an apostle of Jesus Christ through the will of God, and Sosthenes *our* brother,

2 Unto the church of God which is at Corinth, **to them that are sanctified in Christ Jesus**, called *to be* saints, with all that in every place call upon the name of Jesus Christ our Lord, both theirs and ours:

3 **Grace *be* unto you, and peace**, from God our Father, and *from* the Lord Jesus Christ.

Paul is addressing the church of Corinth, but he is not doing so in the general sense. His second statement is an identification of exactly to whom he is directing his comments of guidance. "To them that are sanctified in Christ Jesus". Believers are the only individuals that meet this qualification. He is talking only to the true Christians inside the physical church of Corinth. This is an example of Paul's style regarding several of his documents that are addressed to various churches of God. Each of theses examples include both the identification of to whom he is addressing (genuine believers) and his wish and desire for them to continue in their possession of grace and peace, not salvation itself.

Grace and peace are mentioned by Paul in his opening greeting intentionally in that order, given there can be no peace in an individuals life without first acquisition of God's grace. Since grace is willed by Paul upon individuals who already possess salvation, this is verification that although grace is an important part of the salvation experience, it is not salvation in and of itself. It is the outpouring of God's love directed to the world in relation to God's call for the lost to accept salvation, and the presence of himself in us as believers and our remaining inside that presence which is his will, thereby growing continually closer to him throughout our time in the physical.

2ndCorinthians 1:1-2

1 Paul, an apostle of Jesus Christ by the will of God, and Timothy *our* brother, unto the church of God which is at Corinth, **with all the saints** which are in all Achaia:

2 **Grace** *be* **to you and peace** from God our Father, and *from* the Lord Jesus Christ.

Ephesians 1:1-2

1 Paul, an apostle of Jesus Christ by the will of God, **to the saints which are at Ephesus**, and **to the faithful in Christ Jesus**:

2 **Grace** *be* **to you, and peace**, from God our Father, and *from* the Lord Jesus Christ.

Philippians 1:1-2

1 Paul and Timotheus, the servants of Jesus Christ, **to all the saints in Christ Jesus** which are at Philippi, with the bishops and deacons:

2 **Grace** *be* **unto you, and peace**, from God our Father, and *from* the Lord Jesus Christ.

Colossians 1:1-2

1 Paul, an apostle of Jesus Christ by the will of God, and Timotheus *our* brother,

2 **To the saints and faithful brethren in Christ** which are at Colosse: **Grace** *be* **unto you, and peace**, from God our Father and the Lord Jesus Christ.

The most definitive of Paul's writings concerning this subject is found in a letter he wrote to his former travel companion and ministry partner, Timothy. Being a young evangelist under the guidance of Paul in his younger years, from time to time Paul felt the need or was inspired by the Spirit to impart teachings as well as encouragement to

Timothy. The Church is blessed with this advantage through the possession of that information.

1ˢᵗTimothy 1:1-2
1 Paul, an apostle of Jesus Christ by the commandment of God our Saviour, and <u>Lord Jesus Christ, *which is* our hope</u>; (Jesus, as our "hope", is a critical point inside our teachings of the Rapture).
2 Unto Timothy, *my* **own son in the faith**: **Grace, mercy,** *and* **peace**, from God our Father and Jesus Christ our Lord.

Through Paul's identification of Timothy as his own son in the faith, he makes a declaration that not only is Timothy a believer, but he is a direct "descendant" of Paul's work in evangelism. Timothy's conversion to Christianity was a direct result of God calling Paul to teach and preach the Gospel. Then immediately following this declaration, Paul mentions his usual message of grace and peace with the addition of mercy separating the two in this particular record.

One can not wish and will the grace, mercy, and peace of salvation itself on one that is most definitely already in possession of salvation. Paul is doing so toward Timothy for him to have an abundance of everything that is good in and of God, within the relationship that already exists between him and the Father. This will strengthen Timothy's fellowship (and ours) within the existing relationship, as well as help him grow and mature as a child of God, as should we all.

May we ourselves take to heart the lessons Paul was imparting to Timothy and endeavor to do the same in our own relationship with the Father, through the Spirit, in the name of Jesus Christ. The entire Church of God needs to realize the importance of spending more time (if not walking continually) in the Spirit of God, thereby drawing closer to him in fellowship. Especially considering the times in which we live, it being dusk of the final day of the Church Age. Grace and peace be multiplied to you all.

Chapter Two

The Second Coming

During the thirty-three years I have spent in study of the Rapture I have become painfully aware that almost everyone who is not of the Pre-Tribulational view are adamant in their argument that the term "Rapture" does not appear in the King James Version of the Bible. But in point of fact, it is even more true of the term "second coming". The truth is, the phrase "second coming" does not appear anywhere in the King James Version of the scripture that I have been able to find. I will stand corrected if any one can refer me to such a passage.

I am sure it was the invention of a well meaning theologian somewhere in church history and derived from the obvious teachings regarding the return of Jesus Christ. But the term in and of itself does not appear in the text of the scripture and is therefore unbiblical.

However, the fundamental teaching that the word Rapture conveys can be found in 1ˢᵗThessalonians 4:17 translated from the original Greek into King James English as "caught up", which is derived from the Latin word "Rapere" meaning to seize (sometimes by force) or to snatch away.

1ˢᵗThessalonians 4:17

17 Then we which are alive *and* remain shall be **caught up** together with them in the clouds, to meet the Lord in the air: and so shall we ever be with the Lord.

But the two words "second" and "coming" are not found together in scripture to describe the return of the Lord making the expression "second coming" itself unscriptural when referring to the return of Jesus.

That is not to say there will be no second coming. There most certainly will be. But we must first find it in scripture under another term. This we will do from the passage Hebrews 9:28. The only instance in the entirety of the scripture (that I am aware of) when and where a numerical value is placed within the teaching of a reference to the return of our Lord. Again, If you are aware of any information to the contrary, please, let me know.

When I teach on Hebrews 9:28, I always begin with the preceding verse, Hebrews 9:27. This allows me to point out a substantial misquote leading to a minor misuse of this passage by the Church.

Christen/dumb or Churchianity (as I call them) says, "It is appointed unto man once to die and after this the judgment." This is not a false statement. It is emphatically, most literally the truth. However it is a significant misquote and unfortunate misuse of this passage.

Hebrews 9:27 is actually setting us up for and pointing us to Hebrews 9:28. Together they state, (paraphrased) "And as it is appointed for men once (numerical one) to die and after this (their physical death) the judgment, So Christ (Jesus) was once (numerical one) offered to bare the sins of many, and unto them that look for him will he appear "the second time" (numerical two) without sin unto salvation (the result of his second appearance).

Just as sure as it is true you will die and face God for judgment, Jesus came once (which was the first time) and he will return which will be the next time, which is referred to by this passage as the second time.

This is the only verse in the scripture that directly identifies itself as referring to the second time the Lord Jesus will appear. Not the Rapture, (caught up or "snatched" before the Great Tribulation Period) not the traditional Second Coming (at the end of the Great Tribulation Period) but the next time or "second time" Jesus will make an appearance into this physical world.

This passage alone speaks volumes to the Church if she will listen. But more importantly this passage stands alone to point us to the full explanation of Jesus' return for his Bride. It begins the journey that guides us through all the questions that leads us to all the answers God intended for us to understand concerning the return of our Bridegroom Jesus Christ.

The Word of God, for those who will listen, teaches us,

Hebrews 9:27-28

27 And as it is appointed unto men once to die, but after this the judgment:

28 So Christ was once offered to bear the sins of many; and unto them that look for him shall he appear the second time without sin unto salvation.

It is imperative that the Church begins to listen once again to the Word of God, if in fact it ever has. The truth in him is so assured, it is as inevitable as death and judgment.

The traditional Second Coming of Christ is generally accepted to occur at the end of the Great Tribulation Period. In turn, The Great Tribulation Period, for those who believe in such a time, is said to be a seven year period of near total turmoil separated into roughly two equal segments of three and one half years. We will proceed upon that assumed premise.

The Post-Tribulational Second Coming

Post-Tribulationists believe that the entire body of Christ (the Church) will enter into the Great Tribulation Period with the rest of humanity. It will begin largely unannounced and the Church will gradually become aware that she has crossed its threshold from the signs of the times within.

Predominately the antichrist or beast will become evident to us by his actions described to us through the prophesy of the Old Testament and the details of the New Testament book of Revelation, along with the descriptions by Jesus of that time found in the gospels Matthew, Mark and Luke. The most notable feature will be the signing of the seven year peace agreement with Israel, which will reveal itself to be the seven year Great Tribulation Period in disguise.

In point of fact, the religious world in our modern day recent past has mistakenly thought itself to have already entered this period of future history several times over.

When world events have appeared to indicate catastrophic times of unspeakable horrors, a portion of the religious world would, for a short time, believe that the "end of the world" was nearing or had even arrived. In actuality, The Post-Tribulational view lends itself to suggest this scenario. Since all of history tends to repeat itself with the unfortunate addition of the worst possible horrors imaginable by mankind, upon their approach the Post-Tribulational view has repetitively identified the worst of them to be the Great Tribulation as they occurred.

This view is invariably incorrect each time another worst case scenario presents itself to follow that which was believed to be the worst case scenario that proceeded it. To revisit an old saying from my own youth, "You ain't seen nothing yet". This axiom could be refined today to better reflect my current understanding of future world events by stating, "No one has ever witnessed the like of events that are just beyond our own horizon". This was confirmed by Jesus himself in all three records of the Olivet Discourse.

The Post-Tribulational view also ignores the clear message of escape from this terrible time described to us by the Lord Jesus himself also contained in the Olivet Discourse of Luke chapter twenty-one. Since Jesus implies the possibility of avoiding these tragic events during his description of the events themselves, the subject of an escape in some form must at least be addressed.

Sadly, the Post-Tribulationist simply ignores the connecting phrase inside the passage that clearly contains the teaching of the escape provided to believers at the beginning or just prior to the Great Tribulation Period.

The Pre-Tribulation Rapture

The Pre-Tribulationists insist that millions upon multiple millions of Christians or believers will suddenly at an undisclosed, undetermined, unannounced and unknown time, all instantly disappear on a global scale. The event will result in the leaving behind of unbelieving friends, loved ones and family members just prior to the Great Tribulation Period. The Rapture will, according to the Pre-Tribulationist, in essence usher in this period of Great Tribulation.

This scenario is of course the primary teaching within the fictional story line of the **Left Behind** series of books and accompanying films popularized in recent years. However, with all the publicity generated by the success of these publications and productions making this version of the Rapture clearly understandable and familiar, if not accepted by the majority of the evangelical world, the process has also informed the rest of the populace of the concept.

Even I have acquired a **Left Behind** movie poster which I have displayed on my office wall (for obvious illustration and conversational value). I obtained it just after the release of the first movie. Literally thousands of people have seen it. (My poster, I mean).

But, if every Christian church on the face of our planet were instantly rendered virtually vacant due to a gathering of this magnitude, (to say nothing of all the genuine Christians of the world who fail to attend services) I find it difficult to believe the remaining population will have absolutely no clue as to what might possibly have just occurred. The reality of such an event would suggest the validity of the teaching itself. A close friend of mine and I were having a conversation once concerning another subject unrelated to religious matters. During that discussion he made a comment that I not only deem credible, but impressed me and I believe is worth a mention toward application here. He said, "The world is willfully ignorant, but it's not stupid."

At any rate, due to the Left Behind series (well done guys), The Rapture has been given a semi thorough examination by the Church as a whole that was long overdue. We will simply attempt to finalize that inspection.

Reality?

Even if we had no scriptural support provided to us by God's Word suggesting the approach of a rapture that will be conditional in its scope, I find its scenario much more credible than the all encompassing rapture which is believed and taught by the majority of the Evangelical Christian world today. But if one considers all the evidence found in the scripture supporting the theory of a rapture of any kind, the rapture that reveals itself to the honest investigator is the version containing the attachment of conditions for inclusion. The amount of documentation presenting itself from the scripture concerning these conditions is overwhelming.

According to the scriptural record, such a Rapture is also much more logical and therefore more likely than the simultaneous disappearance of multiple hundreds of millions of believers all over the world. Allow me to explain why this should be true.

The Word of God confirms for us a corridor of escape provided to a select group prior to the Great Tribulation Period (as we will prove) but fails to illustrate, demonstrate, or describe anywhere in its text an event involving such a gathering being accomplished on any monumental scale. A "mass exodus" as it were, fails to appear in the text of God's Word in reference to the Rapture. Only several mentions to an escape can be gleaned from the text, and all but one of these are accomplished through the process of interpretation. (The Spirit interpreting to the believer through The Word, with confirmation of that interpretation through corroborating scripture).

As its teachings suggests, the true Rapture will envelope only the smallest percentage of the actual membership of the Church. The portion that is "left behind" who had been in opposition to the concept of a "partial rapture" before its occurrence, will also be unable to immediately accept that it has taken place. Their idea of the rapture involves the entire Church which will encompass all believers. That belief will even lead them to help the secular world explain the small number of disappearances scattered quite thinly across the globe.

In their opinion, "whatever has happened it can not be the Rapture because I know I am a Christian and I am still here".

For a period of time they will look for alternative explanations, as will the world, who will in addition claim to have solved the mystery. Only later will it be realized by the remaining portion of the Church that was unprepared, they have in fact missed the true Rapture and have become the first members of the group referred to by us today as the tribulation saints.

A Rose, By Any Name

The word Rapture, while not specifically found in the King James Version of the Bible is derived from the Latin equivalent, and as such is found in translation. It appears in Paul's first letter to the church of Thessalonica.

1stThessalonians 4:17
17 Then we which are alive *and* remain shall be **caught up** together with them in the clouds, to meet the Lord in the air: and so shall we ever be with the Lord.

As found in 1stThessalonians 4:17 the Latin word Rapere is translated into the English phrase "caught up". The word Rapture is the English derivative of the Latin, and it is as simple as that.

The word "rapture" is a modern term attached to a first century Biblical teaching for the purpose of describing the event itself. The fact that the word "rapture" does not appear in the scripture, and the phrase "caught up" does, is so insignificant, the argument is not even worthy of this discussion. But there has been such an out cry on the part of Post-Tribulationists concerning this technicality, I am forced to point this out.

Anyone who is of the opinion there will be no Pre-Tribulational Rapture based solely on the fact of the lack of a modern term in an ancient text, in my judgment, has their mind made up regardless of what the facts suggest to be the truth. I have come into contact with many such people during my ministry. And many more when my study of the world around us and the universe that surrounds us is included in the debate. If I had not retained an open mind during those studies, I would have never been blessed by God with the truth.

Agreeing with you that the term Rapture does not appear in the King James Version of the Bible, you have no choice but to agree with me that the teaching of being "caught up" into the clouds to meet the Lord Jesus in the air certainly does.

1ˢᵗThessalonians 4:16-17

16 For the Lord himself shall descend from heaven with a shout, with the voice of the archangel, and with the trump of God: and the dead in Christ shall rise first:

17 Then we which are alive *and* remain shall be **caught up** together with them in the clouds, to meet the Lord in the air: and so shall we ever be with the Lord.

And if I might add, as Paul through the inspiration of the Holy Spirit did,

1ˢᵗThessalonians 4:18

18 Wherefore comfort one another with these words.

In regards to verse eighteen, we would have nothing to comfort each other with (in the physical) without the teaching of the Rapture. If we are not provided an escape (which is documented in description by Jesus himself) in the form of being caught up to meet him in the air (in turn described by Paul) before the commencement of the Great Tribulation Period, we would be predestined to endure that segment of world history. There is no comfort of any kind in such a scenario.

However, if you believe in any shape, form or fashion that the Bible is the Word of God, the "second coming" of

Jesus Christ must be taken as a genuine future event from the time of its documentation. And since we have no record of it occurring from the time of its documentation until the present, we can safely assume it remains a future event. Can we agree on this? (Stay with me now).

Post-Tribulationists and Pre-Tribulationists should both be in agreement with this concept. The question that remains and demands to be answered is, when will the moment we are "caught up" take place? Yes, it is as simple as asking the scripture a question such as this, and allowing it to answer for itself. However, the answer that reveals itself from the Word of God is going to step on a few denominational toes. I do not apologize.

QUESTION :

When will we be caught up to meet Jesus in the air?

ANSWER :

1. When Jesus returns.
   Can we agree on this?

2. When Jesus returns the next time.
   Can we agree on this?

3. The next time Jesus returns will be the "second time" Jesus returns.
   Can we agree on this?

At this juncture I am forced to repeat myself. There is only one passage in the whole of God's Word (to my knowledge) which attaches any numerical value (much less the specific numerical "two") within its text and without any question refers to a coming of the Lord thereby positively identifying itself as the "second time" he will appear. It is, of course Hebrews 9:28, and once again the answer is as sure as death and judgment. Hebrews 9:27.

Hebrews 9:27-28

27 And as it is appointed unto men once to die, but after this the judgment:

28 So Christ was once offered to bear the sins of many; and unto them that look for him shall he appear **the second time** without sin unto salvation.

Hebrews 9:28 does not confirm the Rapture, because it does not mention being "caught up", from whence the word Rapture was derived. It does however provide us with the numerical value which determines its location in the order of Jesus' appearances and verifies this record as his second inside that succession. In addition, it confirms the primary aspect of the Rapture teaching, which is also the other most controversial subject the Church can not agree on.

The only way to continue to believe in either of the traditional comings of the Lord Jesus, (The Pre-Tribulational Rapture or the Post-Tribulational Second Coming) is to deny or at least ignore the clear reading and teaching of God's Word in its entirety.

If you ask the scripture, "who is Jesus going to appear to when he appears the second time"? Taking the Word of God at face value the scripture clearly answers, "unto them that look for him". No one has to accept this phrase to be significant inside the context of the verse, but **that is what it says**. I prefer to believe the Word of God as it is written. You may believe what you wish.

I might take this opportunity to remind all my readers that regardless of what we (you or I) wish or convince ourselves to be true, our personal preferences will not change what is made by God the events that will shape our future and will inevitably become fact. In addition, each of us will stand before the judgment seat of Christ to give account for everything done in the physical. That of course includes our doctrines that each of us teach to anyone who will listen. It better agree with the scripture as best we can comprehend. After this physical world comes to its conclusion, there will be a final exam given by the Almighty himself to see how each of us measures up. We might all keep that thought in mind as we decide through the study of God's Word what we accept and teach to be the truth and why.

Returning to our earlier statement by my elderly black brother, "Let it say what it say" and taking that concept one step farther, my study has consisted of asking the scripture questions and allowing it to answer for itself. It is alive with the Spirit of God after all. God needs no help from us, we need only to listen. I believe this to be the correct procedure taught by the Word of God itself when instructing us on how to "rightly divide the word of truth". The Word can not lead you astray, only man's interpretation of it can.

The appearance of Jesus that is most commonly referred to, has him coming with/or/in the clouds of heaven, in/or/ with great power and great glory (Matthew 24:29-30, Mark 13:24-26 and Luke 21:25-27).

Matthew 24:29-30

29 Immediately <u>after the tribulation of those days</u> shall the sun be darkened, and the moon shall not give her light, and the stars shall fall from heaven, and the powers of the heavens shall be shaken:

30 And then shall appear the sign of the Son of man in heaven: and then shall **all** the tribes of the earth mourn, and **they shall see** the Son of man coming in the clouds of heaven with power and great glory.

Mark 13:24-26

24 But in those days, <u>after that tribulation</u>, the sun shall be darkened, and the moon shall not give her light,

25 And the stars of heaven shall fall, and the powers that are in heaven shall be shaken.

26 And **then shall they see** the Son of man coming in the clouds with great power and glory.

Luke 21:25-27

25 And there shall be signs in the sun, and in the moon, and in the stars; and upon the earth distress of nations, with perplexity; the sea and the waves roaring;

26 Men's hearts failing them for fear, and for looking after those things which are coming on the earth: for the powers of heaven shall be shaken.

27 And **then shall they see** the Son of man coming in a cloud with power and great glory.

These passages paired together in context suggest they speak of the same coming as it is also recorded in Revelation 1:7.

Revelation 1:7

7 Behold, he cometh with clouds; and **every eye shall see him**, and they *also* which pierced him: and **all kindreds of the earth shall wail because of him**. Even so, Amen.

This appearance, that is so obviously the glorious appearing (every eye shall see him) undoubtedly takes place at the end of The Great Tribulation Period (after the tribulation of those days). But, these narratives do not record the numerical value identifying any of them as the second coming, nor do they agree with the description of Hebrews

9:28 that does (unto them that look for him shall he appear "the second time").

The writer of Hebrews records clearly that he will appear to those who are looking for him and defines that appearance as the second time. These two criteria are then associated with the return of Jesus Christ in our future, due to the fact it has not yet occurred. Nowhere else in scripture are we given these two pieces of information attached to a single passage that is referring to an appearance of our Lord Jesus Christ. This is it. Or as my friend and former partner Texas peace officer extraordinaire Dennis Martin would say, "There it is"!

Since the passage of Hebrews is so dissimilar than the text of Matthew, Mark and Luke, the differences in their descriptions suggest there will be two separate events, both of which involve an appearance of the Lord Jesus Christ. The Rapture, (the second time) appearing only to the select few who are looking for his return which will initiate the Great Tribulation Period. Then the traditional Second Coming, when the entire population of the world will see and witness his triumphant glorious appearing which will end The Great Tribulation Period.

Also, if you think about it, how fitting it is for those two events to occur at just those particular times. In the book of Revelation, which is dealing directly with Jesus' teachings on and description of The Great Tribulation, he repeatedly says of himself, "I am the beginning and the end."

But, since this "theory" is derived from the assumption that the Rapture is in fact a biblical teaching from a predetermined Pre-Tribulational perspective, we need scriptural corroboration in order to accept it as truth. Is there a passage of scripture that would help us confirm this "interpretation" of two separate comings of the Lord ? I believe there is, and as it happens, Jesus himself is again the speaker.

Luke 17:20-22

20 And when he was demanded of the Pharisees, when the kingdom of God should come, he answered them and said, The kingdom of God cometh not with observation:

21 Neither shall they say, Lo here! or, lo there! for, behold, the kingdom of God is within you.

22 And he said unto the disciples, The days will come, when ye shall desire to see **one of the days of the Son of man**, and ye shall not see *it*.

The main subject of Luke 17:20 - 21 is the kingdom of God and its coming. We will limit our study within that boundary.

It is also necessary to be conscious of when we are reading in relation to time. Although we are in the Gospel according to Luke contained within the pages of what we refer to as The New Testament, we are not reading within the New Covenant. The Pharisees are asking a question inside the Old Covenant. Jesus, the sacrificial lamb, has not yet given his life for the sins of the world.

In addition, the "caught up" event from the perspective of the Old Covenant was a mystery which was unknown to the Old Testament saints. Therefore, when the beginning of the kingdom of God was the subject of conversation, the only point of reference an early first century Jew had was what we refer to as The Old Testament today, along with any available texts that were of a Jewish religious origin, but not inspired by the Spirit.

He then turns to his disciples, with the subject of the coming of the Kingdom of God still the topic, and makes reference to the days of the Son of man, making the two subjects synonymous. But when he does so, he mentions the days in the plural, and then a time that will come when the disciples will desire to see one of them.

"One of the days of the Son of man" is a direct indication of more than one, confirmed by the rest of the scripture in its descriptions as two, beginning and ending the time known as The Great Tribulation Period. And again, it is fitting that the two appearances of the Lord Jesus Christ should take place at just those times. For,

Revelation 1:8
8 I am Alpha and Omega, the beginning and the ending, saith the Lord, which is, and which was, and which is to come, the Almighty.

There is one more illustration derived through the process of interpretation one can draw from the scripture that is taken from the life of Jesus himself. Of all the types and shadows throughout God's Word of past and future events that have been identified and in turn illustrated by highly qualified theologians, I have never seen this next example exhibited. Therefore, we will do so and share it here.

Post-Tribulationists and Pre-Tribulationists alike will have their mutual disagreements for all the differing reasons that are based on their own interpretational perspectives. But if one was to consider the two main appearances or comings of the messiah inside the life and times of Jesus of Nazareth himself, you would be dealing with his birth and his Triumphant Entry into Jerusalem. Both had been foretold in prophesy, and were being awaited by the proper individuals in perfect portrayal of the Conditional Rapture.

In regards to Jesus' Triumphant Entry into Jerusalem at the beginning of the passion week, all Jerusalem turned out to witness his arrival and be proclaimed by the people as the King of the Jews. It is almost universally accepted by virtually all of Evangelical Christianity that his arrival at and entry into Jerusalem depicts by illustration his Glorious Appearance at the end of the Great Tribulation Period. At that time he will make his first physical entry into the Holy City in almost two thousand years fulfilling, full circle, the promise of the coming messiah.

I absolutely agree with the assessment of the one depicting the other in illustration, and in my professional opinion it would be foolish to believe otherwise. By the same token however, one key significance has been overlooked. If his Glorious Appearing is portrayed by his physical entry into Jerusalem at the beginning of the passion week, should not the teaching of a Pre-Tribulational appearance of Jesus in the form of the Rapture be depicted in scripture as well? This would be logical if the Rapture is an authentic Biblical teaching and a genuine historical event destined in our future. I not only believe it should, I believe it is. What's more, it is done so concerning his physical arrival into this world.

At his birth less than a handful of people were in attendance and witnessed the event we refer to as the nativity. Mary and Joseph (close immediate family, totally committed to the will of God) are the only individuals mentioned by scripture as having been present. Most people like to imagine Joseph providing Mary with at least the minimal traditional help that would or could have been available at the time. This would have consisted of one or more women performing the duties of midwives, assisting one another in encouraging Mary during the birth. The scripture however fails to mention the acquisition of any such assistance. Considering the magnitude of the event (the arrival of the savior of the world) and the lack of such information in scripture, we are forced to assume the absence of that support.

This small number of individuals would adequately represent and would compare "in type" to the teachings of the Conditional Rapture. Just as a handful of God's people witnessed the first appearance of the Lord Jesus Christ at his birth, so will only a handful of God's people be aware and witness his first reappearance after the Church Age is completed.

This illustration is of course interpreted from the scripture by way of an assumed and predetermined Conditional Rapture perspective, but it agrees completely with its teachings through those portrayals. It seems increasingly peculiar how numerous these examples are in scripture, not to mention the ease with which they can be used to portray the Rapture that the scripture teaches so clearly. We will look at several during the course of this study.

This will begin our examination of the Rapture of the Bride of Christ. Thirty-three years of Bible study directed specifically toward this subject has given me a desire to share with the Church as a whole all the relevant information the Lord has provided to me through his Word concerning the return of our Bridegroom Jesus Christ. I pray you will enjoy the journey as much as I enjoy taking you on it.

Really!

Grace and peace be multiplied to you all.

Chapter Three

The Partial Rapture in "theory"

First and Foremost I would like to question the use of the term "partial" to describe something the Father of Glory instituted for the purpose of acquiring a Bride for his only begotten Son. There will be absolutely nothing "partial" about the Rapture of the Bride of Christ. The escape of the Bride provided by her Bridegroom will take place in all its splendor, complete in every detail, according to the Word and will of God. The reason this "theory" was tagged by such a title is obvious when you familiarize yourself with its teachings.

The partial rapture theory teaches only a portion of the true Church is going to be included in the Rapture. The largest majority will be left behind for a number of reasons, depending on who you consult on the conditions necessary for inclusion. Then, as I understand it, some partial rapture theorists teach there are to be several "mini raptures" during and perhaps even throughout the great tribulation as individuals join the family of God through salvation.

What I have just described to you is truly a theory, because a portrayal of such events can not be found inside the Word of God. Allow me an attempt at clarification.

I want to go on record for the purpose of making clear, I do not believe in a partial rapture as it is depicted here. The Word of God does not contain teachings that would resemble this description.

That being said, I can not confess I do not believe in a Rapture that will be partial in its scope from the Churches point of view. If any individual member of the Church is excluded from the Rapture for any reason, it will most certainly take only a portion of the Church. Therefore by definition, from the perspective of that individual or group, it would have appeared to have occurred in a partial manner.

This is, in fact, exactly what the Bible teaches. It is not a new "theory" of the twentieth century, nor derived from a "vision" of the nineteenth. It has been taught since before the birth of the Church, no matter who has told you otherwise. There have been several inconsistent versions of the teaching that have surfaced over the generations, which has resulted in the Church taking a very dim view of any such notion.

The most notable point of interest is that with a complete and thorough study of the subject, no one would wish it to be true. I certainly did not myself. But the truth is always the truth, no matter what we want or convince ourselves to believe. And in mentioning a complete and thorough study of the evidence at hand, I am at a lose to understand why modern scholars refuse to investigate that evidence.

The largest majority of the believing theological world dismisses the subject out right. What's more, it does so in the absence of any examination of what could be called evidence to the proponents of the "theory" itself. It does exactly what the atheistic evolutionary community does in relation to the subject of creation. Denies even the possibility of, based on a predetermined forgone conclusion from biased misinterpretation of supposed evidence in hand. This is unfortunate, for the pursuit of the truth should be the only desire of any honest Biblical theologian.

Most scholars have clearly been sincere in the studies they have performed which have led each to their various beliefs. However, from my perspective, many of their conclusions are a direct result of ignoring key phrases imbedded in the Word of God that have been intentionally connected to the subject matter which, when overlooked, results in a failure to grasp the intricate detail contained in each lesson. These phrases are the means by which God reveals every truth he intended for us to understand in this life, but it is especially true in the case of the escape of The Bride of Christ.

At this time I would like to quote one of my two favorite authors. I have the utmost respect for him and all who teach the traditional Pre-Tribulation Rapture. Hal Lindsey's book The Late Great Planet Earth elevated my interest in eschatology to a new height as a teenager, and was responsible for my purchase of Tim LeHaye's study on the book of Revelation.

Together, in conjunction with other works involving the study of the End Times, they installed within me a hunger and a thirst for searching out the truths which are contained in the Word of God. I have never met either of these fine gentlemen, but it would be an honor. My only regret is that the results of the quest they inspired me to undertake, has now put us at odds with one another on this one issue. But, just for the record Mr. Lindsey and Mr. LeHaye. From the bottom of my heart, thank you both.

In his book, Vanished : Into thin air, Mr. Lindsey describes the various modern views of the Rapture, including the partial rapture theory. In its depiction he dedicates one whole page to explain its fallacies. He writes,

The New Protestant Purgatory

There is a fifth view concerning the Rapture of the Church which also has recently been introduced. It is not widely taught, since it is unorthodox and at considerable variance with the scripture. However, it is a view that could gain some following among those who are weak in their knowledge of the Word of God and strong on experience and human viewpoint.

There are some variations among its adherents, but generally it means the following: When the Lord Jesus comes to snatch away the true Church, only the spiritual believers will be taken. The carnal, or "backslidden" believers will be left to go through the Great Tribulation. It's an interesting position, given the word "backslide" is an Old Testament term. A born again believer doesn't do anything to obtain his salvation, and he can't literally "backslide" to his former state. A more accurate term would be "rebellious believer". Most adherents of this view believe that the partial rapture will occur before the Great Tribulation.

I hope Mr. Lindsey is wrong concerning the gaining of popularity by the partial rapture that he depicts in his book, for anything that can not be substantiated by the scripture should be categorically dismissed. Our beliefs and doctrines should be derived from the Word of God, not incorporated into the scripture to make it appear to imply what we wish to be true. But, he has made his thoughts fairly clear, and I will agree with him on several of his comments. However, a rebuttal is in order on a few points.

I do not believe in the partial rapture that he describes nor did I personally know anyone that believed in the partial rapture at the time I began work on this manuscript. Furthermore, I was unaware of the existence of the "partial rapture theory" at the time the scripture was teaching me what

I was calling **The Conditional Rapture** during the early 1980's. It was not until the mid 1990's that I even became exposed to the teachings of the partial rapture theory, and then only through the opponents of it who taught the traditional Pre-Tribulation Rapture. Through the study of their teachings I received little more than a brief condemnation of the theory.

Through the available sources I learned only the major differences between the partial rapture theory and the true Rapture the Bible teaches so clearly. I continued to call the concepts I believed the Lord was teaching me from his Word The Conditional Rapture even as I began work on the documentation of that information.

Since I am the only individual who has ever heard of the Conditional Rapture (besides a meager hand full of close friends and family members who also disagree with me), it has become increasingly more difficult for me to receive invitations to teach and preach what I sincerely believe to be the truth.

It is not popular to believe what God has allowed me to rediscover. If I was not totally convinced it was the absolute truth, I would not be placing myself in the crosshairs of mainstream Evangelical Christianity. Although I know there is a substantial amount of information that has yet to be revealed through the scripture, the current mountain of evidence is overwhelming and when understood in context, quite undeniable. I look forward to sharing the tip of that iceberg with you.

Which brings me to my ministry. The one thing I love more than teaching is preaching and I leap at every chance. And where I have had opportunity to lecture on the subject, I have done so and will again at every occasion called upon. However, I put the Christian world on notice. I will not argue over the Word of God with anyone. An honest exchange of information out of a genuine Christian love is welcome, but

I have had my fill of heated debate. I have grown weary of my opponents last word concerning the interpretation of a pertinent scripture passage being, "Well, that's not what it means." My closing response to that statement, that the reader of this manuscript will become annoyingly aware of through the process of repetition still stands. **"Well, that's what it says".**

NOTE: I was even told once, "I don't know what it means, but it doesn't mean that".

The Rapture I was taught by the scripture will transpire only once. It has never occurred in the past nor will it repeat itself after it takes place. Although there are examples, types, and teachings in the scripture where the Rapture is portrayed, there is no record in the scripture of any individual other than Jesus being "changed" from mortal to the state of immortality (glorified) which is the transformation process. The Bride of Christ is next in line for that unique procedure which will take place at the time she is "caught up" to meet Jesus in the air.

The reference made in the scripture to any individual being translated is simply movement or travel from one point to another, even if the destination is the spiritual realm of God as was the case with Enoch and Elijah. The transformation process, (of which we know almost nothing, other than it has occurred in the case of Jesus and will occur to the Bride) is regularly confused with translation.

With all due respect to all who oppose me and are of the opinion that the Conditional Rapture is in disagreement with the teachings of the scripture, the Word of God itself will show that assessment to be incorrect. The scripture is where I found it. I was amazed when the implications of it literally jumped out of the pages of the Bible at me upon simply surrendering myself to the truth contained in Gods'

Word. I am inclined to believe it will startle any honest child of God.

The Rapture I see in God's Word has absolutely nothing to do with an individual losing his or her salvation. You can not be a child of the devil after you have been adopted into the family of God.

Through the blood of Jesus Christ we are sealed with the Holy Spirit of promise. We become literally the children of God, the spiritual offspring of our heavenly Father, reborn unto him through the Spirit. The physical equivalent in example would be, my offspring will always be my offspring. There is no process that can change that physical fact. And if God can not keep his children his children, then we as parents have more power over our children in the physical than God has over us in the spiritual. To take such a stand on the issue of salvation places one on dangerous doctrinal ground. Allow me to elaborate briefly with the appropriate passages from the Word of God.

Ephesians 1:4-14
    4 According as he hath chosen* us in him* before the foundation of the world, that we should* be holy* and without blame* before him in love:
    5 Having predestinated *(preordained through his foreknowledge)* us unto the adoption of children by Jesus Christ *(salvation)* to himself, according to the good pleasure of his* will,
    6 To the praise of the glory of his* grace, wherein he hath made us accepted *(past tense)* in the beloved* *(his espoused bride)*.
    7 In whom we have *(present tense)* redemption *(salvation),* through his blood the forgiveness of sins, according to the riches of his* grace *(inside his good favor)*;

8 Wherein he hath abounded toward us in all wisdom and prudence;

9 Having made known unto us the mystery of his* will *(the adoption process whereby we become children of God, which is salvation leading to engagement to Christ under the New Covenant),* according to his* good pleasure which he hath purposed in himself*: *(in Christ)*

10 That in the dispensation of the fulness of times *(plural)* he might gather together in one all things in Christ, both which are in heaven, and which are on earth; *even* in him*:

11 In whom also we have obtained *(past tense)* an inheritance *(it is ours),* being predestinated *(preordained through his foreknowledge)* according to the purpose of him* who worketh all things after the counsel of his own will*:

12 That we should be to the praise* of his glory*, who first trusted in Christ.

13 In whom ye also *trusted,* after that ye heard the word of truth, the gospel of your salvation: in whom also after that ye believed, ye were sealed *(permanently stamped)* with that holy Spirit of promise *(the Holy Spirit of the New Covenant),*

14 Which is the earnest *(receipt of payment)* of our inheritance *(we own it)* until the redemption *(reception)* of the purchased *(bought and paid for)* possession *(it belongs to us),* unto the praise of his* glory.

These passages say much, **much*** more than I have commented on here due to the depth of God's Word, but this suffices to the subject at hand. Needless to say, from the perspective of the Church as a whole, I believe in eternal security of the believer. According to the scripture, every believer should. We will elaborate greatly on this subject later as it is an essential piece of the Conditional Rapture puzzle. It is also most interesting.

Returning to the issue of becoming a child of God, you can join the family of God through the process of salvation but hardly ever or even never obey your heavenly Father. Any such behavior will result in effectively making you a disobedient child.

We all know this to be true in the physical through our own experience as children, and as parents of children for those of us who have made that transition. No amount of disobedience will change who our biological parents are. In point of fact there is no experience or condition that can alter the relationship between parent and child. The relationship is not in question, only our fellowship or the lack thereof. The same is true in the spiritual of our heavenly Father. The physical, with which we are all familiar, is the example provided to us by God in this world which points to the truth in the next, which is the spiritual, wherein awaits our new existence the other side our change.

However, you can become a child of God, then refuse to live the life that your heavenly father intended and expected for you to live. Any rebellious act of this nature on our part results in distancing oneself from the Father and affectively hinders ones growth as a child of God. Many or most Christians never grow into maturity because they are encumbered by this distance that is created by themselves.

This condition is what is being referred to when opponents of the Conditional Rapture use terms like "rebellious believer" or "backslidden Christian" when discrediting the "theory". They are correct to point out that the term "backslidden" is an Old Testament or old covenant term, and correct again in their assessment of a New Testament believers inability to perform the act of backsliding. But the New Covenant has its counterpart under grace within which a true believer can be guilty. It is, however, limited to the inability of causing the loss of ones salvation. That process is referred to in scripture as "draw back".

Hebrews 10:38-39
38 Now the just shall live by faith: but if *any man* **draw back**, my soul shall have no pleasure in him.
39 But we are not of them who draw back unto perdition; but of them that believe to the saving of the soul.

A believer can certainly draw back from everything between his duty and service to the Lord, to his fellowship itself, as well as never attain to the proper fellowship with God that was within his or her grasp during their time in this physical life. The result of such actions on the believers part places an individual in a state the Bible describes as carnal, which some opponents of the Conditional Rapture maintain is also not possible for a believer. The scripture however, begs to differ.

1ˢᵗCorinthians 3:1-3
1 And I, brethren, could not speak unto you as unto spiritual, but as unto carnal, *even* as unto babes in Christ.
2 I have fed you with milk, and not with meat: for hitherto ye were not able *to bear it*, neither yet now are ye able.
3 **For ye are yet carnal**: for whereas *there is* among you envying, and strife, and divisions, **are ye not carnal**, and walk as men?

This lifestyle results in an existence that is centered mainly in this physical world referred to in this passage as "walking as men" which is the equivalent of "walking after the flesh" or the ways of the world. Those actions have the effect of rendering any such believer carnal as this passage points out, complete with all the undesirable attributes. It is this effect that is the primary condition which leads many believers to the various circumstances that will prevent most of the Church from participating in the event we call The Rapture.

As long as a believer remains in ignorance of walking in the Spirit, or worse yet is in direct rebellion to do so, he or she effectively positions themselves in the path of the abundant temptations the world has to offer. Those temptations, when succumbed to, results in a believers indulgence in the lust of the flesh. By walking in the Spirit that indwells us at the time of our spiritual baptism during the rebirth experience, we can avoid the temptations of the world that lead many believers to surrender themselves to acts of disobedience.

Galatians 5:16
16 *This* I say then, **Walk in the Spirit, and ye shall not fulfil the lust of the flesh**.

Colossians 2:8
8 Beware lest any man spoil you through philosophy and vain deceit, after the tradition of men, **after the rudiments of the world**, and not after Christ.

Ephesians 5:6-8
6 Let no man deceive you with vain words: for because of these things cometh the wrath of God upon the children of disobedience.
7 **Be not ye therefore partakers with them**.
8 For ye were sometimes darkness, but now *are ye* light in the Lord: **walk as children of light**:

Disobedience alienates you from the Father and thereby prevents growth toward maturity as a child of God. Spiritual growth is essential for a healthy viable fellowship with the Lord. Outside of fellowship we are at the mercy of the world, and the powers that be in it, namely, the powers of darkness. Being affected constantly by those powers without the fellowship of our heavenly Father, we position ourselves outside his direct assistance. "As" sheep without a shepherd as it were.

"As" means that we do have a shepherd who is observing our actions, or even pleading with us to return to fellowship with him, but we have no "ear to hear". Now that sounds familiar. "He that has an ear let him hear"?

Setting aside, for the moment, the genuine "partial rapture theory" (that I am opposed to myself), we will look at the notion of a rapture in general that could be classified as conditional in its scope.

To insist the teaching is a new concept first created in as early as the nineteenth century, is to also assume no record of any kind can be found anywhere in the entirety of human history of any such belief. Allow me to reword this statement for the purpose of making myself absolutely and unquestionably crystal clear.

If you are convinced and are adamant in the belief, as some I have read are, that the teaching of a rapture of any kind, let alone one that is partial in its scope, is a new concept first created in the nineteenth century, you have committed yourself to declaring for a fact that,

1. No record,
2. Of any kind
3. Can be found
4. Anywhere
5. In the entirety of human history
6. Of any such or
7. Similar belief.

Which, I am delighted to say, is not the case. The argument itself is also irrelevant since knowledge of God's plan, from many aspects of Bible study, has been progressive down through each generation. It would be quite natural for us not to come to a knowledge of the finality of that plan until the last generation has emerged onto the historical scene. But, that truth as it stands, has not been the case with this particular principle since the teachings of the Conditional Rapture are plainly declared by the scripture itself, as we will see and demonstrate.

As I began to realize what the scripture was teaching me, I also understood I could not be the only believer in the whole of Christian history to recognize such a doctrine. Every child of God has the same and equal access through the Spirit of God to acquire all the relevant information required to gain knowledge of God's plan which would lead each of us to the truth as is Gods will for us all. I am not so special as to have been singularly privileged by God with such insights.

Also, as I have pointed out to many of my brothers and sisters in Christ, I personally and individually am not this smart. I could not have concocted this theory out of thin air on my own, and I am very much alone concerning this work (in the physical). I am singularly incapable of twisting so many passages in the scripture to make seemingly appear a doctrine that is truly unbiblical.

Since I found it in the New Testament, the early Church had to have been aware of it. Hence, there would be documentation of that knowledge in Christian manuscripts external of the accepted Spirit inspired scripture.

Although these extra biblical texts are not inspired of God, many were written by legitimate well meaning church leaders and genuine Christian layman who were expressing there true beliefs and doctrines that were circulating in the Christian world during their lifetime. Those texts would reflect what was believed by a portion of the Church, however correct or incorrect the doctrine to be.

This is in no way unfamiliar to us today in relation to our own well meaning Christian authors. Every bookstore with a religious section containing works of a Christian nature will have a number of manuscripts that any one of us would disagree with concerning faith, doctrine or beliefs. But the contents of those manuscripts do contain the faith, doctrine and beliefs of the author. He or she does believe what they have penned however correct or incorrect their understandings to be in relation to the truth regarding the chosen subjects.

The Shepherd of Hermes is one such ancient document.

We will acknowledge first that much of what is recorded in these texts does not agree with the teachings of the scripture. That fact alone establishes the complete set of manuscripts of no doctrinal value. But, setting aside that detail for the moment in order to analyze the contents of these documents, we learn one of the records makes mention of a vision the "shepherd" had of a giant raging beast. This animal made an attempt to charge the shepherd presumably to cause him great harm. The shepherd, however was able to escape by relying on God for protection.

The next vision he encounters is that of a beautiful maiden, identified by the shepherd himself as the Church. She in turn identifies the creature as an illustration of the great tribulation to come, and tells him he escaped it by putting his full trust in God. She then gives him the responsibility of informing all other believers they can do the same, but only if they too put their full trust in the Lord.

This is a very brief look and oversimplification of the content of those manuscripts. But since they have been accepted to have been written in the second century, it is concrete proof that the "concept" of the Rapture in general (as referring to an escape from a future time of great tribulation) and conditions connected to participating in that specific escape existed outside of Biblical text, but inside the body of the Church, to within approximately one hundred years of the physical death of Jesus Christ.

Even if the doctrine is in error, it was a belief of a portion of the membership of the Church, regardless of how few, documented to as early as the second century and there exists earlier evidence. Anyone choosing to deny the clear content of these articles, is blind wishing to remain so. You can honestly choose to believe and thereby continue to teach the doctrine to be in error, but you cannot deny that it was believed by a portion of the early Church. It existed, that is a fact.

There are numerous websites on the Internet that continue to expound the myth that the teaching of the Rapture was not even conceived of until the late 19th or early 20th century. Anyone denying the existence of this doctrine by even the smallest percentage of the early Church should be held suspect concerning any and all doctrines that are put forth by that person or organization.

I will add personally that this is as silly an argument as exists in Christendom since the teachings of The Conditional Rapture, (therefore the concept of a rapture that will be partial in its scope from the perspective of the Church) saturate the scriptures themselves. They are also directly stated by the surface text without the performance of any interpretation on our part whatsoever, as we will see. Anyone surrendering themselves to the clear reading of the Word of God will be amazed at just how they have overlooked these references in the scripture.

My only regret in God allowing me to rediscover these truths is that they have separated me from my Pre-Tribulational brothers and sisters in Christ. I have no "kindred spirit" in the faith as it were. I know of no single denomination which believes as I, and these teachings have alienated me from the denomination in which I grew up. Perhaps this publication will serve to identify myself to such an assembly if it exists. If not an assembly, then individuals who are like minded in the reading of God's Word. These studies and the conclusions to which they have led, have also suggested to me that there may be a grain of truth in an age old saying. Maybe ignorance truly is bliss.

My only comfort in the faith (in the physical, of course) is my small congregation. They understand it is not necessary for us to have the exact same beliefs to love one another as a church family and seem to genuinely enjoy learning of my beliefs even when they are not in full agreement with a particular teaching. This is precisely the attitude I have enjoyed myself for many years.

In my own study of dissimilar denominational beliefs I have attempted to comprehend the differences in doctrines between my own and others in an effort to better understand their positions. I have enjoyed sharing that accumulated knowledge with the members of my congregations. My current congregation being the greatest of those blessings. I wish the Church as a whole could follow their example.

Grace and peace be multiplied to you all.

Chapter Four

The Churches of Revelation

For the purpose of explaining the Rapture, a full length in depth study of the churches of Revelation is unnecessary. However, an overview certainly is, due to specific information inside the letters to the churches dealing with the subject of the Rapture that can be found nowhere else in the scripture, only corroborated.

Also, the beginning of chapter four of the book of Revelation needs to be addressed, as most of the Pre-Tribulational world holds stock in it being a record of John the apostle being caught up into heaven as a picture of the Rapture itself.

One scholar, who's work I was studying years ago, made the comment that John was a fitting example of the Church being translated into heaven. I will not disagree with that view, for the Bible is saturated with models, types, and picturesque illustrations that are unquestionably designed for us on which to build sound doctrine. I fully agree that Jesus may very well have intended for us to accept Johns' experience in just that fashion. It is after all, a perfect fit from a Pre-Tribulational perspective.

I only wish the Church could see and accept other doctrinal truths which are stated by the Word of God directly or which can be established as such through the confirmation of comparable Bible passages. Historically, the Church is notorious for accepting teachings it believes to be correct that unfortunately only exist through the process of interpretation.

John's experience of translation is one such example, in that it can only be seen by interpretation through the preconceived point of view that the Pre-Tribulation Rapture theory is correct. I am not trying to imply that all doctrines which are derived through interpretation are incorrect. In this particular case it happens to be a teaching I am in agreement with. However, it none the less needs to be pointed out it is derived through the process of interpretation.

All information acquired through interpretation leading to the establishment of doctrine must be accompanied by support sources, that are in definitive agreement with that doctrine. All doctrines obtained through all these available sources must then agree with the whole of God's word. Admissions such as this will keep all of our studies and documentary works honest.

The book of Revelation opens with the declaration, "The Revelation of Jesus Christ". This is literally the revealing or "unveiling" of Jesus our Lord in his present and glorified form, which John witnesses in all his splendor. It is perfectly understandable that John was thoroughly overwhelmed by the experience.

The book of Revelation itself declares it was provided to Jesus' servants for the purpose of informing us of things which must shortly come to pass. The phrase "unto his servants" means the true Church or body of Christ. All, but only, genuine believers. This is an important fact to remember, considering many portions of the teachings that are provided to us by the book of Revelation can be (and regularly are by Christendom) misdirected to refer to the physical church in the local sense. Our churches in the physical contain unbelievers who have not yet accepted salvation, and those who believe themselves to possess salvation but unfortunately do not.

Most are well meaning and legitimately sincere, but they are not children of God and therefore not part of the body of Christ. The book of Revelation and the letters to the seven churches contained in it were written to the servants of God alone. Once this principle is understood and applied properly to the teachings of Revelation in general, and to the seven churches specifically, several modern doctrines collapse.

The most remarkable feature of the opening address of chapter one of Revelation is verse three. My initial interest in the book of Revelation was sparked by the explanation of that verse by a visiting evangelist in revival at my home church at the age of fifteen. Looking back I have to confess it was a selfish act on my part, but the process set in motion the means by which I was able to gain insight into the correct interpretation of the verse. The blessings of knowledge that eventually emerged from that course of action were their own reward.

Revelation 1:3

3 Blessed *is* he that readeth, and they that hear the words of this prophecy, and keep those things which are written therein: for the time *is* at hand.

I was told that the Lord would bless all those that made the reading of the book of Revelation a regular part of their Bible study. I therefore, in greedy pursuit of the blessing (I knew not what was) added Revelation to my daily Bible reading. Regardless of where I was in the scripture, a portion of Revelation was included, and after a reasonable amount of time had elapsed (set by myself, of course) I anxiously awaited the fall of the heavenly blessings promised by the Lord God Almighty.

One small problem. During the course of this seemingly ever increasing and extraordinarily extensive delay, I realized I had made the first of many mistakes related to relying on another person to interpret for me, what only the Holy Spirit can explain.

Years passed without the reception of the alleged blessing I had been so patiently waiting for. Through continued Bible study and the Lord teaching me to listen to him through the Holy Spirit, (never neglecting the reading of the book of Revelation) he drew my attention back to that very same passage to correct one of my greatest study errors.

Sure yourself not to make the same failure.

Blessed is he that readeth,

Readeth, - I had gotten that far. This was the only easy part of the equation to get right. The reading of Gods' Word is the first step. We must make a steady flow of it into our lives daily.

But it is only the first step. It does us very little genuine good without the second, and its companion, the third and final step. And this is especially true in regards to the book of Revelation and the truths contained inside its prophesies.

And they that hear the words of this prophesy,

Hearing - This refers to being receptive to, or willing to receive that which is being taught. We can not learn what the book of Revelation is teaching us about our future unless we are willing to submit ourselves to the presence of God in his word and receive. God knows the end from the beginning and wishes us to recognize that he and he alone can guide us down the path of life.

When we attempt navigation on our own, we literally become the proverbial blind leading the blind. That is especially true of eschatology or the study of the end times. God holds the future in his hands, but in those nail scared hands he also holds out and open the book of Revelation to give us a glimpse at what that future entails. It holds the status of prophet in order to forewarn us of the dangers that are awaiting the world inside The Great Tribulation Period that is sure to come.

And keep those things which are written therein: -

Keep those things - This is the most overlooked process of the command of God concerning the receiving of the blessing being promised by him. As we learn of the future from the book of Revelation (and the entirety of the scripture in general), we must apply those truths to our lives as they establish doctrine within our faith. At the same time we must teach and inform one another of each lesson learned from God through Johns' unique experience. The only catch is that we must be correct in our understanding of God's Word in order to apply genuine truth to our lives.

When all three steps are followed and applied according to the Word and will of God, we do receive the blessing promised us by our Lord. After reading, accepting, and applying the truths of Gods' future, foretold to us by Jesus himself, we are blessed beyond the knowledge of that future with the comfort that it and we are in his hands. So, let us comfort one another with those words,

for the time is at hand.

The time is at hand. - This proclamation needs no explanation. It is a statement of fact and quite simply the truth. I need only to add, because the time is at hand now more than ever, since we are closer to the end than we've ever been, we need more so now than any time in history to understand the book in which God reveals to us the events that will shape and conclude the latter days. This revealing is called prophesy. And prophesy is quite literally history future.

God spoke this physical world into existence complete from beginning to end in a moment before time. Through his Word he informs us of our future and how it will take shape. The events that are to take place, will take place, simply because from his Divine perspective they already have. That is what God confirms for us through his Word, his witness, his Son, our Hope, Yeshua.

Revelation 1:4-6

4 John to the seven churches which are in Asia: **Grace** *be* **unto you, and peace, from him which is, and which was, and which is to come**; and from the seven Spirits which are before his throne;

5 And from Jesus Christ, *who is* **the faithful witness,** *and* **the first begotten of the dead, and the prince of the kings of the earth.** Unto him that loved us, and washed us from our sins in his own blood,

6 **And hath made us kings and priests unto God and his Father**; to him *be* glory and dominion for ever and ever. Amen.

Revelation 1:4 begins Johns' greeting to the seven churches of Revelation. Verses five and six includes Jesus in the greeting who is the faithful witness and the "first begotten of the dead". (The first raised from separation from the Father). Jesus goes on to inform us he is prince over the kings of the earth, effectively giving us notice that no one rules that he does not allow. He loved us to the point of death (again, separation from the Father), that he may cleanse us of our sin with his own blood. Through sanctification (the cleansing process / Buried with him (the Spirit) in baptism) he has made us kings and priest unto God the father who has dominion over all.

Revelation 1:7

7 **Behold, he cometh** with clouds; **and every eye shall see him**, and they *also* which pierced him: and all kindreds of the earth shall wail because of him. Even so, Amen.

Revelation 1:7 dramatically describes a coming of the Lord, which is obviously the glorious appearing that will undoubtedly take place at the end of the Great Tribulation Period. At that time all eyes shall behold his triumphant return in the clouds of heaven, which was demonstrated by Jesus in type upon his triumphant entry into Jerusalem at the beginning of the passion week.

Revelation 1:8

8 **I am Alpha and Omega, the beginning and the ending**, saith the Lord, which is, and which was, and which is to come, **the Almighty**.

Verse eight contains the familiar titles Jesus rightfully declares for himself, "I am the Alpha and Omega, the beginning and the end". He later adds to that list the first and the last, a variation of the same.

Revelation 1:9

9 **I John**, who also am your brother, and companion in tribulation, and **in the kingdom and patience of Jesus Christ, was in the isle that is called Patmos, for the word of God, and for the testimony of Jesus Christ**.

Then in verse nine John explains briefly who he is, what he is doing, and where he was when all this took place. He then closes verse nine with the explanation of why. He declares, "for the Word of God, and for the testimony of Jesus Christ".

Revelation 1:10
10 **I was in the Spirit on the Lord's day**, and heard behind me a great voice, as of a trumpet,

There is, within the Church, a tremendous amount of conflict over interpretation beginning with this verse. John was in the Spirit (of God) on the Lords' day. But there is great debate on what precisely he actually meant. He was in the Spirit, but how? Was he filled with the spirit or was he referring to literally being swept into the spiritual realm as some believe.

Does the Lords' day refer simply to the first day of the week (Sunday) on which the Lord rose from the Grave? Or was he literally transported into the future to witness the Day of the Lord, the end of days, first hand. There are many speculations on these matters, and varying opinions. And although each has a bearing on the teaching of the Rapture, conclusions on these inquiries are not necessary for the study of the seven churches, which is our current task. We will address the answers to these questions in this same chapter immediately following our examination of the seven churches when we witness John being caught up into heaven at the beginning of Revelation chapter four.

Revelation 1:11
11 Saying, **I am Alpha and Omega, the first and the last**: and, What thou seest, write in a book, and send it unto the seven churches which are in Asia; unto Ephesus, and unto Smyrna, and unto Pergamos, and unto Thyatira, and unto Sardis, and unto Philadelphia, and unto Laodicea.

In verse eleven, Jesus re-identifies himself and instructs John to document everything he witnesses in a book (which will contain the letters to the churches) and send it to the seven churches.

Revelation 1:12-20

12 And I turned to see the voice that spake with me. And being turned, I saw seven golden candlesticks;

13 And in the midst of the seven candlesticks *one* like unto the Son of man, clothed with a garment down to the foot, and girt about the paps with a golden girdle.

14 His head and *his* hairs *were* white like wool, as white as snow; and his eyes *were* as a flame of fire;

15 And his feet like unto fine brass, as if they burned in a furnace; and his voice as the sound of many waters.

16 And he had in his right hand seven stars: and out of his mouth went a sharp twoedged sword: and his countenance *was* as the sun shineth in his strength.

17 And when I saw him, I fell at his feet as dead. And he laid his right hand upon me, saying unto me, Fear not; I am the first and the last:

18 I *am* he that liveth, and was dead; and, behold, I am alive for evermore, Amen; and have the keys of hell and of death.

19 Write the things which thou hast seen, and the things which are, and the things which shall be hereafter;

20 The mystery of the seven stars which thou sawest in my right hand, and the seven golden candlesticks. **The seven stars are the angels of the seven churches: and the seven candlesticks which thou sawest are the seven churches**.

Then John, from verse twelve through twenty, upon turning to see the voice which is speaking to him, is rewarded with a view of the risen glorified Lord Jesus Christ. Overwhelmed at the sight, John falls at his feet, as if dead. Jesus lays his right hand upon him in comfort, and tells him there is no need to fear and declares once again that he is the first and the last.

John states he witnesses Jesus walking in the midst of seven golden candlesticks. Also he has seven stars in his right hand that we are told are symbolic of the angels of the seven churches. The scripture itself explains these candlesticks to represent the seven churches themselves. If we pay close attention to the scripture as we read and study, it will directly interpret itself more times than not. When it chooses not to do so directly, it always allows or even insists on being cross referenced by other passages where the reader will discover it agrees with itself on any given subject. In which case, scripture at the very least interprets scripture.

There is never a need for us to attempt interpretation ourselves. In fact, the scripture is of divine origin and no member of the human race can understand its essence in the physical. Only God through the Holy Spirit (that still small voice) can explain and interpret its concepts to us after salvation. This is in fact one of the most important duties of the Spirit. It functions as an intercessor between the Creator and his creation.

Romans 8:26-27

26 Likewise the Spirit also helpeth our infirmities: for we know not what we should pray for as we ought: but the Spirit itself maketh intercession for us with groanings which cannot be uttered.

27 And he that searcheth the hearts knoweth what *is* the mind of the Spirit, because he maketh intercession for the saints according to *the will of* God.

The word angel translates into modern English as messenger. Many scholars believe this simply refers to the leader or pastor of the church and not an angelic being watching over the churches in some manner. I agree with that explanation based on the fact the churches are literal and physical, therefore there is no reason (nor evidence in scripture) to believe otherwise of the angels. Also I find no support passages in the scripture to imply they are of heavenly origin. All interpretations of the scripture must agree with the whole.

If the Bible does not say it or at least imply it (and such must be accompanied by corroborating passages) you can not teach it, or in my case preach it. Many denominations today fail in this one respect in that their doctrine contains teachings that are essentially man made. It has the ring of truth (sounds good) but its precepts have no basis in scripture.

Here is where we begin to analyze the churches and their conditions.

From the perspective of what is called Dispensationalism, which refers to the belief that God interacts with his creation through stages or ages in history, the seven churches of Revelation represent more than what they appear in the physical. This belief stems from elements mentioned in the letters to the churches of which they themselves could not physically take part, because they simply would not survive until those stages of history. This leads to the understandable conclusion they are representative of something more than simply the literal and physical churches of Johns' day.

It is believed the illustrations and teachings that they are and possess extend through the whole of history to reach even beyond the modern world we refer to as today. This would allow them to be applied in principle throughout the entirety of the Church Age and into the Great Tribulation itself. I believe this conclusion to be correct.

Jesus has singled these seven churches out because each in their physical condition singularly resemble the stages the actual Church of God has progressed through during the Church Age. The era in question is the span of time from the birth of the Church, (the day of Pentecost, Acts 2) until the "second time" the Lord will appear "unto them that look for him" (the day of the Rapture, 1stThessalonians 4:16-17 and Hebrews 9:28) which will initiate The Day of The Lord known to us as The Great Tribulation.

Pre-Tribulational scholars believe the last two or possibly three phases of the progression described will extend to the close of the Church Age. From historical records related to the Church and the condition of the Church as a unit today, I would also not totally disagree with that assessment. However, there is a third illustration that has been overlooked.

The state in which the churches of Revelation find themselves that Jesus is bringing to their attention also exists in each and every believer today individually. If any Christian wishes to know where they stand in their fellowship with God, (and each should) all that is required is to study the seven churches of Revelation. In doing so you will expose the existing quality of your own fellowship, (or lack thereof) between you and your Bridegroom that is contained inside the descriptions set forth by Jesus himself.

Each, save one, was given a condemnation by the Lord for that which was lacking within their relationship and how to correct it. Each, save one, was given a commendation concerning the faithful service it had performed within their relationship and how to maintain or improve it.

The Church of today is subject to the same rigorous standards set forth by Christ during his ministry which were in turn expanded upon in the Olivet Discourse. Those standards were then painstakingly described in brutal detail of chapters two and three of Revelation in the form of directives to the Church, along with the consequences of failure to comply.

The modern Church is severely lacking in its fellowship with its Bridegroom and needs to take a serious look at the seven churches, for within their combined example is healing for the Church as the Bride of Christ.

In conclusion, the seven churches of Revelation are representative of three things.

1. They were literal physical churches of Johns' day of which six had varying degrees of problems within their structure which were hindering their fellowship in the Lord. Some of these problems were even being denied by the hierarchy of the Church, causing a movement toward the heretical. Serious consequences were to result if repentance was not established within those churches.

John's mission was to document the information provided to him from the Lord, for the purpose of informing the churches of their disobedience thereby allowing them the opportunity to repent of their sins. If executed, this would of course heal their fellowship in the Lord and put them back on the path of righteousness. Failure to comply would result in reception of the penalties established and set forth by Jesus.

2. The seven churches of Revelation represent the stages or phases the Church as a whole has experienced over the course of its lifetime throughout history. We can look back through the historical record and establish the correlation documented by John in the book of Revelation. This has been sufficiently documented in many modern works by several of our best Evangelical Christian authors. The lesson for the modern Church to learn, is to use history as a guide so that we as individual churches may avoid the mistakes made by the Church as a whole throughout that history.

3. The most critical lesson to learn is the spiritual. The seven churches of Revelation are a representation of each and every believer today. The conditions recorded in the churches of Revelation are present in our lives as individual Christians, personally. A look at chapters two and three reveal all the varying fellowships or lack thereof that are possible between us and our Bridegroom. If we lack in fellowship we will suffer in our own future the same consequences that are documented in the seven churches. Some of those consequences are severe in the extreme.

There has been an enormous amount of disagreement directed toward me on this point throughout my ministry. If illustration 3 is valid as it appears, all of the information supplied to us for each of the seven churches is intended to be directed to all believers, with special emphasis on the generation which will witness the events being described. In point of fact, the scripture gives us no indication this is not true, and every piece of evidence found suggests it to be correct.

Revelation 1:1

1 The Revelation of Jesus Christ, which God gave unto him, to **shew unto his servants things which must shortly come to pass;** and he sent and signified *it* by his angel unto his servant John:

The phrase "shew unto his servants" is obviously referring to the present recipients of the information in question, which would be the Church of the first century. The seven churches named in chapter one stand in illustration for the physical Church as a whole. This would constitute the physical application of the message to the Church as a whole in John's day, which would be applied at the time of the delivery of the message.

But the phrase "things which must shortly come to pass" suggests a portion of the Church that would witness first hand the events that will be described. Since the events that are detailed in the text of John's record will not take place until the end of the Church Age and therefore remain unseen by the existing Church of the first century, it is intended to be understood that the last generation of believers before the end of the Church Age are to be accepted as recipients as well.

This would constitute the spiritual application of the message to the Church across time. It would demand the application of all information in the letters to the seven churches to be directed to the entire Church throughout its history with special emphasis of the close of that history involving the last generation of believers making up the modern Church of today.

Through this study we hope to show that it is essential that every Christian examine his and her own fellowship with God through the Spirit of Christ. We recognize and confess that all legitimate Christian denominations would agree with this statement, but it is our belief that the premise of that testimony be applied to the Rapture of the Bride as well. Supplemented with the entirety of the scriptural record, the study of the seven churches of Revelation is the rule provided by God through Christ as recorded by John, by which that measure is established.

Which brings us to Revelation chapter four.

Revelation 4:1

1 **After this I looked**, and, behold, a door *was* opened in heaven: and the first voice which I heard *was* as it were of a trumpet talking with me; which said, Come

up hither, and I will shew thee things which must be hereafter.

The opening of chapter four begins with "after this I looked". Our explanation of the second example the seven churches of Revelation represent, connects to this phrase. If each letter to all seven churches symbolize the progression through all the phases the Church has passed through during its lifetime for the duration of the Church Age, then this statement would be referring to the sequences of events following the completion of that age.

It is true, from a Pre-Tribulational perspective, that John could be envisioned as an appropriate "type" or picture of the Bride being taken up into heaven. The mention of a door that was open in heaven could coincide with the open door promised to the church of Philadelphia by the Lord that he himself would provide.

Revelation 3:8

8 I know thy works: behold, **I have set before thee an open door**, and no man can shut it: for thou hast a little strength, and hast kept my word, and hast not denied my name.

Philadelphia is referred to as The Loyal Church in the circles of Pre-Tribulationalism. Since they were to be "kept from the hour of temptation" it would seem reasonable for this event to take place through the open door mentioned by the Lord. This would agree with John being an illustration of the Church, him being a loyal servant in the Lord, which would in turn be in agreement with the timing of such an event which would also be correct.

Again, I agree with this scenario in regards to its order of events and its timing. However, the Church has again overlooked a critical point of interest that when brought to the forefront, it trivializes at best.

Since John is a picture of the Church in chapter four, and the door he sees and evidently passes through coincides with the same mentioned in chapter three to the church of Philadelphia, through the accumulation of all the available information we have the what, when, where, and how. But the modern Pre-Tribulational view has overlooked the fact we do not yet have two vital pieces of information. The who and the why.

They do insist the "who" is the Church (to them, the Bride of Christ) the "why" is because as the Bride she is promised to be kept from the hour of temptation (escaping the Great Tribulation) noting it is to be understood according to the text. However, again, this is a view based on interpretation from an assumed Pre-Tribulational perspective. I prefer to believe the scripture, and not man's interpretation of it.

If you accept John as an example of the true Church of God and the church of Philadelphia as a representative of that Church by illustration at the end of the Church Age, you have no choice but to accept all the teachings within the directives of the Lord concerning the commendation of that church if you wish to agree with the scripture, as well as be correct within those teachings. They have been overlooked.

Revelation 3:8-10
8 I know thy works: behold, I have set before thee an open door, and no man can shut it: **for thou hast a little strength, and hast kept my word, and hast not denied my name**
9 Behold, I will make them of the synagogue of Satan, which say they are Jews, and are not, but do lie; behold, I will make them to come and worship before thy feet, and to know that I have loved thee.

10. Because thou hast kept the word of my patience, I also will keep thee from the hour of temptation, which shall come upon all the world, to try them that dwell upon the earth.

I would so much enjoy correctly dissecting (rightly dividing) the entirety of these three passages with you, but for brevity and the study of the Rapture we will look at only one train of thought here.

Revelation 3:8-10 is the classic, most widely used passage "proving" the Pre-Tribulation Rapture. Unfortunately, much of the information in this passage is overlooked even by Pre-Tribulationists. Also, it is only a support passage because it does not mention any of the components of the Rapture directly or by name.

The teachings attributed to the Rapture from a Pre-Tribulational perspective are interpreted into the passage by way of the predetermined assumption that the Rapture is a Biblical teaching.

To assume that to be the case, the whole of the text must in turn be accepted as well. The traditional Pre-Tribulationist overlooks the condition for inclusion laid down by the Lord Jesus himself in the very verses they use to point to the Rapture. Allow me to explain.

If the Lord has promised the church of Philadelphia (and he has) he will keep them from the hour of temptation (and he will) then the mention of why he will do so is also valid. It must be accepted as well.

The members of the church of Philadelphia had continually kept the word of his patience. This act is what has earned them the privilege of being kept from the "hour" or time of temptation. Jesus himself verified that fact. It can not be denied. No other church addressed in the letters to the seven churches was observing this particular criteria. When we can define what is being addressed in this accomplishment we will have determined the condition by which it is achieved.

For this reason, John truly is the fitting example "in type" of the Bride of Christ, for he has already stated (through inspiration of the Holy Spirit) that he meets this qualification. In the same respect as John, the existence of the letters to the seven churches being recorded by him as commanded by God, are themselves a testimony to the teachings of the Conditional Rapture. They are corrective in their nature and definitive in their content declaring the lack of that same qualification within the seven churches as a whole, Philadelphia standing by distinction as the sole exception. Then Philadelphia is singled out by Jesus in his recognition of their adherence to this qualification.

In short, they were to be kept by Jesus from the hour of temptation to come, by way of their obedience to keep the word of his patience.

Revelation 1:9

9 I John, who also am your brother, and companion in tribulation, and in the kingdom and **patience of Jesus Christ**, was in the isle that is called Patmos, for the word of God, and for the testimony of Jesus Christ.

John, identifying himself as a brother to the seven churches of Revelation, (also confirming he is not speaking to the lost members of the congregations who just happen to be attendees in the churches) includes that he is a companion in their tribulation. This is significant in regards to where this passage appears, placing it before any mention of the Great Tribulation, making it fall during the Church Age in which all Christians endure tribulation to some degree. Jesus himself in the Olivet Discourse calls this time the "beginning of sorrows", which will become a critical point of interest in another of our illustrations. (Matthew 24:8).

John then, after a reference to the kingdom of God (of which the entirety of the book of Revelation revolves) states he is in the patience of Jesus Christ. This declaration informs us that John meets the necessary requirement set forth by Jesus to the Church as a whole in order to be kept from the hour of temptation.

"In the patience of Jesus Christ" and "have kept the word of my patience" are one and the same. Need you be reminded that Jesus is the Word. In the patience of Jesus Christ, or patiently waiting for/or/on the Lord is referred to throughout the entire Bible and is (or should be) the cornerstone of our "living" Christian faith. We will cover it extensively in its own chapter in the course of this study but for now simply put, it is patiently looking forward to the second appearance of our Lord and Savior Jesus Christ. Literally the "second time" he will appear (Hebrews 9:28). The church of Philadelphia was doing just that and would be rewarded for their faithfulness by being included in, what they waited on.

During his ministry we were told by Jesus, he must return to heaven from whence he came. But assured us in the same manner he would return from heaven to gather us (them that look for him, Hebrews 9:28) unto himself that "where I am there ye may be also" (John 14:3).

The gathering of the Bride unto himself to be taken back to the Fathers house (John 14:1-3) is the singular most spectacular event understandable and to be witnessed by us in the physical.

John 14:1-3
1 Let not your heart be troubled: ye believe in God, believe also in me.
2 In my Father's house are many mansions: if *it were* not *so*, I would have told you. **I go to prepare a place for you.**

3 And if I go and prepare a place for you, **I will come again, and receive you unto myself**; that where I am, *there* ye may be also.

The event in question borders the spiritual life that awaits us in eternity "future" that will be without time for which all believers should be anticipating and joyously looking forward to. It operates as a boundary between the physical and spiritual worlds themselves. He even gave us mention of it in the Lords' prayer.

Matthew 6:9-13
  9 After this manner therefore pray ye: Our Father which art in heaven, Hallowed be thy name.
10 **Thy kingdom come**. Thy will be done in earth, as *it is* in heaven.
11 Give us this day our daily bread.
12 And forgive us our debts, as we forgive our debtors.
13 And lead us not into temptation, but deliver us from evil: For thine is the kingdom, and the power, and the glory, for ever. Amen.

This is virtually the same prayer that Jesus gave his disciples when they had asked him to teach them to pray. They are found in Matthew 6:9-13 in the sermon on the mount to the multitude and Luke 11:2-4 when Jesus was praying in a certain place. When he was finished they came to him and asked him to teach them to pray "as John also taught his disciples".

Luke 11:2-4
  2 And he said unto them, When ye pray, say, Our Father which art in heaven, Hallowed be thy name. **Thy kingdom come**. Thy will be done, as in heaven, so in earth.

3 Give us day by day our daily bread.

4 And forgive us our sins; for we also forgive every one that is indebted to us. And lead us not into temptation; but deliver us from evil.

The Lord's prayer contains all the elements necessary to live a healthy Christian life in full fellowship with the Lord if we sincerely take it to heart and literally apply it to our lives. A complete volume of books the size of an exhaustive encyclopedia set needs to be written on this one subject alone.

But the information we wish to glean from the Lords words here are "Thy kingdom come". The coming of the kingdom of God should be the daily desire of every believer. We should be looking forward to that event with the greatest of joyful anticipation. Inside the Lord's prayer, the final arrival of the kingdom of God is the first thing we are instructed to make mention of when making requests to the Lord. Even our daily bread, and forgiveness of our debts are secondary to the coming of the kingdom of God.

However, if you are waiting on the Lord to appear the "second time", but are convinced that day will not arrive until the end of the Great Tribulation period, you can not be looking directly forward to the day of his return. The Great Tribulation or the Day of the Lord is between you and the coming of the Lord.

Amos 5:18-20

18 Woe unto you that desire the day of the LORD! **to what end** *is* **it for you**? the day of the LORD *is* darkness, and not light.

19 As if a man did flee from a lion, and a bear met him; or went into the house, and leaned his hand on the wall, and a serpent bit him.

20 *Shall* **not the day of the LORD** *be* **darkness**, and not light? **even very dark, and no brightness in it**?

There is no comforting one another with these words. The day of the Lord is the Great Tribulation Period, and will begin with the conclusion of the Church Age which will come to a close upon or soon after the initiation of the Rapture of the Bride of Christ. But, only those who have kept the word of the patience of the Lord by looking forward to his second appearance (Hebrews 9:28) with a constant attitude of watching and praying will "be accounted worthy to escape".

Luke 21:36

36 <u>Watch ye therefore, and pray always</u>, **that ye may be accounted worthy to escape** all these things that shall come to pass, and to stand before the Son of man.

Looking back to the Lords' prayer, there is even a support passage that would also imply this to be true. This thought agrees with the whole of God's Word.

Matthew 6:9-13

9 After this manner therefore pray ye: Our Father which art in heaven, Hallowed be thy name.

10 Thy kingdom come. Thy will be done in earth, as *it is* in heaven.

11 Give us this day our daily bread.

12 And forgive us our debts, as we forgive our debtors.

13 **And lead us not into temptation, but deliver us from evil**: For thine is the kingdom, and the power, and the glory, for ever. **Amen.**

(Paraphrased) Lead us not into (the hour of) temptation, but deliver (or remove) us from evil (the Great Tribulation). This is of course an interpretation from an assumed Pre-Tribulational perspective. But it agrees completely with the teachings that are found throughout the scripture concerning the true Rapture of the Bride of Christ that the Word of God details for us so clearly.

Interpretation of support passages consisting of implied text must agree with the clear teachings of the Word of God in its entirety. I have found that the scripture completely agrees with itself, when studied from The Conditional Rapture perspective.

Most of the members of the Church do not share these sentiments however. After thirty-three years of study focused on the Rapture of the Bride of Christ I am convinced the Church's various doctrines are dependant on what they wish to be true and are almost always drawn along denominational lines. I can not make the same claim. What God has allowed me to rediscover, and I have come to accept as the truth, is not what I would choose to be in store for the body of Christ had I any control over the consequences of her actions myself.

When pressed on the subject, most Christians that claim to believe in the Pre-Tribulational Rapture also maintain to be happily anticipating the return of the Lord. However, after years of close observation they appear to me not to be in a hurry for it to occur. The largest majority of the modern Church is wrapped up in their physical lives and not ready to give up this existence for the promise of the next. I was even told once by a Christian brother, "I know this world is not my home, my home is in heaven, but I'm not yet home sick".

That attitude is rampant in the Christian world today. I am fearful of the consequences of that mind-set. While teaching his disciples the lessons concerning the end of the

Church Age in the Olivet Discourse, Jesus warned against this very attitude.

Luke 21:34-36
34 And **take heed to yourselves**, lest at any time your hearts be overcharged with surfeiting, and drunkenness, **and cares of this life**, and *so* **that day come upon you unawares.**
35 For as a snare shall it come on all them that dwell on the face of the whole earth.
36 **Watch ye therefore, and pray always,** that ye may be **accounted worthy to escape all these things** that shall come to pass, and to stand before the Son of man.

God has every intention for us to enjoy the life he has provided for us within this physicality. His will for us is prosperity inside fruitful lives filled with joy and hope in the physical as well as the spiritual. But this reality we share together is a temporary existence, and Jesus warns us through his disciples in verse thirty-four not to be "overcharged" or burdened with the cares of this life. It is the palest of shadows in comparison to the eternal reality of our true life in him awaiting us the other side our change. If we let this physical life dominate our being, and do not keep our eyes (spiritually speaking) on the return of Jesus and his promises, like a snare "it" (the Great Tribulation, the subject of the Olivet Discourse) will arrive without our notice to engulf us, just as the scripture informs us it will encompass the entire world. Outside obedience we will be caught in its grasp as clearly stated by verse thirty-six.

Verse thirty-six defines the parameters for which he has provided us the means of avoiding the horrors of that time. Watching and praying. These two functions, working in tandem, supply for us the way of escape. Keeping a vigilant watch for the second appearance of our Lord and Savior Jesus Christ, and the performance of habitual prayer keeps us in communication and fellowship with the Father through him (the Spirit). As the Bride of Christ, this is the equivalent of keeping ourselves chaste from the world. The Word tells us that we are in the world but not of it. We are to keep our eyes (spiritually speaking) on the promise of life beyond this physical existence.

The condition that constitutes worthiness to be accepted into the avenue of escape from the Great Tribulation is the removing ourselves from fellowship with world. Unfortunately the majority of the modern Church stands guilty of association with the world at present. It is the result of living a life tied to this physical world which it substitutes for the rich spiritual fellowship the Father wishes us to have with him through the Holy Spirit. The consequences for not doing so are clearly stated by the Word of God.

Disobedience guarantees entrance into The Great Tribulation Period and the burden of enduring the most prolific horrors in scale and intensity the world has ever witnessed. There will be no "escape" from this time once it is entered. The only exit out of the Great Tribulation Period is the door of physical death.

I pray you have taken the proper steps necessary to avoid all these things that are coming upon the world. The Lord has provided for us the means by which we can avoid this terrible time if we will recognize and accept its conditions of compliance. Remain vigilant, continue watching and patiently waiting, while in daily and continual prayer that you will be counted worthy to escape. Grace and peace be multiplied to you all.

Chapter Five

The Great Tribulation Period

Once upon a time, I received a telephone call at work. I happened to be on break at just that moment and had a few minutes. A life long friend of mine which I had enjoyed many years of Bible study with, was on the other end of the line with a search question.

"I need one verse from the Bible that points conclusively from our perspective to the Pre-Tribulation Rapture" he said.

"Well", says I carefully and a bit hesitantly, attempting not to provoke a substantial exchange, "There is only one passage in the whole of scripture that contains precisely what you are looking for, but you can't use it".

"And, why not"? He asked quite defiantly.

"Because", I responded, deciding to throw caution to the wind, "All passages that refer to the Rapture, when taken in that context by those of us who believe in a Pre-Tribulation Rapture, also contain a condition of some sort to be met in order to be included in the event. The Church as a whole has overlooked that truth. You do not believe in the Conditional Rapture. The verse you are looking for, if taken literally in its entirety and at face value, confirms quite adamantly within that context what you do not believe in. You will not even be able to use the portion that verifies that the Rapture is Pre-Tribulational, due to the means by which it is revealed".

I continued, "Every passage in the scripture that contains a Pre-Tribulational Rapture teaching, also confirms the condition by which one is include or excluded. These teachings have simply been ignored or at least overlooked by the Church. Ironically, if one accepts the whole of each passage at face value, the Rapture and the associated conditions cannot be separated from one another. It's as if God by his divine creativity nit them together in his word. That is how I came to refer to it as "The Conditional Rapture".

My friend was not amused. We had spent many years together in Bible study as youths and generally knew where we disagreed with each other when our conversations turned toward doctrine. Especially when the subject was The Rapture, it being my passion since the age of fifteen. Until that moment my teachings had been merely a curious novelty to him. Our disagreements were usually on minor points of interests that would have no bearing on major doctrines regardless which of us were correct. Now, however, they had become a genuine nuisance.

The teachings that are being addressed here are The Rapture, its Pre-Tribulational timing and that Jesus is not coming back to retrieve the entire Church, only the true Bride of Christ that has kept herself chaste and worthy, who is encased inside the Church.

The scripture does confirm that the entire Church as a whole (baring no individual member) is espoused or engaged to Christ at this present time.

2ndCorinthians 11:1-2

1 Would to God ye could bear with me a little in *my* folly: and indeed bear with me.

2 For I am jealous over you with godly jealousy: for **I have espoused you to one husband, that I may present** *you as* **a chaste virgin to Christ**.

But most of the Church has corrupted itself from the simplicity that is in Christ by not keeping itself chaste. Paul, in fact, documented for us that this was his very fear.

2ndCorinthians 11:3

3 **But I fear**, lest by any means, as the serpent beguiled Eve through his subtilty, **so your minds should be corrupted from the simplicity that is in Christ**.

Chastity is what the opponents of the Conditional Rapture are referring to as "spiritual Christians" when discrediting the "theory". These critics have not recognized the correlation between historical Israel's culture and tradition, and the relationship inaugurated by God between he and his mirror image, man. Much of Israel's tradition found in its distant past, for the most part, was derived from its knowledge of (as best they understood) the relationship established by God with his creation.

Through the blood covenant, established with the death of Christ, God instituted the strictest of all agreements between his creation and himself. The Covenant that binds the Church to God is in fact, the ultimate marriage contract.

With the completion of the espousal or engagement period of this marriage proposal, the Lord will return for his Bride to remove her from the body of what is referred to today as The Church, sweeping her from this physical world into the spiritual. This extraction will effectively result in a divorce between the Bridegroom and the unfaithful and adulteress members of this group of believers. What is left of the Church then enters the Great Tribulation Period where it has now become the first members of the group known as the tribulation saints.

This is the reason the Church is not mentioned in the narrative of the Great Tribulation in the book of Revelation beyond chapter four. Not because the Rapture has swept the entire Church to heaven, but upon the completion of the Rapture of the Bride of Christ, the Church no longer exists.

After the departure of The Bride the individuals that remain (which is the largest majority of the Church) enter into the Great Tribulation Period taking their place as the individual saints of the tribulation. They also constitute the first of two groups that are seen by John (Revelation 6:9-11) who are recorded to have come out of Great Tribulation (Revelation 7:13-14).

Revelation 6:9-11

9 And when he had opened the fifth seal, **I saw under the altar the souls of them that were slain for the word of God, and for the testimony which they held**:

10 And they cried with a loud voice, saying, How long, O Lord, holy and true, dost thou not judge and avenge our blood on them that dwell on the earth?

11 And white robes were given unto every one of them; and it was said unto them, that **they should rest yet for a little season**, until their fellowservants also and their brethren, **that should be killed as they *were*, should be fulfilled**.

This narrative takes place during the Great Tribulation Period as confirmed by the elder to John in our next passage. But in verse eleven of chapter six it must be pointed out that the individuals that are given robes, are told they must remain resting yet for a little while until their fellow servants and their brethren that should be killed as they were, should be fulfilled.

Taken at face value, this information tells us that there are two classes of saints inside the Great Tribulation Period. One class is referred to as fellow servants to John, which would constitute those who came to a knowledge of Christ inside The Great Tribulation therefore are fellow servants to him. The other being called brethren indicating they were believers before the arrival of the Great Tribulation therefore direct blood kin to John under the New Covenant but were unprepared at the time of the Rapture. Both classes of tribulation saints will pay for their entrance into this time period of world history with their lives. There is no comforting one another with these words. (1stThessalonians 4:18).

Revelation 7:13-14

13 And one of the elders answered, saying unto me, What are these which are arrayed in white robes? and whence came they?

14 And I said unto him, Sir, thou knowest. And he said to me, **These are they which came out of great tribulation**, and have **washed their robes**, and made them white in the blood of the Lamb.

I also need to point out, found in chapter seven verse fourteen is the mention of the robes of the individuals which came out of Great Tribulation. When a child of God receives their robe it is clean upon reception of it. It is their wedding garment that they are to take care to keep unsoiled. However, it was necessary for these robes to be washed, implying they were soiled at the onslaught of the Great Tribulation Period.

This cleansing process took place during the Great Tribulation as the saints which entered that time gave their lives for their faith after repenting of the sins that cause their entrance into the great day of the Lord in the first place. The garments which have been cleansed then become a testimony of their repentance inside the Great Tribulation.

Toward the end of the book of Revelation the lamb's wife is mentioned and the Bride is mentioned, which are one and the same, but she is never referred to as the Church inside the narrative. Only after the story line is completed and Jesus is speaking to John in the present sense of the first century (at which time the Church does exist as a single entity), does he once again mention the churches in the plural and local sense as well as Johns testifying of these messages and directives to them. (Revelation 22:16).

Revelation 22:16

16 I Jesus have sent mine angel to testify unto you these things in the churches. I am the root and the offspring of David, *and* the bright and morning star.

This short narrative on the chain of events just prior and leading into The Great Tribulation Period is necessary for point of reference. So many denominations disagree with the concepts within these teachings they are incapable of honest investigation of the truth which is contained in God's Word.

It is God's truth, the whole of God's truth and nothing but God's truth I have always been interested in. It is solely his truth I continue to seek today. Our heavenly Father has been, and always will be, persistent in this area of enlightenment to all who seek to be knowledgeable in his truth.

Unlike the phrase "second coming", the term Great Tribulation is mentioned in the scripture directly and by name. Jesus' first mention of the Great Tribulation is documented in the book of Matthew inside the record of the Olivet Discourse. In those passages, which is also recorded in the books of Mark and Luke, Jesus describes future events during a time that are easily recognizable by the disciples as the Time of Jacob's Trouble from the prophetic book of Jeremiah.

Jeremiah 30:7
7 Alas! for that day *is* great, **so that none** *is* **like it**: it *is* even the time of Jacob's trouble; but he shall be saved out of it.

Compare this passage with,

Matthew 24:21
21 For then shall be great tribulation, **such as was not since the beginning** of the world to this time, no, **nor ever shall be**.

There can be no doubt that the two time periods being referred to in these passages are one and the same, since there can not be two separate "such as was not, or ever shall be" events in history. Therefore, we have a reference by which we can trace the Great Tribulation through the scripture and thus through time itself.

Jesus' second reference to the Great Tribulation is recorded in the book of Revelation 2:22, the verse my friend was asking me for, that I knew he could not use. Allow me to explain.

My friend Randy is, as I once was (stated from the heart with the utmost respect and the greatest of Christian Love), a full blooded, dyed in the wool, as convinced as they come, I've got my mind made up don't confuse me with the facts, traditional Southern Baptist Pre-Tribulationist. (And believe it or not we are still friends, "last I checked"). This group of individuals, which at the close of the 20th century made up the majority opinion of the Evangelical world, believe Jesus is coming back before the Great Tribulation, (which is correct) and he is taking the entire Church, lock, stock and barrel, back to heaven with him regardless of their degree of individual disobedience. (Regrettably, I'm afraid not).

The passage most often used by Pre-Tribulationist is Rev. 3:10.

Revelation 3:10

10 Because thou hast kept the word of my patience, I also will keep thee from the hour of temptation, **which shall come upon all the world**, to try them that dwell upon the earth.

This verse, directed to the church of Philadelphia inside the letters to the seven churches of Revelation, makes mention of an hour of temptation, which will come upon the entire world as a whole. Pre-Tribulationist reason that there will only be one time in history when this will be true, The Great Tribulation Period, based on Jeremiah 30:7 and Matthew 24:21, to name just two.

Therefore for them this passage teaches that Jesus, through the open door of verse six, will remove the Bride from this world (which for them means the entire Church) through the process of the Rapture, effectively "keeping thee from" (Raptured) "the hour of temptation" (The Great Tribulation).

What's wrong with this picture? In reality very little. When I take into account all I am familiar with concerning the teachings in the scripture regarding the Rapture of the Bride of Christ, this is very close to the truth. I agree with the majority of this doctrine as it is portrayed. However, it needs be pointed out, it must be interpreted as such. Again, allow me to explain. (Search this passage in comparison with the following information to test "my" teachings, confirming whether "I" am correct. **This is important**).

1 This verse does not mention The Great Tribulation by name.

2 It does not contain a direct reference to the process of being "caught up", but an indirect reference that must be deduced.

3 No mention of the Bride is made in any direct form.

However correct from a general perspective this teaching may be, it is derived through the interpretation of the reader, not stated by the scripture itself. This point seems to be the most difficult concept for the Church as a whole to comprehend.

My objection to the Church is how it can accept an indirect reference (hour of temptation) and establish doctrine upon it, however correct that doctrine to be, while at the same time ignoring a direct reference completely (Great Tribulation).

This practice is prevalent in Christendom for its ability to allow individuals and groups to integrate specific interpretations of acceptable doctrines into their midst which agree with their established denominational beliefs. The direct reference in question in this case is clearly acknowledged by the text contained in an adjacent letter addressed to the church of Thyatira.

If one wishes to study what the Word of God has to say concerning the Great Tribulation, one will have to study, at the very least, the three passages mentioning the Great Tribulation by name. Can we agree on this?

The three references are as follows.

1 Jesus himself teaching of it in Matthew 24:21.

2 Jesus himself making point of it in Revelation 2:22.

3 One of the "elders" explaining to John who is to come out of it in Revelation 7:14.

To overlook or ignore any one of these passages is to deny the teachings they contain. They speak for themselves, as does the entirety of God's Holy Word.

Revelation 2:22
22 Behold, I will cast her into a bed, and them that commit adultery with her into **great tribulation**, except they repent of their deeds.

This is the verse of scripture my friend could not use as a Pre-Tribulation passage although it teaches conclusively that there will be an event which will result in someone avoiding the Great Tribulation Period. Reread the passage and see if you can recognize the reference. I will not apologize for pointing this out to my Post-Tribulational brothers and sisters in Christ, but like it or not, someone is not going into Great Tribulation.

If the teaching of an avoidance of that time is not a confirmation of Jesus' description of an escape of it, I don't know what is. This would only agree with the teaching of a "caught up" event which is Pre-Tribulational, and that is the current definition of the Rapture. Therefore, found in these passages is the scriptural documentation of the Pre-Tribulation Rapture.

Revelation 2:22
22 Behold, I will cast her into a bed, and them that commit adultery with her into great tribulation, **except they repent of their deeds**.

At the same time however, the entrance into the Great Tribulation is documented by the same passage through a connecting phrase making entrance into that terrible time by the same group being addressed undeniable.

Revelation 2:22

22 Behold, **I will cast her** into a bed, **and them that commit adultery with her into great tribulation**, except they repent of their deeds.

Only the presence of the condition makes escape from The Great Tribulation a possibility, it is not a forgone conclusion as traditional Pre-Tribulationists have convinced each other to believe.

Both teachings exist simultaneously in the same passage with the use of the connecting phrase forever linking them together. I do not understand how the Church has missed the presence of them in the scripture. I can only assume since the Church wishes not to believe, it chooses not to accept.

The majority of Pre-Tribulationists take the stand that "all" of the Church is going to be "caught up" and sites scripture to verify that conviction. This belief stems primarily from 1stCorinthians 15:51.

1stCorinthians 15:51

51 Behold, I shew you a mystery; We shall not all sleep, but we shall all be changed,

The mention of the term "all", they claim, means all believers. I have even heard that message preached in revival from that one verse. "All" means all of the Church. They effectively over look the "if's" of the scripture, which defines the "all" of this verse.

A silly argument I once used to make my point within this debate is, why doesn't "all" mean all people, the entire population of the planet, or all mankind throughout the entirety of human history for that matter. The obvious answer is of course that it is to be understood Paul is referring to the Church alone. Again, interpreted from a predetermined assumption.

I believe it is understood he is directing his teachings to the Bride of Christ. I believe this, not because I choose to, but because it is clearly seen in the manner he opens this same chapter, 1stCorinthians 15:1-2 which when combined with 1stThessalonians chapter 4, becomes resurrection central.

1stCorinthians 15:1-2
1 Moreover, brethren, I declare unto you the gospel which I preached unto you, which also ye have received, and wherein ye stand;
2 By which also ye are saved, **"if"** ye keep in memory what I preached unto you, unless ye have believed in vain.

"Quotation marks mine".

The "if's" of the scripture are the most overlooked indicator of truth there exists in the Bible. They are not the most informative, they are not the most plentiful, but they are the most overlooked. We will address the most substantial "if's" of the scripture with their own chapter toward the later portion of this book. They are most interesting and enlightening.

But, because of the "if" contained in this verse, this passage is difficult for the Pre-Tribulationist to reconcile within his doctrine. Most Pre-Tribulationists believe in eternal security of the believer. It is better known as once saved always saved. I have never liked that terminology, although I too believe in eternal security of the believer. Fortunately, God gave me a better term. Once a child of God, always a child of God. This phrase better illustrates and accurately describes the true relationship that exists between each believer and our heavenly "Father".

John 3:3

3 Jesus answered and said unto him, Verily, verily, I say
unto thee, Except a man be born again, he cannot see
the kingdom of God.

John 3:5-7

5 Jesus answered, Verily, verily, I say unto thee, Except
a man be born of water and *of* the Spirit, he cannot
enter into the kingdom of God.
6 That which is born of the flesh is flesh; and that which
is born of the Spirit is spirit.
7 Marvel not that I said unto thee, Ye must be born
again.

When the scripture deals with the subject of eternal life,
also known to some as everlasting life, it always addresses it
in a permanent form. The rebirth experience in the spiritual
mirrors birth in the physical, which is permanent. You cannot
change who your biological parents are. Regardless of what
type of fellowship my children and I have (or do not have),
in relationship they remain biologically from conception my
children. Nothing in this physical world can change that fact.
Another illustration used in the scripture is circumcision.

Romans 2:28-29

28 For he is not a Jew, which is one outwardly; neither *is*
that circumcision, which is outward in the flesh:
29 But he *is* a Jew, which is one inwardly; and circumcision *is that* of the heart, in the spirit, *and* not in the
letter; whose praise *is* not of men, but of God.

Circumcision of the heart in the spiritual mirrors circumcision of the flesh in the physical, which is permanent. Once
surgery is done it is always done. On and on it goes. Once

a child of God, always a child of God. But remember, it is possible to be a disobedient child, which returns our attention right back to the "if's" of the scripture.

1stCorinthians 15:1-2

1 Moreover, brethren, I declare unto you the gospel which I preached unto you, which also ye have received, and wherein ye stand;

2 By which also ye are saved, **"if"** ye keep in memory what I preached unto you, unless ye have believed in vain.

Again "quotation marks mine".

This passage contains a reintroduction to the gospel (good news) that Paul had already preached to the church of Corinth. They had received that gospel and the portion of the Church which had applied those teachings to their life were "standing in" that gospel. Two steps not one. They had not only received but were living faithful Christian lives by way of the good news preached to them. In the face of blatant paganism, I might add. Not all Christians make that transition.

Paul reminded them that it is by this means they are saved, "If" you keep in memory what I preached unto you. If one did not keep in memory (live by) the things that were preached, a Christian is likely to (and will) falter in their Christian walk. The problems documented in Paul's two letters to the church of Corinth attest to the existence of short comings such as this.

The salvation being addressed by Paul is not salvation of the soul from everlasting death unto life eternal, but the salvation from physical death (or separation) through the resurrection of the body at the time of the Rapture. The resurrection, after all, is the subject matter of this whole chapter. He goes on to add, "unless you have believed in vain". Not, unless you have not truly believed, but after you have believed you somehow allow the truth to become useless to you by not having your spiritual sight on the Hope of the Gospel, the Blessed Hope.

The members of the church of Corinth were true believers, but Paul was reminding them that they must remain vigilant in their faith to be included in the resurrection of the dead. Standing in the faith of the "gospel" (good news) of verse one, not just reception of it, is the key to being included in the "all" of verse fifty-one.

The teachings of this passage are somewhat subtle, and do not stand on their own. One would be hard pressed to establish the doctrine that I propose from these few verses alone. I would not even point them out save for the fact they are support passages and they assert credibility to the teachings we find in the letters to the seven churches of Revelation.

But upon a thorough investigation of the truth contained in God's Word, I have found the Church has just as must trouble accepting the clear message of the written Word of God in a blunt form as it does the implied when it contradicts with their established beliefs. The direct message being addressed here is found in the study of the expanded passages of Revelation 2:18-22. Found with this series is the verse, of which my friend could not use.

Revelation 2:18
18 And unto the angel of the church in Thyatira write; **These things saith the Son of God,** <u>who hath his eyes like unto a flame of fire,</u> and his feet *are* like fine brass;

The first thing I would like to draw your attention to is what I call the identifier in the letters to the seven churches. Each church is given a description of the speaker that is addressing them. That description refers directly back to the picture of Christ that John saw and painted for us in chapter one of Revelation.

Here, for the church of Thyatira the identifier is "who hath his eyes like unto a flame of fire, and his feet are like fine brass". That image can be found within the vision of Jesus that John is commanded to record in chapter one. Each church is given a portion of this description of Christ effectively identifying him as the speaker. However, in the case of the church of Thyatira, Jesus identifies himself directly as the Son of God before the identifier appears in the text. This is significant. He does this to no other church.

Only to the church of Thyatira does he identify himself directly by divine title, "These things saith the Son of God" before the identifier is recorded. And curiously, only to the church of Thyatira does he speak of the Great Tribulation directly and by name.

Revelation 2:20-22

20 Notwithstanding I have a few things against thee, because thou sufferest that woman Jezebel, which calleth herself a prophetess, to teach and to seduce my servants to commit fornication, and to eat things sacrificed unto idols.

21 And I gave her space to repent of her fornication; and she repented not.

22 Behold, I will cast her into a bed, and them that commit adultery with her into **great tribulation**, except they repent of their deeds.

The phrase "Which calleth herself a prophetess", tells us that she is not called by God. She is not a former prophet that has been mislead or is somehow deluding herself. She never was. She has elevated herself by deception within the physical church, and to make matters worse, the believers inside the church have allowed it to take place. The text implies the Church has even accepted at least portions of her false doctrine and has begun to practice within those teachings.

The fornication she commits and teaches the servants of God to commit represents disobedient behavior, the result of her false teachings. She is seducing the Church with false doctrines that the Lord has condemned. The Lord has given her a chance at repentance (salvation) but she has rejected it. Her fate is entrance into the Great Tribulation Period at the appointed time, and we can assume under her current spiritual condition, eventually everlasting death (separation from God) in hell.

But notice when Jesus addresses the members of the Church. Even in their acceptance of the false doctrine, he still refers to them as his servants. And when he speaks of their sin against him it becomes adultery, not fornication as is the case with Jezebel. There is a very interesting and important point to be made about the sin of adultery. A person can only commit adultery against their spouse. Just as we, as Christians, are espoused or engaged to Christ as 2ndCorinthians 11:2 confirms, so are the members of the church of Thyatira. This point brings us to the heart of this lesson.

Verse twenty-two tells us Jesus will cast her (Jezebel) into a bed, and the members of the Church that commit adultery with her, he will cast into Great Tribulation. Jezebel, at the very least, represents the teaching of false doctrine.

This is the first pivotal teaching in these passage to be acknowledged. It matters not if the members of the church of Thyatira recognize the teachings being taught as false. It is their acceptance of them that is the crucial issue here. It is every believers responsibility to "study to show themselves approved". We should all remain close enough to God in fellowship so as to allow him to point out false teachings when they are presented to us. Just as each of us are responsible for our own ignorance, so to were the members of the church of Thyatira. (Make and be sure the truth is being preached from the pulpit of the church in which you fellowship. You will be held responsible for the acceptance of false doctrine should you allow it to occur).

The second pivotal teaching is in the last phrase. "Except they (the members of the Church) repent of their deeds". This letter is not directing them to repent of some form of unbelief but repent of disobedient behavior inside the belief and faith they have acquired. The deed or sin of adultery is undeniably the act in question. It is stated clearly and specifically by the Son of God our Bridegroom the Lord Jesus Christ himself. However, if the members of the Church repent of their deeds (the actions which constitute their sin of adultery), the opposite of the consequences of the sin will ensue.

Allow me to put this into perspective. You may deny the obvious if you wish.

If they continue to commit adultery against their Bridegroom Jesus Christ, they will be cast into the period of time identified by the Son of God himself as the Great Tribulation. If they repent of the sin of adultery they will not be cast into Great Tribulation and it is as simple as that.

Someone is not going into The Great Tribulation Period according to the Word of God. The condition for not going into the Great Tribulation Period is to repent of the sin of adultery against the speaker. The violator is espoused or engaged by Gods' biblical standards to the individual responsible for "keeping" them from that time. That individual identified himself personally by divine title as the Son Of God. There can be no question of his identity nor when "rightly divided" the consequences that result from the actions of disobedient Church members.

And allow me to point out one other sobering fact. While Jesus was informing the physical church of Thyatira of all these truths, he knew very well that the literal church of Thyatira, that physically existed in Johns' day, would not survive two thousand years into the future to see The Great Tribulation Period. To say nothing of the individual members of the church themselves. He is speaking through the obvious addressee to the entire Church existing through the whole of the Church Age, but particularly to the last generation that will witness first hand the events portrayed for us in the illustration.

Since Jesus the only begotten of the Father has identified himself directly to the Church through the example of Thyatira in these passages, the espoused Bride of Christ is the only person who would meet the qualifications to be kept from that time.

According to the scripture, there is an escape from the Great Tribulation Period (if you believe the wording of your own Bible), as Jesus himself mentioned in Luke 21:34-36. Jesus uses those words and that exact terminology himself. It is from him we get our information, not false history lessons.

Luke 21:34-36

34 And **take heed to yourselves**, lest at any time **your hearts be overcharged with** surfeiting, and drunkenness, and **cares of this life**, and *so* that day come upon you unawares.

35 For as a snare shall it come on all them that dwell on the face of the whole earth.

36 **Watch** ye therefore, and **pray always**, that ye may be **accounted worthy to escape** all these things that shall come to pass, and to stand before the Son of man.

Verse thirty-four is literally a warning that any child of God should be able to recognize. Jesus says, "take heed". He warns us through the teachings directed to (or more accurately through) his disciples, of living a life too caught up in the worries of this world. We are reminded elsewhere in the scripture, we are in the world but we are not of it. The same line of reasoning is in use here, but it is extended to include the Great Tribulation to come. For as a snare will it come upon all who dwell upon the whole earth. This implies, if we are obedient to the commandments of God concerning the warning of verse thirty-four, we will not suffer the fate of verse thirty-five.

These teachings would all but demand that the Bride of Christ not be present on the earth. The snare mentioned, which is quite obviously the Great Tribulation, will encompass any and all persons present on the earth when it arrives. The Bride would be included in that company were she present. The warning of verse thirty-four implies she is not. But, it is only implied.

Verse thirty-six is a different matter all together. Quite simply, Jesus speaks directly of an escape of the obedient from the time period he has made the subject. The Bride, of course, is not mentioned directly by name but with respect to the subject matter, and Jesus as the speaker, she is the only individual that could meet the necessary qualifications that the text itself demands. I am at a lose to understand how any one can accept these passages in any way other than that in which Jesus clearly states it.

But as the Post-Tribulationist deny anyone will escape the Great Tribulation at all, the Pre-Tribulationist ignores the condition necessary to be met in order to be included in that escape. The requirements necessary are laid out with perfect clarity by the Lord Jesus Christ our Bridegroom. The only requirement for understanding this passage is to accept the lesson as it is recorded.

Watch and pray always (continually) "that" (for the purpose of) you may be accounted worthy. These two tasks are the functions by which the inclusion is achieved. Without obedience to this command one can not be included in the escape.

Without obedience to this command you can not be accounted worthy. It is through obedience to this command one is accounted worthy. If this were not true, this passage (and others like it) would be unnecessary and simply not appear in God's Word. In which case they would be unavailable to anyone like me for "misinterpretation", of which I have been so frequently accused during the course of these studies. Now, wouldn't that be convenient.

Each and every member of the Church is a child of God and a member of his future kingdom. As a result, we are all engaged to the Father's Son, Jesus Christ. It is through chastity we remain members of the future Bride. The Bride is incased inside the Church. The entire Church is espoused or engaged to Christ, but the majority of the Church has defiled itself by not "watching" in great anticipation of the return of her Bridegroom, as well as not "praying always" by which the lines of communication are kept open and through which fellowship is maintained with the Father.

Their resulting condition (attaching themselves to the cares of this present world) is hindering their relationship with their Bridegroom during the engagement or espousal period of the marriage. Israel was divorced by God under similar conditions during her engagement "in type" to Jehovah under the Old Covenant.

If you have not accomplished these tasks, you are not in full fellowship with the Lord. You may be a believer, a child of God. You may genuinely be a Christian but, you are just playing church. You have not applied the truths of God's Word literally into your life and in turn, allowing your life to be governed by them.

What is necessary for a believer to be accounted worthy by the standards set by God to escape all these things that are coming upon the world, is to live separated from and uncontaminated by the world (in it but not of it) continuing in the patience of the Lord Jesus Christ within a rich and fulfilling spiritual life in the Lord. (Spiritual believers you say?)

Correctly put, believers that are walking daily in the Sprit of God instead of after the lusts of the world.

It is God's wish for every individual to come to a knowledge of the truth in Jesus Christ.

1ˢᵗTimothy 2:1-6

1 I exhort therefore, that, first of all, supplications, prayers, intercessions, *and* giving of thanks, be made for all men;

2 For kings, and *for* all that are in authority; that we may lead a quiet and peaceable life in all godliness and honesty.

3 For this *is* good and acceptable in the sight of God our Saviour;

4 **Who will have all men to be saved, and to come unto the knowledge of the truth.**

5 For *there is* one God, and one mediator between God and men, the man Christ Jesus;

6 Who gave himself a ransom for all, to be testified in due time.

Just as it is his desire that every member of his created mirror image come to a knowledge of the truth, so to is it his will that all believers should be "in the patience of Jesus Christ inside the hope of his gospel". This is intended to insure that each would come to the knowledge of the need to remain inside the grace of God and be not moved away from the hope of the gospel waiting for that blessed hope in Christ Jesus our Lord.

Titus 2:11-15

11 For the grace of God that bringeth salvation hath appeared to all men,

12 Teaching us that, **denying ungodliness and worldly lusts**, we should live soberly, righteously, and godly, **in this present world**;

13 **Looking for that blessed hope**, and the glorious appearing of the great God and our Saviour Jesus Christ;

14 Who gave himself for us, that he might redeem us from all iniquity, and purify unto himself a peculiar people, zealous of good works.

15 These things speak, and exhort, and rebuke with all authority. Let no man despise thee.

For as the Old Testament prophet Jeremiah once documented for us,

Jeremiah 17:7

7 Blessed *is* the man that trusteth in the LORD, and whose **"<u>hope</u>"** the LORD is.

All emphasis mine.
Grace and peace be multiplied to you all.

Chapter Six

Engaged to Christ

In order to keep my work honest, I need to confess here, that I found myself in an unexpected dilemma after I became aware of the following support passages and accompanying teachings contained in this chapter. I did not anticipate the negative reactions of the various congregations upon attempting to teach and preach the scripture as I understood them to agree with the Conditional Rapture. I will point out the subject of controversy when we arrive.

2ndCorinthians 11:1-2

1 Would to God ye could bear with me a little in *my* folly: and indeed bear with me.

2 For I am jealous over you with godly jealousy: **for I have espoused you to one husband, <u>that I may present you</u> *as* a chaste virgin to Christ.**

Make no mistake, the entire Church is "espoused", meaning engaged to Christ. In our society, that means we have more or less promised ourselves to a mate. But there is nothing in our culture that demands that we deliver on that promise. We have the option of simply changing our mind, walking away and going about our business.

But in the world of the practicing Jew, by the law of the Old Covenant, the Hebrew had no such option. If he were leading a proper life according to the Law of Moses, the espousal of a Bride to himself was part of the marriage. Although the final wedding ceremony was in the future to be completed, by Jewish law the marriage had begun with the engagement or espousal agreement referred to as the betrothal. If for any reason other than death, the completion of the marriage was not to be fulfilled, it was necessary for a writing of divorcement to be implemented between the two.

Paul is writing his second letter to the Corinthians when he puts this into perspective for us as he explains the relationship between Christ and the Church. This is actually a re-explanation in that it is information he has already covered in his first letter to the Corinthians. We will include those teachings here as well.

With this passage he asks the church of Corinth, (heavily paraphrased) "I would like very much for you to bare with me a moment in my foolish example, really, bare with me".

Paul makes this statement for the purpose of preparing his readers for an illustration that is quite impossible for him to perform himself, but that is essentially true from the perspective of the divine. Inside his example he places himself in the role of the father figure acquiring a bride for his son. The illustration however, turns to serious matters with the mention of a Godly jealousy and the identification of the recipient of this particular Bride being Christ, the Son of God.

He directs their attention to an image of the union of a man and his wife emphasizing the true state of the Church, which is within the engagement process herself to the Lord Jesus Christ. With that position comes great responsibility. A Bride must keep herself chaste and pure for her Bridegroom in order for her to remain acceptable to him as a wife. But, Paul goes on to say,

2nd Corinthians 11:3

3 But I fear, lest by any means, as the serpent beguiled Eve through his subtilty, so your minds should be corrupted from the simplicity that is in Christ.

Without going into all the possible studies that could be dealt with concerning the fall of Adam through his God given wife Eve, suffice to say they fell through disobedience to God, which is by definition all sin is.

Here, Paul makes mentions of the corruption of the mind, which is completed in the flesh. Most of the Church has allowed corruption to take hold in their Christian lives by taking part in and adopting practices exercised by the world that will guide a child of God away from fellowship with their heavenly Father. This process begins with the evil imagination of man that is akin to the corruption of the mind mentioned in this verse. It always leads to disobedience which is the root and reality of all sin. The corruption being addressed here is explained in the next verse.

2nd Corinthians 11:4

4 For if he that cometh preacheth another Jesus, whom we have not preached, or *if* ye receive another spirit, which ye have not received, or another gospel, which ye have not accepted, ye might well bear with *him*.

In short Paul warns against the acceptance of another gospel taught of Jesus that is blatantly inaccurate and therefore apocryphal. The practice is even more prevalent in our modern age with the reintroduction of teachings into our society of Jesus that were heresy in Paul's day. If such gospels are accepted, the receiver is guilty of following a watered down doctrine and thereby pursuing practices that are un-becoming of a child of God.

This example can be seen in its extreme in the church of Thyatira of the seven churches of Revelation. The subject in question was the sin of adultery, of which they were directly guilty. John records in the book of Revelation chapter two verses twenty-two that the penalty for committing such a disobedience against your Bridegroom is exclusion from escape of the Great Tribulation Period. This prohibition results in nothing short of entrance into that very time of horror.

Many scholars do and will continue to disagree that Revelation 2:22 teaches the doctrine that I propose. But, I have considered a number of other possible teachings that have presented themselves from a variety of sources. None of which stand up under a thorough examination.

There are only three passages in the scripture that mention the Great Tribulation by name, this passage being the second, and it appears twice in the book of Revelation which was written to the servants of God to make known unto us all the events which must take place in the future at the end of the Church Age.

It is found first inside the letters to the churches that contain directives on correcting disobedient behavior against the Lord. The disobedient behavior in question in the case of the church of Thyatira is the sin of adultery against the Son of God. These are the facts.

Revelation 2:22
22 Behold, **I will cast her** into a bed, **and them that commit adultery with her into great tribulation**, except they repent of their deeds.

That is what it says.

Paul's first letter to the Corinthians dealt with this same problem on a broader scale when he taught the abstinence from several obvious sins which included fornication, which is the other abomination mentioned in Revelation 2:18-22.

1ˢᵗCorinthians 6:18-20

18 Flee fornication. Every sin that a man doeth is without the body; but he that committeth fornication sinneth against his own body.

19 What? **know ye not that your body is the temple of the Holy Ghost** *which is* **in you**, which ye have of God, and **ye are not your own**?

20 For ye are bought with a price: therefore glorify God in your body, and in your spirit, which are God's.

Every sin that a person can commit has its origins in the imagination of our mind. That is where temptations are contemplated by the child of God and lead to disobedience when surrendered to. The unbeliever is in a constant state of fornication against their creator because they have not yet obeyed the Lord in surrendering themselves to him and accepting salvation.

The sin of fornication is mentioned specifically in these passages, but verse nineteen is directed to the human body which, when referring to a believer, is the temple of God because it houses the Holy Spirit of God. The act of fornication, when committed by a believer, automatically constitutes the sin of adultery.

Paul states specifically "you are not your own, you are bought with a price". In the truest sense of the marriage agreement, like it or not, we do not have control over our own body. Jesus has bought and paid for it with his own self for himself under the New Covenant (the espousal or engagement phase of the marriage agreement). When we knowingly and willfully disobey in regards to binding ourselves to this physical world, it is the most direct form of sin against our Bridegroom Jesus Christ.

Israel made the same mistake against Jehovah (Jesus in his pre-earthly form) under the Old Covenant with disastrous results. The Old Covenant was "in type" a forerunner for the New Testament Covenant we live under today. In reality the Law of the Old Covenant was the physical representation of what was to be fulfilled for us in the Spirit. Paul called it the schoolmaster by which all were to learn, so that it could bring us to Christ.

In actuality the "type" it represented was that of the future marriage through the spirit between Christ and the Church. But, Israel under the Old Covenant was found in violation to the point of being "put away" as bride to Jehovah. Simply put, Israel was divorced by Jehovah as a consequence of her repeated acts of disobedience in direct violation of her marriage agreement and contract, The Old Covenant.

Deuteronomy 24:1-4
1 When a man hath taken a wife, and married her, and it come to pass that she find no favour in his eyes, because he hath found some uncleanness in her: then let him write her a bill of divorcement, and give *it* in her hand, and send her out of his house.
2 And when she is departed out of his house, she may go and be another man's *wife*.
3 And *if* the latter husband hate her, and write her a bill of divorcement, and giveth *it* in her hand, and sendeth her out of his house; or if the latter husband die, which took her *to be* his wife;
4 Her former husband, which sent her away, may not take her again to be his wife, after that she is defiled; for that *is* abomination before the LORD: and thou shalt not cause the land to sin, which the LORD thy God giveth thee *for* an inheritance.

The Law mirrors in the physical what is true in the spiritual. It instructed man through illustration, what was to come. While it was in effect it pointed to the future, to reveal our relationship through Christ to the Father. National Israel under the Law of Moses was "in type" bride to Jehovah, but was incapable of remaining faithful to the Law given to her by God. After repeated acts of idolatry (going after other gods, which is the act of adultery under the blood covenant), Jehovah had no choice but to finally severe that particular relationship with Israel.

Jeremiah 3:1-8

1 They say, If a man put away his wife, and she go from him, and become another man's, shall he return unto her again? shall not that land be greatly polluted? but thou hast played the harlot with many lovers; yet return again to me, saith the LORD.

2 Lift up thine eyes unto the high places, and see where thou hast not been lien with. In the ways hast thou sat for them, as the Arabian in the wilderness; and thou hast polluted the land with thy whoredoms and with thy wickedness.

3 Therefore the showers have been withholden, and there hath been no latter rain; and thou hadst a whore's forehead, thou refusedst to be ashamed.

4 Wilt thou not from this time cry unto me, My father, thou *art* the guide of my youth?

5 Will he reserve *his anger* for ever? will he keep *it* to the end? Behold, thou hast spoken and done evil things as thou couldest.

6 The LORD said also unto me in the days of Josiah the king, Hast thou seen *that* which backsliding Israel hath done? she is gone up upon every high mountain and under every green tree, and there hath played the harlot.

7 And I said after she had done all these *things*, Turn thou unto me. But she returned not. And her treacherous sister Judah saw *it*.

8 And I saw, when for all the causes **whereby backsliding Israel committed adultery I had put her away, and given her a bill of divorce**; yet her treacherous sister Judah feared not, but went and played the harlot also.

The entirety of the Christian world lives inside the permissive will of God because we have failed him in not choosing the perfect will he had planned for us. Israel herself had forsaken the Lord often enough and long enough to constitute God putting her away. He had even taken her back multiple times inside his permissive will which was contrary to his perfect will for her. Many of the ordinances placed in the Law of Moses were supplement to the original Law and not God's perfect will for Israel but permitted by God due to the "hardness of the heart" of Israel. This is even confirmed by Jesus as recorded in the New Testament by the two gospel writers Matthew and Mark.

Matthew 19:3-8

3 The Pharisees also came unto him, tempting him, and saying unto him, Is it lawful for a man to put away his wife for every cause?

4 And he answered and said unto them, Have ye not read, that he which made *them* at the beginning made them male and female,

5 And said, For this cause shall a man leave father and mother, and shall cleave to his wife: and they twain shall be one flesh?

6 Wherefore they are no more twain, but one flesh. What therefore God hath joined together, let not man put asunder.

7 They say unto him, Why did Moses then command to give a writing of divorcement, and to put her away?

8 He saith unto them, Moses **because of the hardness of your hearts suffered you to put away your wives**: but from the beginning it was not so.

Mark 10:2-9

2 And the Pharisees came to him, and asked him, Is it lawful for a man to put away *his* wife? tempting him.

3 And he answered and said unto them, What did Moses command you?

4 And they said, Moses suffered to write a bill of divorcement, and to put *her* away.

5 And Jesus answered and said unto them, **For the hardness of your heart he wrote you this precept.**

6 But from the beginning of the creation God made them male and female.

7 For this cause shall a man leave his father and mother, and cleave to his wife;

8 And they twain shall be one flesh: so then they are no more twain, but one flesh.

9 What therefore God hath joined together, let not man put asunder.

A few verses into chapter seven of 1ˢᵗCorinthians Paul confirms "And they twain shall be one flesh: so then they are no more twain, but one flesh. What therefore God hath joined together, let not man put asunder" under the New Covenant, again through the image of the marriage.

1ˢᵗCorinthians 7:4

4 The wife hath not power of her own body, but the husband: and likewise also the husband hath not power of his own body, but the wife.

When this thought is placed into the context of the marriage of the Church to Christ it reminds us that our physical body, which houses the Spirit of the Lord, belongs to the Lord through that indwelling. We do not have the privilege to do with it as we wish, but are responsible for using it to his honor and glory and to remain prepared for his arrival as we do his will.

This becomes a serious consideration in some believers lives due to the actions some perform in control of their own bodies with no regard to the will of God. All believers will stand before the judgment seat of Christ and give account for everything done in the body. 2ndCorinthians 5:10. Although most believers I have come into contact with through my ministry claim to realize, believe and agree with the teachings of this passage (among many others), the Church as a whole fails to demonstrate by her actions what she claims to believe. Several modern day "old sayings" come to mind every time this is pointed out to me in scripture in relation to the example in practice I see the Church as a whole exhibiting. (Practice what you preach) which is seldom done, (Actions speak louder than words) and (The proof of the pudding is in the eating). All of these axioms illustrate the apparent lack of the Church to be faithful from the heart in obeying and serving the Lord.

This mirrors the true intent of the relationship between a man and his espoused wife as it was established and ordained by God. This can be seen by illustration in the Word of God as it educates us concerning the return of our Bridegroom with the scriptural record of the conception of Jesus himself, as Mary was espoused to and was to be taken as wife by Joseph. (And by the way, we have arrived at the point of contention I mentioned, at the beginning of this chapter.)

Luke 1:24-40

24 And after those days his wife Elisabeth conceived, and hid herself five months, saying,

25 Thus hath the Lord dealt with me in the days wherein he looked on *me*, to take away my reproach among men.

26 And in the sixth month the angel Gabriel was sent from God unto a city of Galilee, named Nazareth,

27 To a virgin espoused to a man whose name was Joseph, of the house of David; and the virgin's name *was* Mary.

28 And the angel came in unto her, and said, Hail, *thou that art* highly favoured, the Lord *is* with thee: blessed *art* thou among women.

29 And when she saw *him*, she was troubled at his saying, and cast in her mind what manner of salutation this should be.

30 And the angel said unto her, Fear not, Mary: for thou hast found favour with God.

31 And, behold, thou shalt conceive in thy womb, and bring forth a son, and shalt call his name JESUS.

32 He shall be great, and shall be called the Son of the Highest: and the Lord God shall give unto him the throne of his father David:

33 And he shall reign over the house of Jacob for ever; and of his kingdom there shall be no end.

34 Then said Mary unto the angel, How shall this be, seeing I know not a man?

35 And the angel answered and said unto her, The Holy Ghost shall come upon thee, and the power of the Highest shall overshadow thee: therefore also that holy thing which shall be born of thee shall be called the Son of God.

36 And, behold, thy cousin Elisabeth, she hath also conceived a son in her old age: and this is the sixth month with her, who was called barren.

37 For with God nothing shall be impossible.

38 And Mary said, Behold the handmaid of the Lord; be it unto me according to thy word. And the angel departed from her.

39 And Mary arose in those days, and went into the hill country with haste, into a city of Juda;

40 And entered into the house of Zacharias, and saluted Elisabeth.

Mary is visited in the sixth month of her cousin Elizabeth's pregnancy by the angel Gabriel. We know Mary is not yet pregnant herself because the scripture records that Gabriel informs her that she will conceive a son and is to name him Jesus. It is obvious that the message which is being delivered is the reason for his visit.

However, she is already espoused or engaged to Joseph at the time of Gabriel's visitation. After a brief question and answer period for the purpose of clarification, Gabriel departs and within a few days (if not the very next day) Mary leaves Nazareth to visit her cousin Elizabeth and actually remains with her for about three months. This would correspond in time to the period just prior or leading up to the birth of John.

However, when she arrives back in Nazareth she is discovered to be with child.

Matthew 1:18-19

18 Now the birth of Jesus Christ was on this wise: When as his mother Mary was espoused to Joseph, before they came together, she was found with child of the Holy Ghost.

19 Then Joseph her husband, being a just *man*, and not willing to make her a publick example, was minded to put her away privily.

Upon Mary's return to Nazareth, after three months, she is discovered to be pregnant. Joseph has not been with her and knows that the child is not his. In the physical (within the limitations of human knowledge at this time in man's history), there can be only one alternative. Early in her journey to see her cousin Elisabeth, during the time span she was absent from Nazareth, someone else had.

The scripture makes plain the fact that Joseph is a just man, implying an unswerving adherence to the Law, making him righteous at least by the standards set by the Old Covenant. But a close examination of his actions recorded by the scripture compared to the ordinances of the Law regarding the offence he thought Mary guilty of will give us an even better view of the mans character and a clearer understanding of his heart.

Deuteronomy 22:23-24

23 If a damsel *that is* a virgin be betrothed unto an husband, and a man find her in the city, and lie with her;

24 Then ye shall bring them both out unto the gate of that city, and ye shall stone them with stones that they die; the damsel, because she cried not, *being* in the city; and the man, because he hath humbled his neighbour's wife: so thou shalt put away evil from among you.

Mary had returned from Elizabeth's pregnant with a child that was not Joseph's. Her only explanation to him for her condition under the circumstances was the truth as she knew it, which was that she had been with no man. We can assume she would have narrated to him the information related to her by the angel Gabriel.

I can not even imagine what Joseph might have been thinking at this time except for the obvious. Any espoused husband in his right mind would not be able to accept such a story as the truth, even if the circumstances were ingrained into their society and lives as a future event ordained by God. According to the record detailed by the scripture, apparently Joseph could not.

From his perspective he could have thought she was simply protecting the guilty party, or attempting to minimize the punishment for the related offence by pleading ignorance or both. In any case, Joseph initially chose a course of action that would illustrate for us his true feelings for Mary. Even though she was carrying another mans child, he did not wish to expose her shame. He decided to "put her away privately" which is to say he would divorce her quietly, and some scholars suggest that it is very likely he also intended to send her away.

In addition to clandestinely divorcing her, sending her away would in fact meet the last criteria of several possible punishments laid down by the Law for several other infractions including this. It would serve to "put away the evil from among you." Mary not being evil herself per say, but the evil by deed that she was accused of by the Law, from Joseph's point of view, in relation to their engagement to one another inside of the marriage agreement.

He could not complete the marriage arrangement and take her to be his wife under such circumstances according to the Law. He would, however, decide to abide by it, albeit loosely from his own interpretational perspective, thereby avoiding any direct violations of the Law himself.

His chosen course of action would however be interrupted by a dream in which an angel informs him of the truth, which was probably already told him by Mary, which would of course confirm her story.

Matthew 1:20-25

20 But while he thought on these things, behold, the angel of the Lord appeared unto him in a dream, saying, Joseph, thou son of David, fear not to take unto thee Mary thy wife: for that which is conceived in her is of the Holy Ghost.

21 And she shall bring forth a son, and thou shalt call his name JESUS: for he shall save his people from their sins.

22 Now all this was done, that it might be fulfilled which was spoken of the Lord by the prophet, saying,

23 Behold, a virgin shall be with child, and shall bring forth a son, and they shall call his name Emmanuel, which being interpreted is, God with us.

24 Then Joseph being raised from sleep did as the angel of the Lord had bidden him, and took unto him his wife:

25 And knew her not till she had brought forth her first-born son: and he called his name JESUS.

The angel in his dream confirms the miraculous circumstances of the virginal conception of God manifested in the flesh. Which in turn completes the entire sequence of events that points to the illustration of the Conditional Rapture.

Throughout my youth during the reading and study of the scripture, a question formed in my underdeveloped understanding. In my mind it was quite a simple inquiry. Why, after the angel Gabriel informed Mary that she would conceive the child, did God not also through Gabriel inform Joseph as well or send another angel at the same time, perhaps Michael, to deliver the joyous, prophesy fulfilling news. An even better question would be, Joseph being the future head and authority over the household of he and Mary, why was he not informed first.

Had any of these alternative actions been done the problem of the questionable circumstances would have never been an issue. Joseph could have then followed all the necessary courses of action without any conflict whatsoever with Mary. There would have been no controversy, had Joseph been informed first or at least, from the very beginning.

As a youth I found it difficult to recruit anyone of any given authority to answer for me why Joseph was not informed from the very start. The answer to that question did not present itself until after the teachings of The Conditional Rapture had jumped out of the pages of the Bible directly into my face. Upon my very next reading of the passages concerning the conception of Jesus, the truth contained inside the storyline vividly presented itself. The answer to the question becomes crystal clear when the scripture is studied from the Conditional Rapture perspective.

Mary is representative of the Church as a whole. In the spiritual she was chosen by God for the purpose at hand. She was over shadowed by the spirit through which the conception of God manifested in the flesh was achieved. In this illustration she is the image of obedience, as is God's intent for every believer.

But in the physical she represents (by illustration only) disobedience. When Joseph is not informed before hand, the act of adultery is introduced into the story line of the scripture (under inspiration of the Holy Spirit, the same presence of which through the very conception was achieved) even though it has not taken place literally. From his perspective, (in the physical) it is in fact the only possibility.

Mary is with child. The child is not his. Therefore the child was conceived outside their betrothal or espousal arrangement to one another. This is a fact. And all this is recorded into the narrative of God's word which is written exclusively under inspiration of the Holy Spirit of God itself. The recording of the questionable circumstances in God's Word confirms the importance for us to understand why the recording of the problematic state of affairs are necessary to appear in the scripture in the first place. However, the reasons become obvious when studied from the perspective of the Conditional Rapture teachings.

In the physical she represents (by illustration only) the members of the Church that have coupled themselves to the world in direct violation of the will of God. The result of their actions effectively make them guilty of adultery against there Bridegroom Jesus Christ, just as Mary initially appears guilty of adultery against her bridegroom Joseph. If this condition is not corrected before the return of the Lord Jesus Christ for his Bride, the individuals guilty of the offense will face the penalty appropriate to the transgression committed according to the Word of God, the Son himself.

Revelation 2:22
22 Behold, I will cast her into a bed, and them that commit adultery with her into great tribulation, **except they repent of their deeds.**

The "her" of this passage is a woman called Jezebel. Many scholars do not believe she was a literal person teaching inside the church, but merely represents false teachings in the spirit of the Old Testament Jezebel. I will not debate that issue, but I find no evidence that she is not an actual person who has acquired responsibilities of instruction inside the church, and is referred to as Jezebel as an illustration of the instruction she is delivering.

At any rate, the <u>servants</u> of God (Revelation 2:20) contained inside the church of Thyatira are guilty of <u>adultery</u> (Revelation2:22) against the speaker, who has identified himself as the <u>Son of God</u> (Revelation 2:18). These are the facts. **That is what it says.** The Bridegroom is identified dramatically and undeniably by his own admission and description by that admission as the Son of God.

Revelation 2:18
18 And unto the angel of the church in Thyatira write; **These things saith the Son of God**, who hath his eyes like unto a flame of fire, and his feet *are* like fine brass;

We commented on this passage earlier to point out the fact Jesus identifies himself directly as the Son of God before the mention of what I call the identifier which points back to chapter one when John witnesses the vision of our glorified Lord. Each church is given a portion of that description for the purpose of identification of the speaker (as if that were necessary). But only to the church of Thyatira does he identify himself directly first by his divine title in regards to his relationship to the Father. Our point to this illustration is this.

If this is the Son of God (and it is) and he is talking to Church members (and he is) which are genuine believers (and they are) and they are guilty of adultery, (which is the very purpose of the condemnation) then there can be only one person they can be committing adultery against, just as there is only one person anyone can commit adultery against, ones own spouse. In this particular relationship, it is Jesus Christ.

The penalty for the offense in question is the denial of being included in the escape provided by God to avoid the Great Tribulation Period. That denial will result in most of the Church entering into and forced to endure the single most horrific period of mans entire history. Which was (adding insult to injury) originally intended only to test the unbelieving world.

If you have not taken the necessary steps to be included in the escape, I pray you will waist no more time in educating yourself in the need to do so.

Grace and peace be multiplied to you all.

Chapter Seven

Noah and Lot

Another major misconception held by Pre-Tribulation-alists is the belief that Lot is used inside the New Testament as an example of the Church, thereby "proving" the Pre-Tribulational Rapture. Depicting the destruction of Sodom and Gomorrah as an illustration of The Great Tribulation Period, some interpret the entire Church being removed out of the world.

This also helps to validate the view that all Christians will be included in the Rapture regardless of the circumstances in which the Lord finds them upon his return. This line of reasoning is derived from the passage in the New Testament informing us that at the time of Lot's removal he was "vexed with the filthy conversation of the wicked".

2nd Peter 2:6-8

6 And turning the cities of Sodom and Gomorrah into ashes condemned *them* with an overthrow, making *them* an ensample unto those that after should live ungodly;

7 And delivered just Lot, vexed with the filthy conversation of the wicked:

8 (For that righteous man dwelling among them, in seeing and hearing, vexed *his* righteous soul from day to day with *their* unlawful deeds;)

Some Pre-Tribulationists mistakenly believe Lot to have adopted at least the vulgar language of the wicked occupants of the city, making him "in type" or an illustration of the disobedient members of the Church. Then, since Lot was spared (one could argue by force) by way of the angels sent by God, he represents for them the proof that the entire Church will be taken in Rapture and all believers will be included.

The text itself does not bare that message. It must be interpreted as such. A closer examination of the passage will reveal some interesting truths. The most notable is found in the word "vexed". It does not suggest that Lot had adopted the language, much less the practices of the inhabitants of Sodom and Gomorrah. Quite the opposite.

In these passages the word "vexed" appears twice in the King James English. In actuality they are translated from two separate words in the Greek that share a common root but have two separate however similar meanings.

Most Christians are unaware this practice happens quite often in the scripture, which leads to many misunderstandings and outright misinterpretations when genuine study work is not done. In these cases, the definitions of the words in the original language must be understood in order to correctly comprehend precisely the context of the passage.

The "vexed" of verse seven is as follows,
* catatonia - to labor down, wear with toil, oppress or harass.

So we discover Lot was oppressed or harassed with the filthy conversation of the wicked. He had not adopted it as his own as some have misunderstood, but was in fact enduring it.

The "vexed" of verse eight is even more enlightening.
* basanizo - pain, toil, torment, to torture.

Here we are informed that Lot dwelling among them, in seeing and hearing, tormented or tortured his righteous soul from day to day with their unlawful deeds.

In reality he saw things he did not wish to see. He heard things he had no desire to hear. And day after agonizing day he tortured himself by exposing he and his family to the iniquity of disobedience in its totality. This was the sole reason for the fall of God's judgment upon them which resulted in their destruction.

Most Christians have the idea that Lot was a resident of the city of Sodom, but the scripture does not confirm this exactly. He was at the gate of Sodom when the two angels arrived to give him warning of the coming destruction, and the scripture confirms he possessed a dwelling in Sodom whether owned or leased. But this could be the case in all the cities of the plain concerning Lot.

Genesis 13:9-12
9 *Is* not the whole land before thee? separate thyself, I pray thee, from me: if *thou wilt take* the left hand, then I will go to the right; or if *thou depart* to the right hand, then I will go to the left.
10 And Lot lifted up his eyes, and beheld all the plain of Jordan, that it *was* well watered every where, before the LORD destroyed Sodom and Gomorrah, *even* as the garden of the LORD, like the land of Egypt, as thou comest unto Zoar.

11 **Then Lot chose him all the plain of Jordan**; and Lot journeyed east: and they separated themselves the one from the other.

12 Abram dwelled in the land of Canaan, and **Lot dwelled in the cities of the plain, and pitched** *his* **tent toward Sodom.**

Lot was the owner of many flocks (sheep) and herds (goats and cattle) as well as most probably donkeys, camels, and some theorize even horses. This great mass would not have been easy to sustain near or much less in a city, but was maintained in the great rich plain of Jordan, between the cities. He undoubtedly housed his workers as Bedouins in tents as they were in care of his livestock, and he probably journeyed from city to city involved in the business of trade, Sodom being made his "central office". He probably acquired living quarters in several, if not all the cities of the plain, since the scripture confirms for us it was in them that he himself dwelled.

But, for whatever reason he chose to live among the wicked inhabitants until the intervention by God's divine hand, the scripture never suggests anything in his character but righteousness. In point of fact, the scripture confirms that very detail in verse eight.

In regards to this information it could be suggested that his presence in Sodom, besides the transaction of trade, was for the purpose of what we would call missionary work or even evangelism today. The Old and New Testaments agree with each other in teaching the cities of Sodom and Gomorrah were quite familiar with Lot's true character. When all of the men of the city demanded he send his guests out to them, "that we may know them" Lot's response was, "do not this wickedness". I believe this reply to be an example of his normal behavior since there is no indication in the scripture of any surprise on behalf of the men of the city, and quite frankly could be interpreted as a testimony to the nature of the man.

At best, Lot could be identified with Israel in that a remnant of national Israel will be protected by God toward the end of the Great Tribulation Period and saved out of it before destruction of the evil forces of the world. Lot does make a perfect example of the remnant of Israel that, we understand from prophesy, God holds in reserve through election under grace. He even makes mention of Sodom and Gomorrah in the process, thereby linking them to the mention of the remnant in prophesy.

Isaiah 1:9

9 Except the LORD of hosts had left unto us **a very small remnant**, we should have been as **Sodom**, *and* we should have been like unto **Gomorrah**.

Isaiah 10:20-22

20 And it shall come to pass in that day, *that* the **remnant of Israel**, and such as are escaped of the house of Jacob, shall no more again stay upon him that smote them; but shall stay upon the LORD, the Holy One of Israel, in truth.

21 The remnant shall return, *even* the remnant of Jacob, unto the mighty God.

22 For though thy people Israel be as the sand of the sea, *yet* **a remnant of them shall return**: the consumption decreed shall overflow with righteousness.

Romans 9:27-29

27 Esaias also crieth concerning Israel, Though the number of the children of Israel be as the sand of the sea, **a remnant shall be saved**:

28 For he will finish the work, and cut *it* short in righteousness: because a short work will the Lord make upon the earth.

29 And as Esaias said before, Except the Lord of Sabaoth had left us a seed, we had been as **Sodoma**, and been made like unto **Gomorrha**.

Romans 11:1-5

1 I say then, Hath God cast away his people? God forbid. For I also am an Israelite, of the seed of Abraham, *of* the tribe of Benjamin.
2 God hath not cast away his people <u>which he foreknew</u>. Wot ye not what the scripture saith of Elias? how he maketh intercession to God against Israel, saying,
3 Lord, they have killed thy prophets, and digged down thine altars; and I am left alone, and they seek my life.
4 But what saith the answer of God unto him? I have reserved to myself seven thousand men, who have not bowed the knee to *the image of* Baal.
5 Even so then at this present time also **there is a remnant according to the election of grace**.

Yes, Lot could be identified with Israel in that a remnant of national Israel will be protected by God toward the end of the Great Tribulation Period and saved out of it before destruction of the evil forces of the world. He does make a perfect example of the remnant of Israel that God informs us through prophesy he holds in reserve through election under the grace of the New Covenant.

There are in fact, several support passages in the Old Testament that speak directly of the end times (or latter days) that promise Israel it will not be destroyed completely or as a nation during this period of world history. All that is necessary is for her to remember God's promises (which during the Great Tribulation will require the recognition by Israel of her true Messiah) seek him out and be obedient to his will.

Deuteronomy 4:29-31

29 But if from thence thou shalt seek the LORD thy
God, thou shalt find *him*, if thou seek him with all
thy heart and with all thy soul.

30 When thou art in tribulation, and all these things are
come upon thee, *even* **in the latter days**, if thou turn
to the LORD thy God, and shalt be obedient unto his
voice;

31 (For the LORD thy God *is* a merciful God;) <u>he will
not forsake thee, neither destroy thee, nor forget the
covenant of thy fathers which he sware unto them</u>.

But Lot is never implicated by the scripture as an
example "in type" of the Church, (or from my perspective,
the Bride) to illustrate a picture of the Rapture. There will
be no destruction at the time of the Rapture as was the case
during the removal of Lot and his family from Sodom.

This depiction does however undeniably demonstrate all
the characteristics of the Glorious Appearing and agrees with
the original account of the story line recorded in Genesis
right down to the sending of angels to collect the righteous at
the introduction of that account. At the time of the Glorious
Appearing, Jesus will send his angels to gather his elect just
as he sent his angels to gather Lot and his family.

Matthew 24:31

31 **And he shall send his angels** with a great sound of
a trumpet, and **they shall gather together his elect**
from the four winds, from one end of heaven to the
other.

"From the four winds" is a reference to the four points of
the compass designating for us a description of a horizontal
gathering of individuals from every corner of the earth, to
the land of their fathers, the nation of Israel. According to

the scripture this assemblage is undeniably accomplished by the sending of God's angels to finalize the gathering of his elect by the "he" of this verse. The individual in question is universally accepted to be the Lord Jesus who is speaking of himself in his own future. The event we call the Rapture, when depicted by God in his Word, is narrated to us in quite a different manner.

1stThessalonians 4:16-18

16 For the Lord himself shall descend from heaven with a shout, with the voice of the archangel, and with the trump of God: and the dead in Christ shall rise first:

17 Then we which are alive *and* remain shall be **caught up together with them in the clouds, to meet the Lord in the air**: and so shall we ever be with the Lord.

18 Wherefore comfort one another with these words.

This gathering will be a vertical event in which Jesus will personally retrieve the righteous himself to himself for himself. There will be no angels doing the collecting of them for him because it will be his Bride he gathers personally for the purpose of carrying her back to the fathers house from whence he had come, in which he had been preparing a place for her. No one can make claim to the Bride but the Bridegroom himself.

The entire misinterpretation in question concerning Lot stems from him being included in another illustration of the New Testament where Noah also appears. Noah is actually referred to "in type" twice in what appears to be, at first glance, the same teaching. Both references are dealing with the end of days, or the last days but they are totally separate in there depictions, as well as the lessons they teach.

Luke 17:27-30

27 They did eat, they drank, they married wives, they were given in marriage, until the day that Noe entered into the ark, and the flood came, and destroyed them all.

28 Likewise also as it was in the days of Lot; they did eat, they drank, they bought, they sold, they planted, they builded;

29 But the same day that Lot went out of Sodom it rained fire and brimstone from heaven, and destroyed *them* all.

30 Even thus shall it be in the day when the Son of man is revealed.

In verse twenty-seven, Noah and his family entered into the ark, then the flood came and destroyed "them" all. Noah and his family were of course spared, therefore it is obvious that it was the rest of mankind that was destroyed as also recorded for us in the Genesis account. Forgive me for having to repeat the obvious but the Rapture will not result in a destruction in any physical form. It will however serve to effectively remove the Bride of Christ from this physical world and initiate the seven year Great Tribulation Period.

There will be many Christians which will lose their lives during the first half of the Great Tribulation, and many members of the state of Israel that will suffer the same fate during the second half, but the world as a whole will continue to exist after the Rapture of the Bride of Christ. It will remain and function, albeit under the influence of the antichrist, throughout the remaining seven years of that particular portion of its history.

Verses twenty-eight and twenty-nine then return our attention to Lot by way of the same illustration. He and his family were spared from destruction by being removed from the city. But the most interesting piece of information in this passage is found in verse thirty. "Revealed" for us in this verse (forgive the pun) is the piece of the puzzle necessary for understanding the context of the passage.

Luke 17:30
30 Even thus shall it be in the day when the **Son of man is <u>revealed</u>**.

Jesus the speaker says of himself that the example of Noah and Lot that he has just given, is an illustration of what is going to take place at the time "the Son of man is **revealed**." The revelation or revealing of Jesus Christ in the physical to the world will not take place until the Glorious Appearing at the end of the Great Tribulation Period. This is not an example or "illustration in type" of the Rapture which will be the second time he will appear (Hebrews 9:28), but a future record of the destruction of evil after or at the end of the Great Tribulation Period. This is the documentation of the third appearance and final return of our Lord and Savior Jesus Christ.

The controversy that has arisen in Christendom concerning these teachings includes the confusion of these passages with others that are similar, but illustrate an entirely different lesson. In our next passage Jesus again makes reference to his return in which the example of Noah is used, but within which he effectively excludes the mention of Lot. In the following instance only Noah and his family are mentioned and upon close examination it bares no resemblance in its content to the previous passages other than both are dealing with the subject of "a" (not "the") coming of the Lord.

Matthew 24:36-39
36 But of that day and hour knoweth no *man*, no, not the angels of heaven, but my Father only.

37 But as the days of Noe *were*, so shall also the coming of the Son of man be.

38 For as in the days that were before the flood they were eating and drinking, marrying and giving in marriage, until the day that Noe entered into the ark,

39 **And knew not until the flood came, and took them all away**; so shall also the coming of the Son of man be.

For as the days of Noah were, so will be the coming of the Son of man. Before the flood they were eating and drinking and giving in marriage until the day that Noah and his family entered into the ark. They were not aware of the time of the floods onset until the moment it arrived and took them all away. The scripture then repeats itself by reinstating "So shall also the coming of the Son of man be". This event described by the Lord and recorded by Matthew is seemingly familiar to us because it is similar in character and comparable in plot to the example given to us by Luke.

But unlike the record of Luke, this passage fails to indicate any type of destruction, nor does it make any allusion to the Lord being revealed.

The individuals which are carried away are Noah and his family, and in truth no mention of the world in general or the wicked in particular are made. The persons who were eating and drinking and giving in marriage were Noah and his family, and is a description of the events taking place in the normal course of their daily lives.

The day that is being referred to in verse thirty-six is said to be unknown to all but the Father alone. Nowhere in scripture is the Glorious Appearing described in such a fashion. The revealing of Jesus Christ in power and great glory will be preceded by several events that the scripture informs us of in great detail. They are documented in the gospel of Matthew, Mark and Luke, as well as the book of Revelation itself.

This reference is also reminiscent of the father of an espoused son being the only individual privy to the knowledge of when he will send his son and the accompanying wedding party to acquire his Bride. Upon his reception of her he will bring her back to his fathers house where he has prepared a place for them to begin their life together, commencing with the final phase of the engagement process, the marriage ceremony itself. Throughout the scripture, the unknown time factor connected to the return of the Lord points continually to two realities for the children of God.

The first is the unidentified and abrupt timing of the event itself. The exact moment is not only unrevealed by scripture, but is confirmed by the Word of God to be purposefully concealed to anyone other than the Father himself. This is confirmation of the existence of the event in human history, and acts as an identifier for us within the scripture.

The second, as just mentioned, is that the Glorious Appearing is preceded by a number of events that are described in such detail as to positively identify it by anyone who is not in conclusive denial of those events and their significance. This distinction alone prohibits the possibility of its arrival to be classified as anything but conspicuous. All passages contained in the scripture making reference to the Glorious Appearing unanimously depict the event as global, thereby encompassing and involving the entirety of mankind and will be the single most publicly viewed event ever witnessed by man.

By contrast, the escape mentioned by Jesus will take place completely unobserved by the physical world, and will occur unannounced even to the Bride herself. There is a very limited amount of evidence in the scripture that could suggest her being aware of its general approach due to the signs of the times indicative of its proximity. Such information would mirror Noah and his family waiting inside the ark for the onset of the flood, knowing beyond any shadow of any doubt it's advent was imminent per God's instruction, but Noah and his family were completely unaware of the actual moment of its onslaught until the instant it arrived. But the information regarding this possibility is minimal and sketchy, the bulk of which is derived by interpretation into the limited passages suggesting its possibility.

Also, she would be required by that evidence to be extremely vigilant and exceptionally knowledgeable in the area of prophesy and the documentation of each and all of those records.

Based on my experience, even the Bride of Christ of the modern Church does not posses the advanced level of knowledge mandatory in this area for such a task. However, the scripture confirms that no one, including The Bride, will be anything but oblivious to the precise moment of its arrival, just as exampled by the Noah illustration described by Matthew.

On this subject, the scripture gives several interesting details of the circumstances surrounding the moment we are to be taken by the Lord, and how it will be observed by our existing society. There is a great misconception on the part of the Church as a whole concerning these passages, and even Pre-Tribulationists who are correct on the timing of the Rapture have misinterpreted the passages which gives description of the actual moment we are to be taken.

These passages are very familiar to the average Christian but they contain some very informative insights if one is willing to delve into their depths.

Matthew 24:39-44

39 And knew not until the flood came, and took them all away; so shall also the coming of the Son of man be.

The manner in which Jehovah saved Noah and his family, is stated to be the same manner in which he will arrive at the time of his second appearance (Hebrews 9:28) and retrieve his Bride. Noah and his family knew nothing of their carrying away until the moment it took place. In the same fashion concerning the retrieval of the members of the Church,

> 40 Then shall two be in the field; the one shall be taken, and the other left.
> 41 Two *women shall be* grinding at the mill; the one shall be taken, and the other left.

Then the very next verse gives a clear warning from the speaker (Jesus) to the listener (in the physical the disciples, in the spiritual the Church) to be ever watchful for the coming of our Lord, for we do not know precisely at what moment he will arrive. We do not want to be caught off guard.

> 42 Watch therefore: for ye know not what hour your Lord doth come.

This is a very critical verse and teaching. Jesus is not informing the world of his reappearance into the physical. He clearly states, "Watch, for you do not know when **your** Lord is to come. Jesus is not Lord to the world or the lost, but to all the members of the Church. This seemingly short passage is saturated with the implication that it is necessary for the servants of the Lord to be watchful in order to be included in the event of being taken at the time of the coming of the Lord. In fact, no mention of the world or the lost are referred to in any discernable manner. Any teachings that one would put forth to such an end would first have to be interpreted into the passage by way of a predetermined assumption, since the passage fails to make mention of them itself. He goes on to finalize his teachings with,

43 But know this, that if the goodman of the house had known in what watch the thief would come, he would have watched, and would not have suffered his house to be broken up.

44 **Therefore be "ye" also ready**: for in such an hour as ye think not the Son of man cometh.

Once again, before further expounding upon the premise in continuing verses, he reemphasizes the need for his listeners (readers, believers) to be watchful, insinuating the need to do so in order to be included in what is to follow the appearance of the Lord. The event to follow is of course the gathering of the one (who was watchful) and the leaving behind of the other (which was not).

Matthew 24:46

46 Blessed *is* that **servant**, whom his lord when he cometh shall find so doing.

This verse also defines the individual which is the subject and illustration. Jesus himself calls this individual a servant. No mention of the lost, or members of the unbelieving world are referenced. Any teachings regarding this doctrine are interpreted out of the passage by the reader through a preconceived notion of their own. It is not mentioned or taught by the scripture itself. The same is true of the next passage in similar as well as reverse fashion.

Luke 17:34-36

34 I tell you, in that night there shall be two *men* in one bed; the one shall be taken, and the other shall be left.

35 Two *women* shall be grinding together; the one shall be taken, and the other left.

36 Two *men* shall be in the field; the one shall be taken, and the other left.

For one short Sunday afternoon, these passages were a point of contention in relation to the teachings of the Conditional Rapture. I had taught that Sunday morning along the lines of these lessons that had been included in our Adult Sunday school class. I had brought with me some of my own notes and had included them with our lesson.

Upon quoting Luke 17:34-36, one of the class members (which happened to be a skeptic to the teachings of the Conditional Rapture) noticed and mentioned their position in the scripture, which I have always noted myself when such appeared to be relevant (a study technique they had learn directly from me). I am an honest teacher. If I am wrong I wish to be corrected. My only prayer is to be in agreement with the scripture.

The student correctly pointed out that these verses appear immediately following the aforementioned example of Lot,

Luke 17:29

29 But the same day that Lot went out of Sodom it rained fire and brimstone from heaven, and **destroyed *them all***.

An obvious reference to Lot in example of Israel being saved from destruction before the end of the Great Tribulation Period, with the closing statement,

Luke 17:30

30 Even thus shall it be in the day when the **Son of man is revealed**.

Just as obviously a direct mention of Jesus' Glorious appearing to the entire world at the end of the Great Tribulation. The scripture goes on to say,

Luke 17:31-33
31 In that day, he which shall be upon the housetop, and his stuff in the house, let him not come down to take it away: and he that is in the field, let him likewise not return back.
32 Remember Lot's wife.
33 Whosoever shall seek to save his life shall lose it; and whosoever shall lose his life shall preserve it.

This is a clear description of the Great Tribulation Period (in that day, the day of the Lord) and the events which will involve Israel immediately after she recognizes the antichrist for who he truly is. The day of the Lord is initiated by the Rapture or at least commences upon its completion, at least by Pre-Tribulational teachings and the Conditional Rapture Theory. The location of our verses describing one taken and the other left, are the very next subject mentioned. This seems out of place in relation to both these views.

It is true many of the events described by the scripture are not in chronological order (out of sequence). But, these particular verses placed in this particular position in the scripture, if location is significant in this case, posed a problem in regards to the Rapture being a Pre-Tribulational event, which would include the teachings of Conditional Rapture. Not to mention "my" teachings regarding Lot not being an example of the Church in relation to the destruction of Sodom and Gomorrah. Although on the surface at first glance this appears to be the case, this disagrees with other clear passages to the contrary.

I was concerned to say the least, and a serious study of the material and a prayer session was very much in order.

I spent that afternoon between services engulfed in both. Prayer and study. I have learned since then that events such as this can be provoked by the Almighty for the sole purpose of God wishing us to spend time occupied in just this past time. Prayer and study. He killed at least three birds with that one stone that day. We spent the afternoon together, he taught me something, I taught that something to my students.

After God revealed the critical phrase for understanding the context of these passages, I also realized I was studying in the book of Luke. He regularly places material and lessons in reverse order of their occurrence, working back to front, or makes mention of an event toward the end of a sequence when the event actually occurs inside the progression. It is very much his style of writing. It would not have intrigued me except for the fact of the subject matter, my passion associated with the Rapture and the teachings of conditions attached to it.

That is very much the case here. It can be easily seen with a thorough reread of the passages that Luke is writing from the end of the story line back to the beginning. However, that is not how the Lord exposed the lesson.

Luke 17:28-33

28 Likewise also as it was in the days of Lot; they did eat, they drank, they bought, they sold, they planted, they builded;

29 But the same day that Lot went out of Sodom it rained fire and brimstone from heaven, and **destroyed** *them* **all**.

30 Even thus shall it be in the day when the **Son of man is revealed**.

31 **In that day**, he which shall be upon the housetop, and his stuff in the house, let him not come down to take it away: and he that is in the field, let him likewise not return back.

32 Remember Lot's wife.

33 Whosoever shall seek to save his life shall lose it;
and whosoever shall lose his life shall preserve it.

This is very much a description of the Great Tribulation
Period. Lot is an illustration of Israel during that time and
Israel per Lot's example will be saved as a nation out of it
when she turns back to its true Messiah. Destruction of the
wicked will take place last which is mentioned first, after
which in the narrative Jesus makes mention of him revealing
himself to the world, which will actually precede the destruction in real time events. "In that day" is the reference to the
entire day of the Lord which began seven years earlier after
the Rapture of the Bride of Christ.

Luke then points to that event in the very next verses.

Luke 17:34-36

34 I tell you, **in that night** there shall be two *men* in
one bed; the one shall be taken, and the other shall
be left.

35 Two *women* shall be grinding together; the one shall
be taken, and the other left.

36 Two *men* shall be in the field; the one shall be taken,
and the other left.

To the average modern day American Christian incased
in the society in which we have been raised the phrase "in
that night" can be misleading. We think of a day beginning
with the rising of the sun or "as the day dawns". This is the
time our activities begin for the majority of our population,
even though we know the actual day inside its twenty-four
hour time frame began with the stroke of midnight. This is
not the case with the Jewish society of Jesus' day.

The arrival of the next day began with the setting of the
sun, and a day spanned from sun set to sun set. This is the

reason Jesus and the thieves were taken down from their crosses hurriedly before the setting of the sun because the next day was the Sabbath, being the Sabbath of the Passover, making that particular Sabbath an "high day". Their bodies could not remain on the cross at that time.

John 19:31

31 The Jews therefore, because it was the preparation, that the bodies should not remain upon the cross on the sabbath day, (for that sabbath day was an high day,) besought Pilate that their legs might be broken, and *that* they might be taken away.

The Jewish day beginning at sun set, or in the evening stems all the way back to the creation by Jehovah of the physical itself. The scripture records that upon the creation of the physical, the evening preceded the morning as per God's command.

Genesis 1:5

5 And God called the light Day, and the darkness he called Night. **And the evening and the morning were the first day**.

Genesis 1:8

8 And God called the firmament Heaven. And the **evening and the morning** were the second day.

Genesis 1:12-13

12 And the earth brought forth grass, *and* herb yielding seed after his kind, and the tree yielding fruit, whose seed *was* in itself, after his kind: and God saw that *it was* good.

13 And the **evening and the morning** were the third day.

Genesis 1:18-19

18 And to rule over the day and over the night, and to divide the light from the darkness: and God saw that *it was* good.

19 And the **evening and the morning** were the fourth day.

Genesis 1:22-23

22 And God blessed them, saying, Be fruitful, and multiply, and fill the waters in the seas, and let fowl multiply in the earth.

23 And the **evening and the morning** were the fifth day.

Genesis 1:31

31 And God saw every thing that he had made, and, behold, *it was* very good. And the **evening and the morning** were the sixth day.

(I know it was unnecessary for me to list each one of these but I couldn't help it).

Therefore, we have the record of Luke informing us in the following passage.

Luke 17:34

34 I tell you, **in that night** there shall be two *men* in one bed; the one shall be taken, and the other shall be left.

"In that night" is mentioned last in the sequence of events by Luke who has listed those events in reverse order. That would place our subject of this particular "night" first in the sequence of events. This would situate the occurrence of the one taken and the other left before all events mentioned and squarely before The Great Tribulation Period. When positioned into its rightful place inside its correct context in regards to "the day of the Lord" or the Great Tribulation Period, "in that night" would refer to a prior event before the activities of the Great Tribulation itself in teaching and in its location, through position and description. And in truth Jesus himself gives us a glimpse of this concept in one passage when teaching on his return.

Mark 13:35-37

35 Watch ye therefore: for ye know not when the master of the house cometh, at **even**, or at **midnight**, or **at the cockcrowing**, or **in the morning**:

36 Lest coming suddenly he find you sleeping.

37 And what I say unto you I say unto all, Watch.

Jesus is actually letting us know when the carrying away of the Bride is going to occur in relation to the Great Tribulation Period. Nowhere in scripture are we given dates or even specific event markers that would enable us to determine the exact time the "caught up" event will take place, but here we are given enough information, in accompaniment with support passages to know it will occur before "the day" of the Great Tribulation.

Each one of the references Jesus lists are hours of darkness. The time of darkness before "the light of day". Even the time mentioned of "in the morning" is before the rising of the sun as can be seen in the gospels in the record of the morning of the resurrection which is also absolutely appropriate due to the subject matter.

John 20:1

1 The first *day* of the week cometh Mary Magdalene early, **when it was yet dark**, unto the sepulchre, and seeth the stone taken away from the sepulchre.

Luke 24:1

1 Now upon the **first** *day* **of the week, very early in the morning**, they came unto the sepulchre, bringing the spices which they had prepared, and certain *others* with them.

Mark 16:2

2 And **very early in the morning the first** *day* **of the week**, they came unto the sepulchre **at the rising of the sun.**

Matthew 28:1

1 In the end of the sabbath, as it **began to dawn toward the first** *day* **of the week,** came Mary Magdalene and the other Mary to see the sepulchre.

All of these references to that morning (and all Jewish mornings concerning the day) would confirm, very early in the morning the first day of the week, while it was yet dark at the rising of the sun just as it began to dawn "in" that day, Mary Magdalene came with the other women to the sepulcher.

Every piece of information we can glean from the scripture supports (where it does not out right confirm) the Rapture of the Bride of Christ being a Pre-Tribulational event, and that event having connected to it conditions of inclusion.

Therefore, we all need to remain watchful for we do not know when the master of the house is going to arrive, at **even**, or at **midnight**, or **at the cockcrowing**, or **in the morning**. Otherwise upon his abrupt and unexpected arrival he finds us asleep and unprepared. And what he has said through his disciples he intends to be received by us all, Watch.

Grace and peace be multiplied to you all.

Chapter Eight

Worthy ?

The next objection held by opponents to the Conditional Rapture is the argument concerning the manner of separation in which we anticipate the Rapture to take place. In their judgment it is invalid on the basis that it divides the body of Christ, the Church. "God would not do that," I have frequently been told.

My first response is to point out, that is an opinion. What's more, it is an opinion based largely on a predetermined assumption and not on the teachings of God's Word. The scripture itself will illustrate by example this assumption to be false.

The scriptures primary purpose is to instruct. In that capacity it informs God's mirror image (man) on the subject of his creation as a whole. In addition it gives us insight as to our place inside that creation. The advocate of such a position is suggesting a knowledge of the mind of God, claiming to know what he would and would not do from the perspective of the divine.

Man has no capabilities of divinity outside the influence of the Holy Spirit of God. Only through the Holy Ghost can man acquire any knowledge of the magnificence of the plan of God which he merely spoke into existence. God reveals to us bit's and pieces of his plan through his Word that is alive with the very presence of him, the Holy Spirit.

I prefer to rely on the Spirit of God through the text that was given to us by him for the express purpose of explaining those very bits and pieces to us as only God can. We are the creation of Jehovah (God's own hand) in the very image of Elohiym (in the plural, three persons) and he alone as creator knows the limitations of our comprehension.

My second line of defense is to simply point out what has always been obvious to me, that the Church is already divided at the present time and has been so for almost two thousand years. Every saint of God who no longer physically lives, is separated from the living by physical death. That is, in fact, what death is. Separation.

For example, the scripture tells us we, as believers, are dead to sin. (The "singular" sin of unbelief.) A Christian can not be guilty of unbelief. A believer is by definition a believer. He or she simply is and can be nothing else. In order for a believer to return to their former state of unbelief it would be necessary for them to reject what they "know" to be the truth taught by the Word of God through the Holy Spirit.

1stJohn 5:13

13 These things have I written unto you that **believe** on the name of the Son of God; **that ye may know** that ye have eternal life, and that ye may believe on the name of the Son of God.

It is impossible for an individual to return to a former state of unbelief in anything they now know to be the absolute truth. Once you are privy to a fact that has proven itself to be a reality, you have been made aware of that particular truth. It can no longer be anything to you but the truth. This is especially correct in regards to the lessons taught to us by the scripture.

Furthermore, the entity we refer to as the Bride, is not married to Christ at present, but merely espoused to be his wife. She is, in fact, only engaged to Christ. It is crucial that every believer has an understanding of this concept at least from the point of view of Jewish culture and Hebrew tradition. It has begun, as we can clearly see by the example of Mary and Joseph as recorded for us in the gospels, Mary and Joseph being espoused to one another. The same is true of the Bride of Christ in that the marriage ceremony to the Bridegroom has not yet been completed.

In the physical, which is the created mirror image of the spiritual by the hand of Jehovah himself, she must be accounted worthy at the time the Bridegroom comes to receive her as his Bride. Only after this declaration can she be taken back to the fathers house to ultimately take her place as the lambs wife.

The subject of worthiness is an irrelevant point to the die hard mainstream Pre-Tribulationist, since being saved and being worthy holds the same meaning for them. The scripture teaches emphatically that salvation is not the equivalent to being found worthy. We will see from this study, that they are not the same thing.

This point of interest can be found repeatedly throughout the entirety of the New Testament, especially inside John's recording of the letters to the seven churches of Revelation which are corrective in nature. In the same fashion, much of the material contained inside the letters of Paul takes the form of constructive criticism for the purpose of pointing out necessary modifications in the behavior of the churches and individuals he addresses in the text of those documents.

In the book of Revelation, recorded by John for example, Jesus is speaking directly to the seven churches primarily of their shortcomings. Even in his mention of acts that are in illustration of faithfulness, he includes directives that point down a path of progress which implies the existence of imperfections in the manner a portion of their service to the Lord is being performed.

Faithfulness is commended along with instructions for improvement for six of the seven churches. Shortcomings are condemned and the associated penalties for disobedience are described for the guilty who refuse to repent and correct their rebellious attitudes and actions.

What the modern Church does not want to understand or admit is that the seven churches of Revelation collectively represent the body of Christ as a whole throughout its complete history. That history will come to its conclusion with the last generation at the completion of the Church Age.

All of the information found in the second and third chapters of Revelation can be found inside the Church today. In fact, every single believer can find his or her own personnel condition of fellowship (or the lack thereof) between espoused Bride and Bridegroom inside the combined examples of the seven churches.

After all, as the Word of God has already confirmed, the book of Revelation itself was written,

Revelation 1:1

1. The Revelation of Jesus Christ, which God gave unto him, **to shew unto his servants** **things which must shortly come to pass**; and he sent and signified *it* by his angel unto his servant John:

The Revelation of Jesus Christ was written to the servants of God. We as his servants, are expected to communicate and emphasize that message to everyone we come into contact with. That would naturally include a lost and dying world that God is calling to repentance, yearning for it to come to a knowledge of salvation through Jesus Christ.

But the book of Revelation was written to God's servants specifically, not to the world. It was also not written to the unbelievers who were ignorantly attending services in the local churches and associated with those memberships solely through their attendance. Once that concept is understood and accepted, the lessons contained inside the book of Revelation can be seen clearly in a blinding new light.

For Example:

Revelation 3:4
4 Thou hast a **few names** even in Sardis which **have not defiled their garments**; and they shall walk with me in white: **for they are worthy**.

I have always been struck in loving awe of God by their ability to teach a lesson through the omission of information. It will never cease to amaze me. This passage is a direct reference to the relationship between Christ and his Bride. In this instance it is recorded that there were a few of the servants of God in the church of Sardis who had not defiled their garments. The mention of the "few" who had not defiled their garments establishes the presence of the "many" members of the Church who had. The wedding garment of the espoused Bride of Christ is the subject.

Also, it should be obvious to the modern Christian that any and all members of the congregation of the church of Sardis being addressed by Christ are believers for the simple fact that unbelievers do not have garments to defile.

There are several passages in the scripture that make mention of performing actions on the behalf of the kingdom of God for the purpose of making ourselves worthy of that kingdom. These teachings are not discussing salvation. Salvation is a gift provided to us by the Lord that he has purchased himself with his own blood. It is paid for and the only requirement for reception of that gift is the acceptance of it. Surrender and submission to God is the only prerequisite.

Another example can be found in Paul's second letter to the Thessalonians. In this case he informs them he thanks God continually for their growth in the faith, (they were maturing as they should) and their love shown one for another was also increasing in the Lord toward all the brethren.

2ⁿᵈThessalonians 1:1-4

1 Paul, and Silvanus, and Timotheus, unto the church of the Thessalonians in God our Father and the Lord Jesus Christ:

2 Grace unto you, and peace, from God our Father and the Lord Jesus Christ.

3 We are bound to thank God always for you, brethren, as it is meet, because that your faith groweth exceedingly, and the charity of every one of you all toward each other aboundeth;

4 So that we ourselves glory in you in the churches of God for your patience and faith in all your persecutions and tribulations that ye endure:

He commends them on their actions of faith and love which are a reflection on Paul and his party as their efforts through evangelism was God's tool of conversion for the church of Thessalonica. This church was literally a compliment to Paul and his companions work and ministry. But in verse four Paul mentions he glories (rejoices) in all the churches of God, which would include the church of Thessalonica, concerning their patience and faith in all their persecutions and tribulations which they endure.

2ndThessalonians 1:4-5

4 So that we ourselves glory in you in the churches of God for your **patience and faith** in all your **persecutions and tribulations that ye endure**:

5 *Which is* **a manifest token** of the righteous judgment of God, **that ye may be counted worthy of the kingdom of God**, for which ye also suffer:

But the reader needs to notice that he adds in verse five that it is by these means they are accounted worthy of the kingdom of God. **That is what it says**. Not by your works are you saved but by your works are you accounted worthy. The "works" addressed here by Paul are their patience on, and faith in the Lord while enduring the persecutions and tribulations in this physical world. This is a declaration and description of the actions in which the entire Church should be occupied as a whole.

In essence one is saved through their belief in and surrender to the Lord Jesus Christ as their savior. Through the baptism of the Holy Ghost we are adopted into the family of God and through the blood of Jesus Christ we become blood kin to the Creator. But we can only be accounted worthy concerning our place inside the kingdom of God through our patience and faith. Paul is again readdressing an earlier teaching from his first letter to the church of Thessalonica.

1stThessalonians 1:2-3

2 We give thanks to God always for you all, making mention of you in our prayers;

3 Remembering without ceasing, your work of faith, and labour of love, and patience of hope in our Lord Jesus Christ, in the sight of God and our Father;

Faith is their belief and worship, which is correct and includes their doctrine on which it is built, that is sound.

As believers their love is true and is directed properly to all those around them.

Then Paul makes mention of one of two factors (prayer being the second) that together constitute the most important aspect of a Christians life. "Patience of hope in our Lord Jesus Christ". Hope in our Lord Jesus Christ is referring to none other than the "Blessed Hope" of Titus 2:13.

Titus 2:11-14

11 For the grace of God that bringeth salvation hath appeared to all men,

12 Teaching us that, denying ungodliness and worldly lusts, we should live soberly, righteously, and godly, in this present world;

13 **Looking for that blessed hope**, and the glorious appearing of the great God and our Saviour Jesus Christ;

14 Who gave himself for us, that he might redeem us from all iniquity, and purify unto himself a peculiar people, zealous of good works.

The "hope" of the gospel on our part is the act of looking forward to, in joyous anticipation of, the second appearance of our Lord and Savior Jesus Christ as Bridegroom returning to take possession of his beloved. Literally the second time he will appear (Hebrews 9:28), the most important of which will include our change from mortal to immortality for those of us who are alive at the time of its occurrence.

The "Blessed Hope" on Jesus' part is the event itself in which he will take possession of his Bride after her transformation to immortality and translate her back to the Father's house. This event is the literal fulfillment of the promise he made to his Bride through his disciples that is documented for us by the apostle John in the fourteenth chapter of his record of the gospel.

John 14:1-3

1 Let not your heart be troubled: ye believe in God, believe also in me.

2 In my Father's house are many mansions: if *it were* not *so*, I would have told you. I go to prepare a place for you.

3 And if I go and prepare a place for you, **I will come again, and receive you unto myself** ; that where I am, *there* ye may be also.

This is the record of the promise made by Jesus himself in his own words and documented by the apostle John.

The same John who was also present at the Olivet Discourse when Jesus was teaching his disciples of the coming time he called the Great Tribulation.

The same John that was called upon to witness those events first hand, then commanded to observe and record in the book of Revelation everything that he was shown.

The same Great Tribulation that Jesus makes mention of an escape from, if one keeps themselves accounted worthy of that escape.

Luke 21:36

36 Watch ye therefore, and pray always, **that ye may be accounted worthy to escape** all these things that shall come to pass, and to stand before the Son of man.

The escape mentioned by Jesus from The Great Tribulation Period is the event we term The Rapture today, and will take place at the time of his second appearance into this physical world.

Hebrews 9:28

28 So Christ was once offered to bear the sins of many; and unto them that look for him shall he appear **the second time** without sin unto salvation.

This event will include the change of the living Bride from mortal to immortality which is mentioned in 1stCorinthians chapter 15:50-54. Also addressed in 1stCorinthians is the change of the departed believers who have fallen asleep (who are the "dead in Christ" Of 1stThessalonians 4:16-17) who will be raised from that sleep during their transformation from the corruption of that death into the glorious state of incorruption. The Lord through the apostle Paul states he wishes us not to be ignorant of the fact and reality of these events that are predestined to take place in our future.

1stThessalonians 4:13

13 **But I would not have you to be ignorant, brethren, concerning them which are asleep,** that ye sorrow not, even as others which have no hope.

1stThessalonians 4:16-17

16 For the Lord himself shall descend from heaven with a shout, with the voice of the archangel, and with the trump of God: and **the dead in Christ shall rise first**:

17 Then we which are alive *and* remain shall be caught up together with them in the clouds, to meet the Lord in the air: and so shall we ever be with the Lord.

1stCorinthians 15:50-54

50 Now this I say, brethren, that flesh and blood cannot inherit the kingdom of God; neither doth corruption inherit incorruption.

51 Behold, I shew you a mystery; We shall not all sleep, but we shall all be changed,

52 In a moment, in the twinkling of an eye, at the last trump: for the trumpet shall sound, and **the dead shall be raised incorruptible, and we shall be changed.**

53 For this corruptible must put on incorruption, and this mortal *must* put on immortality.

54 So when this corruptible shall have put on incorruption, and this mortal shall have put on immortality, then shall be brought to pass the saying that is written, **Death is swallowed up in victory.**

Hebrews 9:28, as we stated in an earlier chapter, is the only passage in the scripture that places any numerical value (much less the value of two) into a reference to an event which is dealing with an appearance of the Lord Jesus Christ involving the fulfillment of his promise to return.

Hebrews 9:28

28 So Christ was once offered to bear the sins of many; and unto them that look for him **shall he appear the second time** without sin unto salvation.

While at the same time deliberately defining precisely to whom Christ Jesus is going to appear to when he returns the second time which will include the resurrection of the dead in Christ.

Hebrews 9:28

28 So Christ was once offered to bear the sins of many; and **unto them that look for him** shall he appear the second time without sin unto salvation.

In their individual records the scripture gives us related, as well as vital information regarding this event through the churches located in Corinth and Thessalonica. These two churches collectively were each given descriptions and accompanying teachings addressing the subject of our being "caught up", the event we call The Rapture today.

1stThessalonians 4:16-17

16 For **the Lord himself** <u>shall descend from heaven</u> **with a shout**, <u>with the voice of the archangel</u>, and **with the trump of God**: and **the dead in Christ** <u>shall rise first</u>:

17 Then **we which are alive *and* remain** <u>shall be "caught up" together</u> **with them in the clouds**, <u>to meet the Lord</u> **in the air**: and **so shall we ever be with the Lord**.

1stCorinthians 15:51-52

51 Behold, **I shew you a mystery**; <u>We shall not all sleep</u>, but **we shall all be changed**,

52 **In a moment**, <u>in the twinkling of an eye</u>, **at the last trump**: <u>for the trumpet shall sound</u>, and **the dead shall be raised incorruptible**, and **we shall be changed**.

The scripture teaches it is toward this event we should be looking and striving in our Christian walk and life, for the purpose of our being included through obedience to the "hope of the gospel".

Colossians 1:21-23

21 And you, that were sometime alienated and enemies in *your* mind by wicked works, yet now hath he reconciled

22 In the body of his flesh through death, **to present you holy and unblameable and unreproveable in his sight**;

23 **"If" ye continue in the faith** grounded and settled, **and *be* not moved away from the hope of the gospel**, which ye have heard, *and* which was preached to every creature which is under heaven; whereof I Paul am made a minister;

We will look at these passages again under the appropriate chapter, but I wanted to point out what should be obvious to any honest child of God but apparently has been ignored or at least overlooked by the majority of the modern Church.

The recipients of this letter from Paul were the "<u>saints</u> and <u>faithful brethren</u> in Christ which were at Colosse."

Colossians 1:1-2

1 Paul, an apostle of Jesus Christ by the will of God, and Timotheus *our* brother,

2 To the **saints and faithful brethren** in Christ which are at Colosse: Grace *be* unto you, and peace, from God our Father and the Lord Jesus Christ.

First, Paul was addressing only believers. One can not be a saint or a faithful brethren without first being a child of God. Also, even after this is realized, most of the members of the Church today consider the two descriptions referring to the same entity, meaning the Colossian Christians as a whole unit. I would like to point out that every faithful "brethren" in Christ is most definitely a saint. However, it is possible for one to be a brother (believer), but not be faithful. Being an unfaithful brethren would make an individual simply a saint of God, which by sheer coincidence is exactly the term used by Paul.

Brothers and sisters in Christ can (and regularly are) neglectful in our service to God. Every believer that has ever lived has known another brother or sister in Christ that were not dedicated in any real way to the work of the Lord, at times even ourselves. Paul is addressing all the saints of Colosse. The dedicated as well as the unfaithful. This is bore out in verses twenty-one through twenty-three. As we have already stated, most of the contents of Paul's letters to the churches, and John's letters to the seven churches of Revelation, are predominately corrective in nature which follows a reoccurring theme for the entirety of God's Word as a whole.

Paul records that God through his Son had reconciled them to himself (as he has all believers) through his own body through death (separation) for the purpose of eventually presenting them holy and blameless. But, Paul teaches they can only achieve the condition which constitutes one worthy of this presentation "if" they continued in the faith grounded and settled, and did not remove themselves (be not moved away) from the "hope of the gospel" (verse twenty-three).

By stating they needed to continue (or remain) in the faith, and not be moved away from it, he establishes that they had genuinely received and accepted the truth which includes the hope of the gospel (our change at the time of The Rapture). But it was essential for them not to be swayed from the establishment of that truth in their life. **That is what it says.** He confirms for the entire Church (which includes the modern Church of today) that it is possible to be moved away from the hope of the gospel (excluding oneself from the Blessed Hope) if one does not continue to be faithful.

If there is any doubt left in anyone's mind that Paul is pointing to this as a truth, let me point out he documented the concept twice to two separate churches. It is impossible to be faithful and not be a child of God, but it is possible to be a child of God and not be faithful.

Ephesians 1:1-2

1 Paul, an apostle of Jesus Christ by the will of God, **to the saints** which are at Ephesus, and **to the faithful** in Christ Jesus:

2 Grace *be* to you, and peace, from God our Father, and *from* the Lord Jesus Christ.

Several other examples of this teaching exist in scripture that the Church has overlooked. I can only hope it has been overlooked of course, for I would pray it has not been a conscience act of deliberately ignoring what I consider to be obvious. If that were the case I would have to also assume it being done for the purpose of remaining comfortably inside each branch of Christianities own denominational doctrine which, inside our society constitutes what we refer to as our comfort zone.

The Church as a whole considers certain phrases contained inside key passages insignificant that it should recognize as clearly connected to the subject matter and message being conveyed. Failure to accept the truths contained and supplied by these phrases occur regularly when such a phrase implies a teaching that conflicts with ones current beliefs. The Church as a complete unit can not continue the practice of "selective acceptance" without suffering the consequences. Some of these consequences, as we have already observed, are severe in the extreme.

One of the best examples of this flawed interpretational practice is the rejection of phrases inside the same passage of scripture by two of the major groups of eschatology. Let us re-examine these two positions from another perspective in order to address the tendency individual denominations have to overlook a variety of biblical teachings.

The first is the Pre-Tribulationists which insist, based on their understanding of the scripture, there will be a Rapture before the Great Tribulation Period. The second is the Post-

Tribulationists which are just as adamant in their belief that the teachings regarding a Pre-Tribulational Rapture are at best in error. It has even been proposed that the original teachings of The Rapture constitute an out right deception that has been accepted by a large portion of the Church by way of wishful thinking.

It is also important to remember that the Word of God contains many compound applications within its structure. The Divine has compressed an inexhaustible amount of information into his message to his creation by embedding the Spirit of himself into the message itself. This is the reason the Word of God is fresh and new every day. The scripture we are blessed with through our possession of it is literally alive with the presence of God. Through him (his presence, the Holy Spirit) we are given the opportunity to refresh ourselves continually, day after day.

That being said, the Church should take this lesson to heart and accept at face value every single word contained in The Word of God. Every denomination will agree with the statements of this passage on its surface, then point to every other denomination with claims of all others failing to do just that. With this simple example we will determine who is not relying completely (and I do mean completely) on the Word of God.

Luke 21:36
36 Watch ye therefore, and pray always, **that ye may be accounted worthy to escape** all these things that shall come to pass, and to stand before the Son of man.

In my professional opinion this passage (this one verse, that stands on its own in teachings, lessons and doctrine), is very clear and needs no interpretation. In truth neither you nor I can interpret God's Word in the first place. No mere human can. God's Word is of Divine origin, and only he can interpret it to us. The scripture itself declares that no prophesy of the scripture is of any "private" interpretation. (2ndPeter 1:20-21). Holy men of God spoke as they were moved by the Holy Ghost. In the same fashion in reverse order the Holy Spirit is the component in presence critical for our understanding the message being conveyed.

In our study passage of Luke chapter twenty-one verse thirty-six Jesus is informing all believers through his disciples of an event that is located in our future which he defines as an escape. (His words, not mine. **That is what it says.**) This escape is provided to us for the purpose of avoiding the terrible time he has just described which he tells us will encompass the entire world.

He gives this terrible time in history a name, The Great Tribulation (Matthew 24:21, see also Revelation 2:22, and Revelation 7:14). Since it is the future he is informing the Church of, this passage meets all the qualifications of prophesy and as such can not be "interpreted" by us (as is the case with all of God's Word). It must be accepted at face value as the truth (especially coming from God manifested in the flesh himself) and interpreted to us by him (the Spirit) in the manner described to us by scripture itself. Rightly dividing. (2ndTimothy 2:15).

This is related to the phrase and practice of study that was taught to me in my youth, the use of description was scripture interprets scripture. This is very close to the truth. A more accurate representation would be, The Word interprets the word.

Both Pre-Tribulationists and Post-Tribulationists deny teachings that are clearly presented in the phrasing of this passage. The Post-Tribulationists deny there will be an escape "from" The Great Tribulation, sighting the text can just as easily be interpreted "out of" which would confirm their belief of the nonexistence of a Pre-Tribulational Rapture.

However that interpretation conflicts with all other scripture which confirms for us the fact that someone will not enter the Great Tribulation. The most significant of these passages being Revelation 2:22.

The Pre-Tribulationists will look at the same passage and claim the mention of "being accounted worthy" has no bearing on the teachings Jesus is attempting to convey since this phrase for them is the equivalence of salvation therefore is just the mention of the experience in a varied term. This interpretation is incompatible with the statements made by Jesus concerning the offence the members of the church of Thyatira were guilty, also contained in Revelation 2:22, and directly conflicts with the subject matter addressed in both passages, which is disobedience.

The mention of being accounted worthy found in Luke 21:36 implies the compliance to a set criteria and is directly related to the repentance from the sin of adultery against the speaker of Revelation 2:22.

Revelation 2:22
22 Behold, I will cast her into a bed, **and them that commit adultery with her into great tribulation**, except they repent of their deeds.

The sin of adultery is being committed against the speaker by the individuals he identifies as his servants. But the passage also clearly states, if they repent of the sin of adultery the penalty for their transgression will be withdrawn. If adhered to, this will result in the members of the Church avoiding the punishment they are in fact deserving of, as are we all.

To reiterate on the original premise of this chapter, one objection held by opponents to the Conditional Rapture is the argument concerning the partial manner in which we anticipate the Rapture to take place. In their judgment it is invalid on the basis that it divides the body of Christ, the Church. "God would not do that," I have frequently been told.

On the next higher level of controversy, there also exists (as has been "explained" to me) the next point of contention. "God would not separate into two groups, a single collection of believers of which all members have in common a belief that constitutes their faith in the one true God".

Yep, that's what someone actually told me. With a straight face and the absence of any scriptural basis whatsoever, which again is an opinion based predominantly on a predetermined assumption and not on the teachings of God's Word.

Furthermore, what if I were to inform you the scripture actually records for us, in the text of your own Bible, the literal (actual) separation of a collection of believers into two groups that has already occurred. Would you be interested in the investigation of such an event. If not, you may refrain from finishing the reading of this chapter and subsequently the skipping, in its entirety, the next.

However, I can assure you, it was as fascinating a study that was ever shown me by God through his Word short of the revealing of his pre-creational self and nature in three persons, and his creation of mankind after that very image.

This event took place at the singularly most significant time in history for believers (and for the world for that matter), the results of which point directly to The Conditional Rapture. This record appears in your own Bible, (for you to deny at your own leisure).

Matthew 27:50-54
50 Jesus, when he had cried again with a loud voice, yielded up the ghost.
51 And, behold, the veil of the temple was rent in twain from the top to the bottom; and the earth did quake, and the rocks rent;

52 And the graves were opened; and many bodies of the saints which slept arose,

53 And came out of the graves after his resurrection, and went into the holy city, and appeared unto many.

54 Now when the centurion, and they that were with him, watching Jesus, saw the earthquake, and those things that were done, they feared greatly, saying, Truly this was the Son of God.

Now, Jesus, when he had cried again with a loud voice (it is finished), yielded up the ghost (The Holy Spirit). And the veil of the temple was ripped in two from the top to the bottom (a humanly impossible feat); and there was an earthquake, which included the boulders in the area that were cracked and broken, and various tombs in the area that were breached.

As a result, the graves were opened; and many bodies of the saints which had been dead rose from their physical death back to life. They then emerged from their graves and went into Jerusalem, and appeared unto many people.

Now when the centurion and they that were with him, observed Jesus' actions, then witnessed the earthquake coincide with his death, and the things that accompanied it, they were overwhelmed by a tremendous fear. Then the centurion, who was moved to an understanding of the truth confessed, "Truly this was the Son of God".

In my oppositions defense, I could pointed out, there seems to be only a limited amount of information given in verses fifty-two and fifty-three concerning the saints that rose from the dead after the resurrection of Jesus. But, in truth, it only appears to be the case with only a casual read of the text. In actuality there is an enormous amount of discernible facts that can be gleaned from these very few statements as is true with the entirety of the Word of God, especially when cross referenced with the rest of the scripture in regards to Jesus' actions at this same "time" in the spiritual.

I have been told one can not interpret what I claim to believe is the truth concerning these individuals due to the lack of information supplied. We will investigate this passage in detail in the next chapter but first, we will respond to my opponents original argument of, "God would not separate into two groups, a single collection of believers of which all members have in common a belief that constitutes their faith in the one true God".

My opposition overlooks the facts that are found on the very surface of the plain text of these passages. It is futile to argue that something can not take place after the scripture records that it in fact actually has.

The individuals that were raised from the dead are identified in the text itself as saints. Since they were raised immediately after the resurrection of Jesus due to the opening of the graves at the moment of his death, they had to have been Old Testament saints. These believers were formerly being held in paradise along side a number of others similar to themselves.

This can be determined by the means in which the group that is mentioned is identified. Verse fifty-two states that many of the saints that slept, arose from their sleep. By confirming this resurrection of a described many, but not all, the scripture voluntarily omits the mention, but confirms the existence of another group not resurrected. I have mentioned before, but it bares repeating that it is a continual fascination to me how the scripture defines, makes point of, and explains truth after truth, by a simple omission of information.

The spirit/souls of the Old Testament saints that were not reunited with their bodies through this resurrection were escorted by Jesus back to heaven. It is generally accepted that at some point during or after the resurrection of Jesus, he emptied the compartment in which the Old Testament saints were being held, referred to as paradise. This compartment was separated from the punishment side of hell by a great gulf.

Ephesians 4:8-10
8 Wherefore he saith, **When he ascended up on high, he led captivity captive**, and gave gifts unto men.
9 (Now that he ascended, what is it but that he also descended first into the lower parts of the earth?
10 He that descended is the same also that ascended up far above all heavens, that he might fill all things.)

These two records paired together confirm one group of believers that had a common belief that constituted all being held together in captivity (Paradise). But for reasons unknown to the majority of the Church, at the time of the resurrection of Jesus they were separated into two distinct groups. The first group was reunited with their bodies and raised back to life in the physical. The other was taken from "captivity" and ascended with Jesus "far above all heavens" to take their place in the spiritual to await there own physical resurrection at a later date.

This confirms the likelihood of a similar process connected with the teachings of the Conditional Rapture. Since an event of the same nature has already been recorded to have taken place in the case of the Old Testament saints by the scripture itself, it can not be denied that a division of the Church into two groups at the time of the Rapture is at the very least not an impossibility.

Even if the teaching is in error and the separation is destined not to take place, the statements regarding what God would and would not do are unfounded. To put this point into simple Twenty-first century language, since the scripture confirms it has taken place in the past, there is no reason to believe a similar event could not reoccur in the future.

I continue to pray for every member of the human race to come to a knowledge of Jesus Christ as their Savior, as is the call of the convicting Spirit of God to the whole of the unbelieving world. But, the majority of the membership of the Church is in severe need of a wake up call, "lest the Lord find them sleeping" upon his return. I sincerely believe this manuscript "not" to be that alarm, but in just fashion, if it initiates a field of interest and a course of study that can act toward that goal, my calling will have been fulfilled and complete.

Grace and peace be multiplied unto you all.

Chapter Nine

Divine Exclusion

The concept of divine exclusion was taught to me by the Holy Ghost through the Word of God. In the simplest terms it is anything that was initially intended by God to be included inside select sections of his plan, (if not his entire plan as a whole) but was excluded in advance through his foreknowledge. These omissions can be due to disobedience which was anticipated by the Creator, or in the example of our first illustration, born from the necessity for such an omission to illustrate a truth inside the plan of God itself.

Because the exclusion was predestined, though it was originally intended to be included, the end product is complete in every detail due to its omission. At the time of this writing two primary examples of this process pointing to the teachings of the Conditional Rapture have been identified in New Testament scripture but I suspect there to be several.

(I could use a little help here, by the way. All of this is right there in your own Bible).

This model is not stated by scripture directly, but is portrayed and therefore implied through the recording of two events which appear in key locations inside God's Word. The events themselves can not be denied by the Church since they are recorded in every believers Bible regardless of the version one uses. However, the significance of each and the connection between the two can easily be discounted and dismissed by the Church as misinterpretation. I fully expect them to be rejected by the majority of the Christian world since the examples they illustrate completely agree with the "theory" of The Conditional Rapture and depict to the point of perfection the truth contained inside its teachings.

This model can be most easily seen by illustration in the salvation experience itself.

One can not deny the existence of this concept when the scripture is accepted at face value. Our Bibles tell us Jesus came to seek and to save that which was lost. That includes everyone if taken literally. He also died for the sins of the whole world. Taken in the same manner that also includes everyone. You can see these teachings in practice in the literal sense in areas other than we will expose here. For example,

1st Timothy 2:1-5

1 I exhort therefore, that, first of all, supplications, prayers, intercessions, *and* giving of thanks, be made for all men;

2 For kings, and *for* all that are in authority; that we may lead a quiet and peaceable life in all godliness and honesty.

3 For this *is* good and acceptable in the sight of God our Saviour;

4 **Who will have all men to be saved, and to come unto the knowledge of the truth**.

5 For *there is* one God, and one mediator between God and men, the man Christ Jesus;

It was God's original intent for every individual member of the human race, whom he created in his own mirror image to receive redemption, and to be reunited in fellowship with him by way of the relationship provided through the salvation process. After the fall of Adam through his neglect of responsibility concerning his wife Eve, God put in motion the plan of redemption that was willed by him to be advantaged by all of humanity.

Unfortunately, the largest majority of his creation has rejected the free gift that he provided for the whole of mankind through himself. Past and current generations have rejected God's plan of salvation, and if the Lord tarries, future generations will continue to do the same. As a result, most of mankind is destined for the depths of hell wherein awaits everlasting fire and torment, which was originally prepared for the devil and the score of angels that followed him in rebellion against God and his plan of creation.

Matthew 25:41
41 Then shall he say also unto them on the left hand, Depart from me, ye cursed, into everlasting fire, **prepared for the devil and his angels**:

It is heart wrenching to know that many of our family members will not be enjoying the pleasures of the next life by our sides. They will have robbed themselves of not only the peace, love and joy of everlasting life itself, but the very presence of God emanating from every molecule (if there are any) of that existence through the presence of the Holy Spirit.

Many reading this book, however, are no doubt assured in their knowledge, and therefore relieved in their thinking that, "All of my family is saved. We are all going to be together in heaven".

That is a wonderful thought, and I am utterly thrilled to know it, but that is only your immediate family. The lineage of every person that draws breath (if you truly believe your Bible) goes back through Noah and his wife, then ultimately back to Adam and Eve. Every single solitary one of us are distantly related to each and every single solitary other one of us, like it or not.

Modern science, through the advances in DNA research has finally correctly determined (this is several years ago now) that there is a singular female in the past that is responsible for the existence of every single "race" on our big blue planet today. They "theorize" that somehow all possible branches of the human race family tree were unable to survive the journey down through all past ages of history, save one. The sole survivor is responsible for all human life on earth. They call her Mitochondrial Eve.

Well now, how about that. DUUH.

Also, the concept of "race" is man made. The Bible refers to tribes, and peoples, nations, tongues and everything else. But never "races". That is because there is only one race. The human race. Get used to it. Get used to the concept of getting used to getting along with all other "peoples".

Setting aside for a moment the concept of "race", are you uncomfortable in the company of individuals that are from a different "background" as yourself? Or, on the other hand, do you know someone you really don't care for in general regardless of their background and prefer to avoid extended contact or even lengthy conversations. Do any of these individuals profess to be believers, and even you would consider them to be a Christian, beside the fact you do not care to be in their company?

Well, you do not have to like them, but you have no choice when it comes to having a love for them (if you wish to remain in the grace of God), and you better find a way to begin enjoying their companionship because your going to be spending an "awful" lot of "time" with that individual and many others akin to them in the "future", like it or not. Oh yea, I forgot, your going to like it, like it or not, its going to be "heaven", like it or not. See how foolish this can get. But, I have begun to ramble. (Forgive me. All preachers chase a rabbit every now and again).

My point here is, God intended for all of mankind to accept redemption through the process of salvation. Many have rejected God's grace, and many others will continue to do so.

An unbearable unfortunate reality, but true.

However, regardless of the number of individuals that will not be included in the kingdom of God because of their rejection of God's grace, that kingdom will be complete in every detail according to the foreknowledge of God. He knows the end from the beginning, and he is aware of precisely who will and who will not choose to become a member of the family of God. The family will be complete (is complete), with not a soul lost.

Now, Let's get to it.

Matthew 27:50-54

50 Jesus, when he had cried again with a loud voice, yielded up the ghost.

51 And, behold, the veil of the temple was rent in twain from the top to the bottom; and the earth did quake, and the rocks rent;

52 And the graves were opened; and many bodies of the saints which slept arose,

53 And came out of the graves after his resurrection, and went into the holy city, and appeared unto many.

In the last chapter, we merely pointed out that the Old Testament saints that were being held in captivity in paradise were divided into two groups. This account negates the argument that leads many to the assumption that God would not separate into two parties a single collection of believers that basically are of the same beliefs. One group, recorded here by Matthew, was resurrected back to life in the physical. In witness to the event, they were seen by many people as they entered the holy city of Jerusalem after the resurrection of Jesus.

My opponents are quick to point out that these passages do not state these individuals were raised back to physical life. Let me use this passage to explain the proper practice of gathering evidence and the investigation of that evidence, scriptural or otherwise. In this case of course, it is in the form of documentation.

In law enforcement, evidence in document form is a very efficient means by which to prove or disprove a given thing. However, there is one significant difference between the case we are investigating in comparison to the same in the secular world. Assuming there to be no deceptions (and I have witnessed such), or a defendant is not being railroaded into a conviction, in a court of law it must first somehow be established that whatever documentation that is being presented as evidence for or against the accused is genuine or otherwise authentic.

We do not have that stipulation to deal with. If our documentation (The Word of God) is not accurate or otherwise trustworthy, absolutely none of this matters anyway. All bets are off, and each of us are literally on our "eternal" own.

By the way, to be clear on this one thing. God's Word has proven itself to me beyond any shadow of any doubt, to be exactly what he claims it to be. That proof can be found in the fulfillment of prophesy time after time. And I mean this in the most literal manner you are able to receive it. The Creator has identified himself to his creation through the documentation of events destined to take place in history, past, present, and future. God's Word (The Bible) is the only document in the history of all time that has been, is and will be 100% accurate 100% of the time in its original form and message.

Matthew 27:51-54
51 And, behold, the veil of the temple was rent in twain from the top to the bottom; and the earth did quake, and the rocks rent;
52 And the graves were opened; and many bodies of the saints which slept arose,
53 And came out of the graves after his resurrection, and went into the holy city, and appeared unto many.

The veil of the temple being ripped from the top to the bottom is a physical occurrence, as is the earthquake which caused the rupture of rock formations in the area. The mention of the graves being opened, which are tombs in the vicinity of the crucifixion, coincides with the earthquake that "rents the rocks" in at least the local region. Through all of these descriptions we are given the impression that even though we know a supernatural influence is at work because of the death of the Son of God, its influence is acting directly upon life in the physical.

The bodies of the saints which rose from their sleep, not only are mentioned in the physical by them being identified as bodies, but the sleep they are aroused from is understood to be the sleep of death since they are being raise literally from their graves. If raised from death (and that is the implication), this would have to be understood to mean back to physical life. Also, it should be noticed, that if they were being raised into or toward a type of mystical or spiritual state, there would be no reason whatsoever for the opening of the graves in the literal physical sense in the first place.

Every piece of information we are given concerning the saints that are raised (out from under the Old Covenant, a point which will become critical) suggests it was accomplished in the physical.

In addition, there is no evidence given to us in these passages, or others I am aware of, to suggest otherwise. We can accept what seems to be the obvious due to lack of information to the contrary, which in this case appears to be none. In any "honest" court of law in the country, this preponderance of evidence would overwhelmingly favor the side in possession of that evidence. Due to the sheer lack of any documented conformation to the contrary, the opponents of that evidence have virtually "no leg to stand on" from any position of legality or otherwise.

Note: This continues to be a problem within denominations today. Speculating beyond the available facts leads to theoretical assumptions that are accepted into belief systems when conclusions from such speculations agree with established doctrines that have been concocted from the imagination of an "authority" firmly established as such within the denomination..

Our Scientific community is profuse in this practice. As a result, it is in a continuous state of correction due to the majority of the community's refusal to accept any logical argument for the origins of life, save spontaneous generation leading to the "theory" of evolution. These corrections are not updates in formerly known facts, but current proof of errors and even deceptions to present evolution as fact. It even denies to the general public information concerning the true scientific procedures that it itself can not abide by if it is to cling to the evolutionary theory. These procedures are as follows.

The truth in scientific study is found only through,

1. Observation (a subject of study must be detectable)
2. What can be observed must also be calculable (study of the subjects properties must be measurable),
3. What can be observed and therefore subject to calculation must also be replicable (results of study leading to conclusions concerning the subject must be repeatable).

The theory of Evolution can perform or demonstrate none of these functions. Therefore by definition it is just as much a belief system (faith or religion) as any other. More so in fact, as we can see, measure, and repeat this short list of procedures when observing the incredible complexity of Creation itself, spoken into existence by Jehovah.

This publication was not written for the purpose of discussing the evolution vs. creation debate, but I predict in our future (I pray I live to see it) the realization (which already exists) and admission by the atheistic scientific community of the impossibility of the spontaneous generation of life from lifeless inorganic material. Although atheistic science has <u>absolutely</u> (and I choose specifically that word intentionally, you can look it up) <u>no proof or even evidence of its occurrence</u>, its emergence is essential before the evolution of such life can even begin its climb up the evolutionary ladder. What it does possess is only speculation and wishful thinking leading them to a faulty theory, of which also science has <u>zero evidence</u> which constitutes proof. Until then we must put up with being ridiculed by educated idiots, and I am being kind. (God refers to them as fools. Ps. 14:1, and Ps. 53:1).

Continuing our study of the resurrected Old Testament saints based on this premise, the next question to be asked is what happened to them after their physical resurrection back to life. The scripture fails to give us that information directly, but we can reason within the facts we are given and our knowledge of life in the physical.

If these saints are raised back to physical life, what we know of life in this physical world suggests their final end would be physical death once again at the end of that life. Whereas this might appear to some to be unlikely or even somehow unfair, (a person called upon by God to experience physical death more than the once we are familiar with) it has actually been documented by suggestion several times in the scripture.

Jesus raised several individuals back to physical life during his ministry, as well as the occurrence of it taking place as recorded for us in the Old Testament. Each one of these instances would logically result in the individuals in question living out the physical life they were raised back to. That life would ultimately end in physical death once again. In that respect we are looking at the same or at least a similar situation here.

These facts, however, become a critical point of interest concerning the Old Testament saints raised back to life at the time of Jesus' death and resurrection. The timing of the event affords us a unique insight into the condition of these believers and the event itself points directly to the teachings of the Conditional Rapture.

These saints passed from this life originally before the death of Jesus Christ and therefore died under the Old Covenant. They were in attendance with the rest of the Old Covenant saints in paradise (there was no other place for them to be kept) until the arrival of Jesus "to the heart of the earth" when fulfilling the sign of Jonas.

Matthew 12:40

40 For as Jonas was three days and three nights in the whale's belly; so shall the Son of man be three days and three nights in **the heart of the earth**.

All of the available information provided, presents us with a rather controversial dilemma. If these individuals were saints (and they were) and their resurrection was physical (asserted by the available evidence) and they were to die in the physical again (and they would), then this would put that physical death after the resurrection of Jesus and consequently firmly fixed under the New Covenant. This would transfer a portion of Old Testament saints (however small a number) into and under the blood of the New Covenant making them full members of the Church of God during the Church Age itself.

Through the sheer appearance of this event in scripture, which is inspired by the Holy Spirit, we not only have the example of a single group of believers being separated into two assemblies (an occurrence of which my opponents insist God would not have a hand in doing), but of which now stands unprecedented in its occurrence.

A translation (movement or transfer from one point to another) of a people from death under the Old Covenant through resurrection back to life into the New. This incident should act as a flag or flare to draw our attention to the study of all available information concerning both sets of saints involved in this unique experience. We must allow the scripture to explain to us why it appears in the narrative. Upon a thorough investigation we will find that with the mention of their translation comes the representation it reflects that will stand "in type", testimony and direct illustration of the Conditional Rapture.

Ephesians 4:8-10

8 Wherefore he saith, **When he ascended up on high, he led captivity captive**, and gave gifts unto men.

9 (Now that he ascended, what is it but that **he also descended first into the lower parts of the earth**?

10 He that descended is the same also that ascended up far above all heavens, that he might fill all things.)

The first group of Old Testament saints which were excluded from resurrection in the physical at this time, were taken by Jesus to heaven in the spiritual. Why was the second group of saints denied transport to heaven along with them during the initiation of the Church Age?

Ephesians 4:10

10 He that descended is the same also that ascended up far above all heavens, **that he might fill all things**.)

That he might fulfill all things in the most literal sense. Right down to leaving, within the recording of the event itself, the picture of the Conditional Rapture. Allow me to explain.

At the time of the death of Jesus, all of the physically departed Old Testament saints were being held in (because of their faith in the promised messiah and their subsequent resurrection through that promise) the bosom of Abraham, referred to by Jesus while on the cross as paradise. Upon his death on the cross the Spirit of Jesus (The Holy Ghost) descended into the lower parts of the earth (the upper chamber of hell, again paradise) wherein were being held all the Old Testament saints.

After his resurrection, two distinct events took place directly involving the entire company of Old Testament saints that were being held in the bosom of Abraham. The first group was removed from the "heart of the earth" and taken by Jesus to heaven to be presented to the Father, just as the Bride of Christ at the end of the Church Age will be taken by Jesus back to the Fathers house.

The second group was "left behind" (if you will allow) alive, where they entered into the time described by Jesus in the Olivet Discourse as the "beginning of sorrows", just as the remainder of the Church excluding the Bride after the Rapture will enter into the Great Tribulation.

Through this illustration we have one group of believers being led by Jesus to heaven, where they avoid what the second group of believers are forced to face. The picture or example of the Conditional Rapture could not be more clear.

Any opposition to the depictions made by these events can only be argued on the grounds of coincidence or a misrepresentation of the same, at best. I will repeat, I am continually amazed at how frequent these illustrations appear in the scripture, and at the ease in which they can be used to depict our "Hope" in Christ. Coincidence? I think not.

And yes, I have been accused of reading too much into the Word or (God forbid) direct manipulation of it. In truth, my own will is not in question here. To be brutally honest, given the choice, the traditional Pre-Tribulational Rapture, of which I was raised believing, is my personal preference. Inside its version, all past believers are resurrected from the dead. All believers still alive are "caught up" to meet Jesus in the air. The entire Church is taken by Jesus lock, stock and barrel back to the Father's house. "Death" of the entire Church is "swallowed up in victory", and all this takes place in one fell swoop. Everybody goes, everybody wins, happy ending. It could not be more simple. Except for the fact it is very simply not the truth.

I suppose the Church has overlooked these teachings in this case due to its location and the timing of the events in the scripture. If one has not allowed themselves to be made aware of the existence of the teaching of the Conditional Rapture in the Word, its appearance here is easily overwhelmed by the events of the crucifixion and resurrection themselves. Also, its portrayal in general can be easily overlooked if one is not searching, or is deliberately searching not for its existence.

I have an advantage over the Church in this respect, in that the Lord has disclosed to me (as he will anyone willing to perceive through the Holy Spirit) enough information concerning the Conditional Rapture that it is a simple matter to identify its presence within a given passage over an individual previously unaware of its presence in those particular verses. I have been studying this concept for a sufficient amount of time that I am allowed by the Lord to recognize it almost as regularly as it appears.

But again, I could use some help here. Let me assure you, all that is necessary for identification of such information is the willing heart of acceptance. Anyone relying on the Spirit of God for insight and instruction is capable within the will of God to receive. No believer truly needs another's instruction, although we are capable of enjoying such through the process of fellowship and the sharing of information obtained through individual study, but such is not necessary for our advancement of knowledge in the plan of God.

1 John 2:27

27 But the anointing which ye have received of him abideth in you, and **ye need not that any man teach you**: but as the same anointing teacheth you of all things, and is truth, and is no lie, and even as it hath taught you, ye shall abide in him.

I trust my God, through the Holy Spirit to teach anyone the truth, just as he has shown it to me. And on that note, that brings us to our second example of divine exclusion. This one "blew me away".

Revelation 3:14

14 And unto the angel of the church of the Laodiceans write; These things saith the Amen, the faithful and true witness, the beginning of the creation of God;

I always thought several things strange about the letter to the Laodicean church. First it being the last church mentioned in the series of the seven churches seemed to be out of place. I felt the church of Philadelphia was the fitting church to wind up the series, with its reference to being kept from the time of temptation through the open door provided by God.

By Pre-Tribulational interpretation Philadelphia represents the members of the Church who will experience the Rapture which would complete the Church Age, and we witness John being called up into heaven in the beginning of the very next chapter of Revelation.

Laodicea appeared to me to be missed placed in the sequence. It was as if the records were pointing to the Lord having one last problem do deal with concerning the Church after the initiation of the snatching away of her to be presented to the Father. From a traditional Pre-Tribulational perspective, such a suggestion made no logical sense. Of course now, from the Conditional Rapture perspective, it makes perfect sense. (The entire Bible agrees with itself if studied from the Conditional Rapture perspective).

Revelation 3:15-16

15 I know thy works, that **thou art neither cold nor hot**: I would thou wert cold or hot.
16 So then because thou art lukewarm, and neither cold nor hot, I will spue thee out of my mouth.

Verse fifteen establishes the fact that Laodicea is neither completely void of fellowship with the Lord nor is it "on fire" for God. The description given us suggests a relationship that is severely lacking in fellowship, which parallels in portrayal the Conditional Rapture teachings.

I had been taught in my youth that the church of Laodicea represented the members of the church that had no real commitment to the Lord, or had lost the commitment they had once possessed inside their faith. As a result of the Lords observation of their "neutrality", he was stirred by their actions into a condition of (spiritually speaking) nausea. In the simplest terms, I was told, they were making him sick to his spiritual stomach. In reality, that is not what the scripture states.

Revelation 3:16
16 So then because thou art lukewarm, and neither cold nor hot, **I will spue thee out of my mouth.**

The context of the passage usually defines the usage of the word when translated, since most words have multiple applications. Except in a case such as this when the word has only one meaning, then the context is forced to be determined by the definition of the word.

Translation: KJV: spue, Modern: spew, Greek : emeo English: to vomit.

(Paraphrased) Therefore, because you are lukewarm, and nether cold nor hot, I (Jesus) will vomit you out of my mouth.

Jesus states, because of their disobedient behavior, he is going to forcefully vomit them out of his mouth. The statements made by Jesus mentions nothing of the Laodiceans giving him a spiritually queasy stomach, nor does he say that they have brought him to a condition of illness (spiritually speaking). He states quite clearly that he is going to expel them from a portion of his body. In this case, his mouth.

This being the final church in the series of the seven churches of Revelation, would depict the condition of the modern Church of today at the time of transition from the Church Age to the Great Tribulation Period. The majority membership of the Church today fits the description given by Jesus of the church of Laodicea, and would stand excluded from the Rapture. But, it is not as simply as that.

Laodicea being the final church mentioned in the series makes it the seventh church, which is God's numerical reference to completeness. With the addressing of the final church, all events stand accomplished with the expulsion of the portion of the Church which Laodicea appears to represent. Therefore, we have all the elements present by example that suggest agreement with The Rapture of the Bride of Christ taking place in exactly the manner taught throughout each chapter of this publication.

But, it is only suggested or can be interpreted as such. Inside the depiction illustrated to us by the scripture, there is no concrete information. This was an irritation to me. To be shown (assumingly by the Holy Spirit) a passage of scripture with so much promise of possible confirmation of the Conditional Rapture, but with none forth coming outside my own preconceived opinion which had been acquired through the accumulation of teachings to date.

When these passages were brought to my attention, I saw the subtle suggestions that appeared laced inside the text that can be interpreted as have been presented to you from the perspective of the Conditional Rapture. I could not bring myself to argue over the implications of the context, but this illustration was nowhere near as definitive as were the other passages studied and presented in the previous chapters.

In my spirit, I was convinced and content with what I considered to be the truth, this information being in agreement with that truth, but only through the process of interpretation. This piece of the puzzle appeared sufficient only for myself. I was not comfortable with including it in my presentation. That is, until the Spirit lead me back through the scripture on my very next pass. There is a much deeper lesson to learn from the church of Laodicea. This is not a depiction or illustration. We are being given information leading to an actual event involving the Word of God itself in its most literal sense.

This should put the fear of God into all the most honest of his children.

The Word of God has only one message, it has only one thing to say, the truth. But it has a dual nature (the physical and the spiritual) that has been blessed by God with his presence (the Holy Ghost). In addition, through his presence this allows the text the ability to be utilized in multiple applications in the life of the Church in general, and its members specifically.

The dual nature of the scripture can be easily seen through out its length by any believer when observing any given writer addressing a group or individual (in the physical), but the modern Church clearly understands the content and lesson (in the spiritual) that is directed to the Church as a whole throughout its entire life. Each of these lessons have unlimited applications in the lives of each individual member of the Church.

It is believed the illustrations and teachings that the churches of Revelation are and possess extend through the whole of history to reach even beyond our modern world. This would allow their combined examples to be applied in principle throughout the entirety of the Church Age and into the Great Tribulation itself. The letter to the church of the Laodiceans is the final addressed in this record.

The state in which the churches of Revelation find themselves that Jesus is bringing to their attention exists inside the modern Church today. Each, save one, was given a condemnation by the Lord for that which was lacking within their relationship and how to correct it. Each, save one, was given a commendation concerning the faithful service it had performed within their relationship and how to maintain or improve it.

The Church of today is subject to the same rigorous standards set forth by Christ during his ministry which were in turn expanded upon in the Olivet Discourse. Those standards were then meticulously described in deliberate detail of chapters two and three of Revelation in the form of directives to the Church, along with the consequences of failure to comply.

Just as the church of Philadelphia is the sole mention and benefactor of the open door that is reserved for those who have "kept the word of his patience", so Thyatira is the sole recipient of the condemnation and curse of being cast into the Great Tribulation for the sin of adultery against her Bridegroom. Four of the remaining five churches are just as worthy of study by way of the instruction they receive from the Lord, but Laodicea stands in a unique light all its own that will come into direct contact with the teachings of the Rapture.

In each of the other six churches, a clear line of instruction to the local church (in the physical) and the implication of that teaching directed toward us at the end of the Church Age (in the spiritual) is easy to detect. However, in the case of Laodicea, it is not immediately apparent.

The spiritual application that would presumably be directed to the modern Church at the end of the Church Age, is the teaching of being nether cold nor hot as was the local church, and the call to repentance by all the means mentioned by Jesus. Being vomited out of his mouth could be interpreted as a reference to being rejected by him in the face of the open door, mentioned in the case of Philadelphia, with John about to be called up to heaven at the beginning of chapter four presumably (by interpretational illustration) through this same means.

What is missing in the case of the church of Laodicea, is the literal application of being vomited out of the mouth of the Lord (in the physical). No such example appears inside the text for the identification of such an actual occurrence in John's day as is the case with the other churches. All that is forthcoming after completing the study of the passage is the reference itself.

What is the literal meaning of the condemnation (in the physical) to the church of the Laodiceans. How are they to be vomited out of the mouth of Jesus Christ due to their disobedience, and where is the occurrence to be found, if not here?

History tells us Laodicea was the chief city of Phrygia Pacatiana, and it is believed that Paul wrote his first letter to Timothy from this location. Laodicea is mentioned only twice in the scripture itself. The second is recorded for us in the book of Revelation which includes them inside the listing of the seven churches, and the first being Paul's letter to the Colossians.

When we cross reference this material with the condemnation to the church of Laodicea found in Revelation, a startling concept presents itself, and with it comes the controversial teaching of divine exclusion pointing to yet one more confirmation of the Conditional Rapture.

Divine exclusion is the direct acknowledgement or representation of anything that was initially intended by God to be included inside select sections of his plan, (if not his entire plan as a whole) but was excluded in advance through his foreknowledge. In this case the exclusion is the result of disobedience, which in essence is an accurate explanation of predestination.

Colossians 1:1-2
1 Paul, an apostle of Jesus Christ by the will of God, and Timotheus *our* brother,
2 To the saints and faithful brethren in Christ which are at Colosse: Grace *be* unto you, and peace, from God our Father and the Lord Jesus Christ.

Paul writing his letter of encouragement and correction to the church of Colosse, makes reference to the church of Laodicea in chapters two and four of this same letter.

Colossians 2:1
1 For I would that ye knew what great conflict I have for you, and *for* **them at Laodicea**, and *for* as many as have not seen my face in the flesh;

Colossians 4:12-13
12 Epaphras, who is *one* of you, a servant of Christ, saluteth you, always labouring fervently for you in prayers, that ye may stand perfect and complete in all the will of God.
13 For I bear him record, that he hath a great zeal for you, and **them** *that are* **in Laodicea**, and them in Hierapolis.

One can study the contents of the letter to the Colossian Christians carefully (which we should do regardless of our study here) and see the concern Paul had for them as he did for all congregations. Laodicea was in the vicinity of the city of Colosse, and they would have had regular contact as a people and community, socially and economically. With a population of believers present inside the inhabitants of both societies, there would naturally be regular interaction that would have taken place between the congregations of the churches themselves.

One of Paul's desires was for the Colossians to "stand perfect and complete in all the will of God" which was asked for in fervent prayer by Epaphras another servant in the Lord who is also mentioned in this letter. We can assume this to be his will toward Laodicea as well, as they are referred to in conjunction with Colosse inside Paul's letter.

Then upon the closing of the letter Paul gives instruction (under the inspiration of the Holy Spirit, as all scripture is conceived) for this document to also be read in the church of the Laodiceans. If these directives are carried out both churches would benefit immediately by applying the appropriate corrective procedures that are derived from the instructions supplied by God through the apostle Paul which accompany the words of encouragement in the form of compliments concerning their faithfulness.

Colossians 4:15-16

15 Salute the brethren which are in Laodicea, and Nymphas, and the church which is in his house.

16 And when this epistle is read among you, **cause that it be read also in the church of the Laodiceans**; and that ye likewise read the *epistle* from Laodicea.

The act of acceptance of the letter to the Colossians by both congregations, and the reading of it by the first century Church with the intent of obedience to it, fulfills the literal application of God's intent of instruction (in the physical). The survival of the letter unto the present resulting in its being included in the scripture by canonization into our Bible, makes it possible for the twenty-first century Church to fulfill by extension this same application (in the spiritual).

We know it is God's will for us to read, study, and apply his truths to our life as was his will to the first century Church. Though he makes no direct reference to the Church of the future in the text, it is understood. God's Word is recorded and made available to all believers for the benefit of the entire Church.

Then Paul gives one last directive in the physical. This directive has its own spiritual counterpart as all scripture does.

Colossians 4:16

16 And when this epistle is read among you, cause that it be read also in the church of the Laodiceans; **and that ye likewise read the *epistle* from Laodicea**.

Paul gave instructions to the church of Colosse to also read the letter that he had written to the church of Laodicea. This exchange of information, besides being beneficial to both churches, would no doubt have been done in Paul's day and would again fulfill the literal purpose intended by God (in the physical). But there is a problem in the completion of the extended application of this directive (in the spiritual) which was originally intended by God to be fulfilled by the modern Church.

There is no letter written by Paul addressing the church of the Laodiceans included in the canon of our Bibles today. The letter that we know was written, as recorded by Paul, has been omitted and is not available for our consumption, spiritually speaking. In the strictest sense it has been preemptively expelled. Hello!

It has been divinely excluded in advance by God himself by way of his foreknowledge through his omnipresence in the spiritual due to disobedience in example of the Conditional Rapture. It has literally been spewed (vomited, discharged) out of the mouth of Jesus (The Word) because of noncompliance to his word and instruction.

Revelation 3:15-16
15 I know thy works, that thou art neither cold nor hot: I would thou wert cold or hot.
16 So then because thou art lukewarm, and neither cold nor hot, **I will spue thee out of my mouth.**

Jesus' are the hands and he is the mouth piece of God. He is literally God manifested in the flesh. He is also the Word of God, and his spirit is imbedded in the text of his Word, being his literal word and message to his creation.

John 1:1-3
1 In the beginning was the Word, and the Word was with God, and the Word was God.
2 The same was in the beginning with God.
3 All things were made by him; and without him was not any thing made that was made.

What was initially intended by God to be included (documented by inspiration of the Holy Spirit through Paul), has been excluded due to disobedience. It is no coincidence that the condemnation of Revelation 3:16,

Revelation 3:16
16 So then because thou art lukewarm, and neither cold nor hot, **I will spue thee out of my mouth.**

foreshadows the fact of a missing epistle written by Paul to the exact same church, in exactly the manner the condemnation describes.

Colossians 4:16

16 And when this epistle is read among you, cause that it be read also in the church of the Laodiceans; **and that ye likewise read the** *epistle* **from Laodicea.**

Laodicea 1:1-?

1 ??? ?? ??? ??;

2 ?? ??? ?? ???.

This exclusion was divinely preordained through God's foreknowledge by way of his omnipresence. God has fore-knowledge of every moment of what we refer to as "time". The entirety of physical history was spoken into existence by God through Jehovah complete from beginning to end in a moment before the creation of what we refer to as time. I truly wish I had more of that time to "learn of him". God's plan is not only more magnificently complex than we are able to imagine, God's plan is more magnificently complex than we could ever hope to imagine.

Grace and peace be multiplied to you all.

Chapter Ten

The Patience of Jesus Christ

John 14:1-3

1 Let not your heart be troubled: ye believe in God, believe also in me.

2 In my Father's house are many mansions: if *it were* not *so*, I would have told you. I go to prepare a place for you.

3 And if I go and prepare a place for you, I will come again, and receive you unto myself; that where I am, *there* ye may be also.

Jesus promised during his ministry that upon his departure from this world, he would surely return at some point in what we refer to as the future, to gather the faithful portion of the Church himself, unto himself, for himself, for the purpose of removing them (her) from this world to transport them (her) back to the Father's house in which he had prepared a place for them (her). The Pre-Tribulation Rapture is the only "theory" which agrees with this passage of scripture.

The Post-Tribulational view has the Church meeting Jesus in the air at the traditional second coming of Christ at the end of the Great Tribulation Period, then returning immediately to the earth (apparently from the air, in which it had just met him) without any reasonable explanation of the mention of Jesus' preparation of a place in the Fathers house or why, if not to be utilized at that time per Jesus' promise.

New Jerusalem is not brought down out of heaven to be placed and reside forever on the earth until after the thousand years are accomplished and the devil and his angels are confined at their final incarceration for all eternity future in hell.

Again, by illustration, this also makes perfect sense from the perspective of Jesus as a new husband shielding his beloved Bride from all the powers of darkness throughout both the Great Tribulation as well as the end of his thousand year reign when the devil is released from his one thousand year confinement. Not that the shielding of the Bride is necessary, only that it is the manner in which the Lord has chosen through promise to his Bride to conduct the sequence of events inside the marriage to her.

1stThessalonians 4:17

17 Then we which are alive *and* remain shall be caught up together with them in the clouds, to meet the Lord in the air: **and so shall we ever be with the Lord**.

Revelation 20:7-10

7 And when the thousand years are expired, Satan shall be loosed out of his prison,

8 And shall go out to deceive the nations which are in the four quarters of the earth, Gog and Magog, to gather them together to battle: the number of whom *is* as the sand of the sea.

9 And they went up on the breadth of the earth, and compassed the camp of the saints about, and the beloved city: and fire came down from God out of heaven, and devoured them.

10 And the devil that deceived them was cast into the lake of fire and brimstone, where the beast and the

false prophet *are*, and shall be tormented day and night for ever and ever.

And in truth, New Jerusalem will not be placed into permanent residence on the earth until after its renovation, and the wording of this record suggests the Bride of Christ (believed by many incorrectly to be the entire Church) is already residing within its interior.

Revelation 21:1-2
1 And I saw a new heaven and a new earth: for the first heaven and the first earth were passed away; and there was no more sea.
2 And I John saw the holy city, new Jerusalem, coming down from God out of heaven, **prepared as a bride adorned for her husband.**

The mention of John witnessing New Jerusalem coming down out of heaven being prepared and adorned as a Bride for her husband lets us know the city of God is already occupied, and in fact (from the perspective of the physical) has been so for just over one thousand years. It has been the dwelling place of the Bride of Christ ever since the Rapture which initiated the Great Tribulation Period in the first place, just as was promise upon the departure of Jesus.

Acts 1:9-11
9 And when he had spoken these things, while they beheld, he was taken up; and a cloud received him out of their sight.
10 And while they looked stedfastly toward heaven as he went up, behold, two men stood by them in white apparel;
11 Which also said, Ye men of Galilee, why stand ye gazing up into heaven? **this same Jesus**, which is

taken up from you into heaven, **shall so come in like manner as ye have seen him go into heaven**.

The two men standing by them in white apparel asked and said, "You men of Galilee, why do you stand here gazing up into heaven? This same Jesus which is taken up from you into heaven will return in just this same fashion that you have seen him go". This is confirmation of Jesus' own words to his disciples, which is meant for the last generation of the Church Age to heed.

John 14:3

3 And if I go and prepare a place for you, I will come again, **and receive you unto myself; that where I am,** *there* **ye may be also**.

Jesus left the physical world at that time and reentered the spiritual from whence he came. He returned to the Father's house (New Jerusalem) wherein is located the very throne of God. Inside New Jerusalem Jesus has been preparing dwelling places for his Bride which he will collect himself upon his return to the physical world. (I believe this preparation is related to our performance in regards to the level and extent of our faithful service).

I have been interrogated in the past concerning Jesus' preparation of the Father's house for his Bride. On this subject the question has arisen, "Why does Jesus need two thousand years to prepare anything"? The answer is quite a simple one. He doesn't. Also this response answers a host of other questions and puts God's plan into a new perspective. Allow me to explain.

2ndPeter 3:8

8 But, beloved, be not ignorant of this one thing, that one day *is* with the Lord as a thousand years, and a thousand years as one day.

Many individuals have incorrectly used verse eight to justify several modern ideas and even attempt to integrate some into the wording of the scripture. The most common is the subject of creation. Since the scientific community has "proved" (and it ain't done it) the earth to be billions of years old, Christianity has succumbed to the idea and used this verse in an attempt to appear in agreement with current science that the earth was formed (by God) in long periods of ages, referred to in the scripture as days, since a day is as a thousand years, or even thousands of years to the Almighty. That is not what is being explained to us by God.

Each phrase of this passage cancels the time frame of the other. One day is as a thousand years to the Lord and a thousand years is as one day. What we are told by God through Peter can be comprehended by us, but not fully understood in our current location in the space of time in which we physically reside. It can only be understood fully in the spiritual. Time only exists in the physical through the process of God's creation of it.

Outside of this physical world (in the spiritual) there is no time. Only a series or sequence of events. As verse eight verifies, there is no difference to God (or anyone existing in the spiritual) between a day and three hundred and sixty five thousand two hundred and fifty days. They are the same. This makes no sense to us in the physical, but it makes perfect sense in the spiritual. Here is an illustration and a means by which to contemplate this concept.

My grand parents and one uncle have passed on. They all passed at various times in my life beginning at the age of seven. My mother passed away in 1981, her mother (my last surviving grandmother) and my nephew followed her several years later. My father passed away December of 2006, and one of my brothers followed him just a few months later. (My fathers oldest sister past into the spiritual at the time I was writing this chapter).

My point is that in the spiritual where there is no time, each saint of God who passes through the door of physical death, does so into the waiting arms of their loved ones who had gone on before them. Even though there were almost twenty six years separating my mothers departure from this world from my fathers, upon her arrival in the spiritual she only had the opportunity to be welcomed by her own departed family members prior to turning and greeting her own mother and grandson (my nephew, Karl) before my father, her husband was standing behind him. One continuous joyful uninterrupted family reunion that I would not take from any of them and look forward to myself with the greatest anticipation. (I loved, and still love and miss, all of my family members, my mother being at the top of that list. But my father became my best friend in the physical after I became an adult. His passing left a huge void in my life).

Time did not even exist until God (Jehovah) spoke the physical world into existence, and will cease to exist after God merges the spiritual with the created physical after the completion of the one thousand year reign of Christ immediately following the final defeat and eternal damnation of satan and his forces.

But concerning the return of Jesus Christ, there are those that question why he tarries. The scripture of 2ndPeter answers this also.

2ndPeter 3:9

9 The Lord is not slack concerning his promise, as some men count slackness; but is longsuffering to

us-ward, not willing that any should perish, but that all should come to repentance.

He simply wishes for all to come to the knowledge of salvation. Not all will, but God through his foreknowledge knows those that are his children to be, and is waiting for that moment in our future when they will be baptized into the family of God. When the last child of the Church Age is "born" into the family of God, he will bring this stage or age of history to a close by sending Jesus the Son to collect his Bride. This will fulfill the promise to the waiting Church (for those who are truly waiting patiently on that promise) and is the subject of the patience of Jesus Christ. Waiting patiently on his return.

Revelation 1:9
9 I John, who also am your brother, and companion in tribulation, and in the kingdom and **patience of Jesus Christ**, was in the isle that is called Patmos, for the word of God, and for the testimony of Jesus Christ.

John, who is also our brother and companion in tribulation was in the isle of Patmos when he recorded what he witnessed and was commanded by the Lord Jesus Christ to write in a book everything he was to see and send that information to the seven churches specified. Our point of reference here in verse nine of Revelation chapter one is the fact that John was in the patience of Jesus Christ. He is declaring himself to be in the attitude of patiently awaiting the return of Jesus to the physical in fulfillment of his promise. John will not see that return himself, but by remaining in the spirit of anticipation and expectation, he guarantees his participation in the associated resurrection and thereby the change from corruption to incorruption.

The entire Church should have been in constant anticipation of this event since its birth. Even though the event itself was approximately two thousand years in its future, it was meant for each generation to teach the next to live inside an attitude of eager expectation.

Living ones life in a manner of expectancy draws us continually closer to the one we are to be directing our spirit of anticipation to. Imagine for a moment what the Church would be like today if it had spent the last two thousand years drawing closer to one another and the Lord for the duration of that period of time in full anticipation and expectancy of the return of the Lord Jesus Christ.

(PAUSE, a moment of quiet reflection.)

WOW, now that's some picture.

But, the varied teachings of the Church today suggest a failure on its part in this task. Many denominations today proclaim a denial in the coming of the Lord manifesting itself in a Pre-Tribulational appearance as taught by the scripture. These denominations by these descriptions as defined by the scripture are simply not in the patience of the Lord Jesus Christ. They are waiting on something else besides the appearance of the Lord.

Their anticipation is directed to the day of the Lord as they themselves understand it or the Great Tribulation Period. Some are awaiting the identification of the anti-christ or any number of other events that are genuinely future historical considerations but will all take place after the Rapture of the Bride of Christ at the time of the fulfillment of Jesus' promise to those waiting patiently for that specific event.

1ˢᵗThessalonians 1:3

3 Remembering without ceasing your work of faith, and labour of love, and **patience of hope in our Lord Jesus Christ**, in the sight of God and our Father;

The hope mentioned here is the Blessed Hope, and the act of true believing Christians of the church of Thessalonica patiently awaiting the hope of their resurrection (their change from corruption to incorruption) at which time will take place the "catching up" of the saints of God (from mortal to immortality) who will be alive at the end of the Church Age to witness the event.

Hebrews 6:9-15

9 But, beloved, we are persuaded better things of you, and things that accompany salvation, though we thus speak.

Verse nine of this passage verifies that there are things which accompany salvation itself. There are things promised the children of God continually throughout the scripture. They in themselves validate the teachings of the Conditional Rapture in that God only promises the lost of the world salvation alone, if they repent of their unbelief and accept Jesus as their Lord and Savior. Every other promise offered by God with the integral of "if" are to his children upon faithful service and everything that faithful service to God entails.

Hebrews 6:10-15

10 For **God *is* not unrighteous to forget your work and labour of love**, which ye have shewed toward his name, in that ye have ministered to the saints, and do minister.

God will not forget any work or labor that is accomplished by us out of a true love for serving him, in obedience to his will.

Hebrews 6:11-15

11 And we desire that every one of you do shew the same diligence **to the full assurance of hope unto the end**:

Through all the work and labor that we perform (that should always be undertaken out of love and not for the expectation of a reward), must always be done with full assurance of the "hope" (fulfillment of promise) unto the end of our physical life or the event of the Blessed Hope itself at the end of the Church Age. The scripture repeatedly makes mention of continuing in the grace of God or remaining in faithful service. None of which can be accomplished without a believer being ever wary to "walk in the Spirit". Here we are told through the directives given to the Hebrew converts to show the same diligence that is being exampled, inside our own lives with full assurance of (the Blessed) hope (throughout all our generations) unto the end (of the Church Age).

Hebrews 6:12-15

12 That ye be not slothful, but followers of **them who through faith and patience inherit the promises**.

This verse should imply to the Church that the slothful (idle or inactive) will not inherit the promises being made mention of since the faithful and patient are the subject matter of the reception of them. It is through faith and patience we inherit the promises assured us by the Lord. Every member of the Church should be searching out brothers and sisters of our heavenly family who are faithful and patient in their service and be looking toward them as examples in our own life to do the same and even surpass them. **That is what it says.** God wishes all his children to be included in this reception. The Lord through the writer goes on to say,

Hebrews 6:13-15

13 For when God made promise to Abraham, because he could swear by no greater, he sware by himself,

14 Saying, Surely blessing I will bless thee, and multiplying I will multiply thee.

15 And so, **after he had patiently endured, he obtained the promise**.

I will reiterate: After he had patiently endured, he obtained the promise. Abraham in receipt of his promise by God is our example in the reception of our own.

Hebrews 6:16-18

16 For men verily swear by the greater: and an oath for confirmation *is* to them an end of all strife.

17 Wherein God, willing more abundantly to shew unto the heirs of promise the immutability of his counsel, confirmed *it* by an oath:

18 **That by two immutable things**, in which *it was* impossible for God to lie, **we might have a strong consolation, who have fled for refuge to lay hold upon the hope set before us:**

The two immutable (unchangeable, unchallengeable, or absolute) things mentioned in this passage have already been defined in the previous verses. Faith in and patience for that in which we are waiting on. What makes these two things absolute is that they are promised by God, and it is impossible for him to lie making the promises unchangeable and unchallengeable. Namely, the promised return of our Lord and Savior Jesus Christ for to carry us back to our new home where we will reside with him in the Father's house that he has been preparing special for us, his Bride. "If" we are faithful in belief of this promise and patient in awaiting its occurrence, our participation is secure by the promise itself by oath of God.

And I do mean especially prepared, with all the trimmings. I have no idea personally first hand what awaits us, but I do know it will be glorious beyond our wildest imaginations. It will not only be the singular most spectacular experience and existence we can image, but will be more magnificent than we ever could imagine. And even though all readers of this manuscript will agree on this one thing if nothing else, no one realizes the significance of those statements.

You see, Jesus is looking even more forward to our reunion and rejoining than we who are faithfully and patiently awaiting for him to return.

Hebrews 12:1-2

1 Wherefore seeing we also are compassed about with so great a cloud of witnesses, let us lay aside every weight, and the sin which doth so easily beset *us*, **and let us run with patience the race that is set before us,**

2 Looking unto Jesus the author and finisher of *our* faith; **who for the joy that was set before him endured the cross**, despising the shame, and is set down at the right hand of the throne of God.

All he suffered, he endured for us, continually looking into the future through the Spirit to the moment he would sweep us up out of the physical, into the spiritual to be taken back to the Father's house to be presented to the throne of God as his Bride. He looks forward to that moment more so than the most diligent of us.

He, for the conclusions brought by his act of sacrifice, laid down his life willingly in joyful anticipation of the reunion which was made possible and preordained through his sacrifice.

James 5:7-8

7 **Be patient therefore, brethren, unto the coming of the Lord**. Behold, the husbandman waiteth for the precious fruit of the earth, and hath long patience for it, until he receive the early and latter rain.

8 **Be ye also patient; stablish your hearts: for the coming of the Lord draweth nigh**.

With every passing day, the Blessed Hope draws ever closer, and our time inside the Church Age measures ever shorter. But there are so many members of the Church of God who are not prepared for that day. It will catch the vast majority by surprise and spiritually asleep.

Several Hebrew and Greek words translated into English as wait, hope, and trust are very much related in their meaning and usage. For example;

Job 13:15

15 Though he slay me, yet will I **trust** in him: but I will maintain mine own ways before him.

KJV - trust / Hebrew - yachal a prime root; to wait; by implication to be patient, hope (cause to, make to) hope, be pained, stay, tarry, trust, wait.

Again, the context defines the usage of the word in the form in which it is translated when it has more than one usage as exampled in this instance, as opposed to other words which have only one usage in which case the context is determined by the word as we saw in the case of the translation of emeo into "spew"- to vomit.

I suppose in quoting from the scriptures all the references to make point in each of these chapters, there are more mentions of patiently waiting on and having continual hope in the Lord, our change, or our resurrection than any one other thing. Perhaps because it is the one most important duty of a believer, you think?

Here are just a few.

Job 14:14

14 If a man die, shall he live *again*? **all the days of my appointed time will I wait**, till my change come.

Psalm 2:11-12

11 Serve the LORD with fear, and rejoice with trembling.

12 Kiss the Son, lest he be angry, and ye perish *from* the way, when his wrath is kindled but a little. **Blessed *are* all they that put their trust in him**.

Psalm 4:3-5

3 But know that the LORD hath set apart him that is godly for himself: the LORD will hear when I call unto him.

4 Stand in awe, and sin not: commune with your own heart upon your bed, and be still. Selah.

5 Offer the sacrifices of righteousness, and **put your trust in the LORD**.

Psalm 9:8-10

8 And he shall judge the world in righteousness, he shall minister judgment to the people in uprightness.

9 The LORD also will be a refuge for the oppressed, <u>a refuge in times of trouble</u>.

10 **And they that know thy name will put their trust in thee**: for thou, LORD, hast not forsaken them that seek thee.

Psalm 25:5
5 Lead me in thy truth, and teach me: for thou *art* the God of my salvation; **on thee do I wait all the day.**

Psalm 25:20-21
20 O keep my soul, and deliver me: let me not be ashamed; for I put my trust in thee.
21 Let integrity and uprightness preserve me; **for I wait on thee.**

By the way, Hope maketh not ashamed. Romans 5:5.

Psalm 27:13-14
13 *I had fainted*, unless I had believed to see the goodness of the LORD in the land of the living.
14 **Wait on the LORD**: be of good courage, and he shall strengthen thine heart: **wait, I say, on the LORD.**

Psalm 37:7-9
7 **Rest in the LORD, and wait patiently for him**: fret not thyself because of him who prospereth in his way, because of the man who bringeth wicked devices to pass.
8 Cease from anger, and forsake wrath: fret not thyself in any wise to do evil.
9 For evildoers shall be cut off: **but those that wait upon the LORD, they shall inherit the earth.**

Psalm 37:34

34 **Wait on the LORD, and keep his way**, and he shall exalt thee to inherit the land: when the wicked are cut off, thou shalt see *it*.

Psalm 52:9

9 I will praise thee for ever, because thou hast done *it*: and **I will wait on thy name**; for *it is* good before thy saints.

Psalm 62:5-8

5 **My soul, wait thou only upon God**; for my expectation *is* from him.

6 He only *is* my rock and my salvation: *he is* my defence; I shall not be moved.

7 In God *is* my salvation and my glory: the rock of my strength, *and* my refuge, *is* in God.

8 **Trust in him at all times**; *ye* people, pour out your heart before him: God *is* a refuge for us. Selah.

Psalm 145:13-17

13 Thy kingdom *is* an everlasting kingdom, and thy dominion *endureth* throughout all generations.

14 The LORD upholdeth all that fall, and raiseth up all *those that be* bowed down.

15 **The eyes of all wait upon thee**; and thou givest them their meat in due season.

16 Thou openest thine hand, and satisfiest the desire of every living thing.

17 The LORD *is* righteous in all his ways, and holy in all his works.

Proverbs 3:5-7

5 **Trust in the LORD** with all thine heart; and lean not unto thine own understanding.

6 In all thy ways acknowledge him, <u>and he shall direct thy paths</u>.

7 Be not wise in thine own eyes: fear the LORD, and depart from evil.

Proverbs 20:22

22 Say not thou, I will recompense evil; *but* **wait on the LORD**, and he shall save thee.

Proverbs 8:32-36

32 Now therefore hearken unto me, O ye children: <u>for blessed *are they that* keep my ways</u>.

33 Hear instruction, and be wise, and refuse it not.

34 <u>Blessed *is* the man that heareth me</u>, **watching daily at my gates**, **waiting at the posts of my doors**.

35 For whoso findeth me findeth life, and shall obtain favour of the LORD.

36 But he that sinneth against me wrongeth his own soul: <u>all they that hate me love death</u>.

Obtaining favor of the Lord is a direct reference to being in God's good favor or "grace".

Proverbs 14:32

32 The wicked is driven away in his wickedness: **but the righteous hath hope in his death**.

Isaiah 8:15-17

15 And many among them shall stumble, and fall, and be broken, and be snared, and be taken.

16 Bind up the testimony, seal the law among my disciples.

17 **And I will wait upon the LORD**, that hideth his face from the house of Jacob, and **I will look for him**.

Isaiah 12:2-4

2 Behold, God *is* my salvation; **I will trust**, <u>and not be afraid</u>: for the LORD JEHOVAH *is* my strength and *my* song; he also is become my salvation.

3 <u>Therefore with joy shall ye draw water out of the wells of salvation.</u>

4 And in that day shall ye say, Praise the LORD, call upon his name, declare his doings among the people, make mention that his name is exalted.

Isaiah 25:9

9 <u>And it shall be said in that day</u>, Lo, this *is* our God; **we have waited for him**, and he will save us: this *is* the LORD; **we have waited for him**, <u>we will be glad and rejoice in his salvation</u>.

Isaiah 26:4

4 **Trust ye in the LORD for ever**: for in the LORD JEHOVAH *is* everlasting strength:

Isaiah 30:18

18 <u>And therefore will the LORD wait</u>, <u>that he may be gracious unto you</u>, and therefore will he be exalted, that he may have mercy upon you: for the LORD *is* a God of judgment: **blessed** *are* **all they that wait for him**.

Isaiah 40:28-31

28 Hast thou not known? hast thou not heard, *that* the everlasting God, the LORD, the Creator of the ends of the earth, fainteth not, neither is weary? *there is* no searching of his understanding.

29 He giveth power to the faint; and to *them that have* no might he increaseth strength.

30 Even the youths shall faint and be weary, and the young men shall utterly fall:

31 **But they that wait upon the LORD shall renew** *their* **strength**; they shall mount up with wings as eagles; they shall run, and not be weary; *and* they shall walk, and not faint.

Isaiah 64:4

4 For since the beginning of the world <u>men</u> <u>have</u> <u>not</u> <u>heard, nor perceived by the ear, neither hath the eye</u> <u>seen</u>, O God, beside thee, *what* **he hath prepared for him that waiteth for him**.

Jeremiah 14:22

22 Are there *any* among the vanities of the Gentiles that can cause rain? or can the heavens give showers? *art* not thou he, O LORD our God? **therefore we will wait upon thee**: for thou hast made all these *things*.

Jeremiah 17:7-8

7 Blessed *is* the man **that trusteth in the LORD**, and **whose hope the LORD is**.

8 For he shall be as a tree planted by the waters, and *that* spreadeth out her roots by the river, and <u>shall not</u> <u>see when heat cometh</u>, but her leaf shall be green; and shall not be careful in the year of drought, neither shall cease from yielding fruit.

Lamentations 3:22-25

22 *It is of* the LORD'S mercies that we are not consumed, because his compassions fail not.

23 *They* *are* new every morning: great *is* thy faithfulness.

24 The LORD *is* my portion, saith my soul; **therefore will I hope in him**.

25 The LORD *is* good **unto them that wait for him**, to the soul *that* seeketh him.

26 *It is* good that *a man* should **both hope and quietly wait** for the salvation of the LORD.

Daniel 3:28

28 *Then* Nebuchadnezzar spake, and said, Blessed *be* the God of Shadrach, Meshach, and Abednego, who hath sent his angel, and **delivered his servants that trusted in him**, and have changed the king's word, and yielded their bodies, that they might not serve nor worship any god, except their own God.

Micah 7:7

7 Therefore I will look unto the LORD; **I will wait for the God of my salvation:**
my God will hear me.

Nahum 1:7

7 The LORD *is* good, a strong hold in the day of trouble;
and **he knoweth them that trust in him**.

Acts 23:6

6 But when Paul perceived that the one part were Sadducees, and the other Pharisees, he cried out in the council, Men *and* brethren, I am a Pharisee, the son of a Pharisee: **of the hope and resurrection of the dead** I am called in question.

Acts 24:14-16

14 But this I confess unto thee, that after the way which they call heresy, so worship I the God of my fathers, believing all things which are written in the law and in the prophets:

15 And **have hope toward God,** which they themselves also allow, **that there shall be a resurrection of the dead,** both of the just and unjust.

16 And herein do I exercise myself, to have always a conscience void of offence toward God, and *toward* men.

Acts 26:4-7

4 My manner of life from my youth, which was at the first among mine own nation at Jerusalem, know all the Jews;

5 Which knew me from the beginning, if they would testify, that after the most straitest sect of our religion I lived a Pharisee.

6 And now I stand and am judged **for the hope of the promise made of God** unto our fathers:

7 Unto which *promise* our twelve tribes, instantly serving *God* day and night, **hope to come. For which hope's sake**, king Agrippa, I am accused of the Jews.

Acts 28:16-20

16 And when we came to Rome, the centurion delivered the prisoners to the captain of the guard: but Paul was suffered to dwell by himself with a soldier that kept him.

17 And it came to pass, that after three days Paul called the chief of the Jews together: and when they were come together, he said unto them, Men *and* brethren, though I have committed nothing against the people, or customs of our fathers, yet was I delivered prisoner from Jerusalem into the hands of the Romans.

18 Who, when they had examined me, would have let *me* go, because there was no cause of death in me.

19 But when the Jews spake against *it*, I was constrained to appeal unto Caesar; not that I had ought to accuse my nation of.

20 For this cause therefore have I called for you, to see *you*, and to speak with *you*: **because that for the hope of Israel I am bound with this chain**.

Romans 8:18-21

18 For I reckon that the sufferings of this present time *are* not worthy *to be compared* with the glory which shall be revealed in us.

19 For the <u>earnest expectation</u> of the creature **waiteth for the manifestation** of the sons of God.

20 For the creature was made subject to vanity, not willingly, but by reason of him **who hath subjected** *the same* **in hope**,

21 <u>Because the creature itself also shall be delivered from the bondage of corruption into the glorious liberty of the children of God</u>.

The teachings and mentions of waiting patiently on our hope is a very prominent theme throughout the New Testament letters. They are far too numerous to continue to list here, and in fact I refrained from quoting many of the Old Testament references. Anyone can do a word search through the entirety of the Bible (but especially through the New Testament) and the blessings from that study will thoroughly overwhelm any honest child of God.

What our heavenly Father has laid up in store for us inside our hope is truly magnificently awesome. I have been for years inside these studies, attempting to put into words the jest of emotions that are stirred within me each time I am led through these lessons. There are no words in any language to express those understandings. The Word of God, and his still small voice is the only true articulator.

Romans 15:4

4 For whatsoever things were written aforetime were written for our learning, that we **through patience and comfort** of the scriptures **might have hope.**

2ndThessalonians 3:4-5

4 And we have confidence in the Lord touching you, that ye both do and will do the things which we command you.

5 And the Lord direct your hearts into the love of God, and **into the patient waiting for Christ.**

James 1:4

4 **But let patience have *her* perfect work**, that ye may be perfect and entire, wanting nothing.

James 5:7

7 **Be patient therefore**, brethren, unto the coming of the Lord. Behold, the husbandman **waiteth for the precious fruit** of the earth, and **hath long patience for it,** until he receive the early and latter rain.

8 **Be ye also patient**; stablish your hearts: for the coming of the Lord draweth nigh.

Habakkuk 2:2-4

2 And the LORD answered me, and said, Write the vision, and make *it* plain upon tables, that he may run that readeth it.

3 For the vision *is* yet for an appointed time, but at the end it shall speak, and not lie: **though it tarry, wait for it**; because it will surely come, it will not tarry.

4 Behold, his soul *which* is lifted up is not upright in him: but the just shall live by his faith.

Zephaniah 3:8-9

8 **Therefore wait ye upon me**, saith the LORD, until the day that I rise up to the prey: for my determination *is* to gather the nations, that I may assemble the kingdoms, to pour upon them mine indignation, *even* all my fierce anger: <u>for all the earth shall be devoured with the fire of my jealousy.</u>
9 For then will I turn to the people a pure language, that they may all call upon the name of the LORD, to serve him with one consent.

Revelation 14:12

12 **Here is the patience of the saints**: here *are* **they that keep the commandments of God, and the faith of Jesus.**

Jeremiah 17:7

7 Blessed *is* the man **that trusteth in the LORD, and whose hope the LORD is.**

Grace and peace be multiplied to you all.

Chapter Eleven

The Blessed Hope

Years ago, during my youth, there were a number of pubic service announcements that aired regularly during the programs that boys and girls of that age were in habit of viewing. Their purpose was to promote the practice of abstinence from the use of illegally controlled substances. There were several variations and themes, all of which made perfect sense, "hoping" (pardon the pun) to get that age group to refrain from the use of the obvious subject matter if they had been exposed or in the future were it to take place. Several were very well orchestrated and remain vivid in my memory. (I watched far too much of television back then).

One of these featured two young actors depicting adolescents between the ages of approximately twelve to fourteen. The older was attempting to talk the younger into sampling a "joint" of marijuana, assuring him no one would become aware of their actions. The conversation between the two went back and forth with the younger expressing an attitude of disinterest in participating in the activity the older took for a fear of being caught.

The younger finally implied his reluctance was not due to a fear of the substance specifically or the possibility of being discovered, but the uselessness of the ingestion of the substance itself. His final comment to the older teenager was, "Why do you think they call it "dope". (I still laugh in reflection of the simplicity in the clear logic).

The term "dope head" was already in use at that time, but its application was expanded upon and reinforced due to the obvious insinuation. It also attached itself in tandem to another illustration of an egg being introduced by an individual onto a preheated skillet. The premise of that illustration was (the egg) this is your brain, (the egg placed onto the hot skillet) this is your brain on drugs.

The reference to "dope" in this chapter has nothing to do with its similarity of spelling or pronunciation with the word "hope". Those two factors are merely a coincidence within the language. The commonality they share in depicting what they portray is the subject at hand being, "why do you think they call it that".

Titus 2:13

13 **Looking for that blessed hope**, and the glorious appearing of the great God and our Saviour Jesus Christ;

This passage is interpreted by Pre-Tribulationists as making mention of the Rapture by it being referred to as the Blessed Hope. I agree with that assessment in that it is referring to the event in which the Rapture (being caught up) will be included, but the subject of the passage is the resurrection. This raises another question. Why do you think the Bible calls the resurrection hope?

We intend to clarify for you the actual meaning of the term "hope" when referring to the coming of the Lord. Placed into the context in which it was meant to be taken, it takes on a life all its own that the Church as a whole should have recognized long ago.

All believers should be looking forward to the return of our Lord and Savior, Jesus Christ. He is our hope (1ˢᵗTimothy 1:1), which when stated in this manner most believers understand the term to be referring to his return. However, it is not only his return that we should be anticipating, but the fulfillment of promise he brings with him which is the change from our current state of mortal to our new existence of immortality through him, and the life eternal which will come with our change.

When a child of God claims to believe in, and to be looking forward to the Blessed Hope, their attitudes and actions in their physical life should be reflecting the very meaning of the word.

KJV - hope / Greek: elpis from elpo - To anticipate, usually with pleasure. Expectation, confidence, faith, hope.

This is the word most commonly used in the Greek to describe the event all believers should be "anticipating", inside the context of hope. It does, of course have several other applications when describing other subjects, but all are done within these parameters. Within these boundaries we can expand our understanding of the teachings offered to us by the scripture.

The definition of the word denotes an attitude of anticipation toward an upcoming event. Anticipation implies a foreknowledge of the event by the potential participant. This foreknowledge is derived from the study of information contained in the scripture through which is taught several aspects of the events details, besides its mere arrival. What does hope bring with it upon its coming?

Psalm 16:9-10

9 Therefore my heart is glad, and my glory rejoiceth: my flesh also shall **rest in hope**.

10 For thou wilt not leave my soul in hell; neither wilt thou suffer thine Holy One to see corruption.

KJV - hope / Hebrew - betach - a place of refuge or safety, both the fact (security) and the feeling or emotion (trust). Assurance, boldly, careless (care free), without care, confidence, safe, safely, safety, secure, surely, hope.

Verse nine confirms several teachings for us. Relevant to our subject here is the speakers affirmation that his body shall reside in the grave in anticipation and expectation of his resurrection. The appearance of this assertion in the Old Testament (only one of many) verifies for us the hope awaited by this individual is the ultimate coming of the Lord and the resurrection he brings with him. The Rapture itself (the reference to our being caught up) can not be the subject here since it, in its specifics, was a mystery to the Old Testament Saints.

Verse ten, of course contains the prophetic foreshadowing of God informing us he will not leave the body of Jesus in the grave to experience the effects of physical deterioration, but that promise appears in the latter portion of the verse. King David is the writer or speaker, which is confirmed by the New Testament record pointing us to the fulfillment of this prophesy.

Acts 2:25-27

25 For **David speaketh concerning him**, I foresaw the Lord always before my face, for he is on my right hand, that I should not be moved:
26 Therefore did my heart rejoice, and my tongue was glad; moreover also my flesh shall **rest in hope**:
27 Because thou wilt not leave my soul in hell, **neither wilt thou suffer thine Holy One to see corruption.**

David said, "**I** foresaw the Lord continually before **my** face, for he is on **my** right hand, that **I** should not be moved. Therefore **my** heart rejoiced, and **my** tongue was glad. Moreover, in addition, **my flesh shall rest in hope.** Because thou will not leave **my** soul in hell (paradise), neither will you allow your **Holy One to see corruption.**

David was assured in his spirit by the Lord that his spirit self and life soul (spirit/soul) would not remain separated from his physical body, but would be rescued from paradise and eventually be reunited with his body through the resurrection. Here the word hope by definition refers to the expectation of the future resurrection.

King David was assured in his knowledge that his physical body would rest in the grave with expectation of his resurrection. He was in full assurance that the experience promised by God would be delivered. God offers, in proof of this truth, the physical resurrection of his Holy One, Jesus the Son of God himself. As he was raised, so will we be raised. As he was changed, so will we be also.

Romans 6:4-5

4 Therefore we are buried with him by baptism into death: that like as Christ was raised up from the dead by the glory of the Father, even so we also should walk in newness of life.

5 For if we have been planted together in the likeness of his death, **we shall be also** *in the likeness* **of** *his* **resurrection:**

Verse five also confirms the teaching of eternal security of the believer in that if you have been planted into the likeness of his death (immersed by spiritual baptism, into the Spirit of God who tasted death for every man) you will most certainly be resurrected at sometime in the future in his likeness, whenever that particular resurrection takes place. And that is a Divine promise.

The lost of the world will eventually experience "a" resurrection, but it will not be in his likeness, and it will be a resurrection unto death and everlasting separation. This also corroborates the teaching that the world or the lost of the world (who are without Christ) are without, or have no "hope" as was once the case with each believer before we believed.

Ephesians 2:12
12 That at that time ye were without Christ, being aliens from the commonwealth of Israel, and strangers from the covenants of promise, **having no hope**, and **without God in the world**:

As long as an unbeliever rejects the call of the Holy Spirit to repentance, they are without any hope of salvation from everlasting damnation, and the resurrection to life eternal.

Titus 2:11
11 For the grace of God that bringeth salvation hath appeared to all men,

Verse eleven of Titus chapter two states that the grace of God has appeared to all men. This is a confirmation of the convicting nature of the Holy Spirit, and God making his presence known through the Holy Ghost in some manner to every lost individual at some point in their lives. Whether that awareness is multiple in nature or takes place only once, God is faithful that every single person comes face to face with the reality of his or her own knowledge of a condition of separation between themselves and the creator.

Psalm 51:4-5

4 Against thee, thee only, have I sinned, and done *this* evil in thy sight: that thou mightest be justified when thou speakest, *and* be clear when thou judgest.

5 Behold, I was shapen in iniquity; and in sin did my mother conceive me.

The writer of Psalms fifty-one is referring to the condition in which we are conceived. We have committed no sin ourselves, nor has the writers mother (in example of all mothers) done so inside the act of conception itself, but all are conceived inside a condition of separation from God because of the disobedience of Adam, his fall, and the state of disconnection from God handed down by him. Every person is conceived and therefore born into this condition of separation or death from the creator. If a person remains in this condition their entire life until their physical death, they will die inside this spiritual death, lost. They will depart this physical world without God, without "hope", doomed to an existence of everlasting separation from him.

Each individual who is not a part of the family of God is "without hope". But now, being believers we have hope in him of the future state we are promised to be overshadowed and blessed with.

Romans 5:1-2

1 Therefore being justified by faith, we have peace with God through our Lord Jesus Christ:

2 By whom also we have access by faith into this grace wherein we stand, and **rejoice in hope of the glory of God**.

There are several passages in the scripture which confirm this promise concerning our change. Each believer should be continually rejoicing in the hope (expectation) of the glory of God that we are ultimately "clothed" in at our change. The change to immortality is the transfiguration process that will mirror Jesus' own. It will be accomplished literally through the putting on of the Glory (Holy Spirit) of God.

Philippians 3:20-21
20 For our conversation is in heaven; from whence also we look for the Saviour, the Lord Jesus Christ:
21 Who shall **change our vile body**, that it may be fashioned like unto his glorious body, according to the working whereby he is able even to subdue all things unto himself.

1ˢᵗCorinthians 15:51-52
51 Behold, I shew you a mystery; We shall not all sleep, but **we shall all be changed,**
52 In a moment, in the twinkling of an eye, at the last trump: for the trumpet shall sound, and the **dead shall be raised incorruptible, and we shall be changed**.

2ⁿᵈCorinthians 3:17-18
17 Now the Lord is that Spirit: and where the Spirit of the Lord *is*, there *is* liberty.
18 **But we all**, with open face beholding as in a glass the glory of the Lord, **are changed into the same image** from glory to glory, *even* as **by the Spirit of the Lord**.

But, if one claims to be looking forward to the change that takes place at the time of our being caught up, as most believers do, it is important not to overlook the physical evidence concerning the expectancy that the scripture details must be present in each believers life who is truly watchful and anticipating the event. If those factors are not present in a believers life, they are deluding themselves by way of the false instruction given to them by others, which is usually denominationally based.

Titus 2:11-15
11 For the grace of God that bringeth salvation hath appeared to all men,
12 Teaching us that, **denying ungodliness and worldly lusts, we should live soberly, righteously, and godly, in this present world**;
13 Looking for that blessed hope, and the glorious appearing of the great God and our Saviour Jesus Christ;
14 Who gave himself for us, **that he might redeem us from all iniquity, and purify unto himself a peculiar people, zealous of good works**.
15 These things speak, and exhort, and rebuke with all authority. Let no man despise thee.

If the qualities found in these passages are not reflected in the physical life of the believer who claims an anticipation for the Blessed Hope (which is the resurrection/change to the state of immortality at the time of our being caught up), they have successfully deceived themselves into the belief of being future participants of the resurrection which will include the Rapture. They do have reserved in their future a resurrection from physical death to life everlasting, but it will not take place at the time the Bride of Christ is caught up to meet Jesus in the air.

2ndCorinthians 1:3-7
3 Blessed *be* God, even the Father of our Lord Jesus Christ, the Father of mercies, and the God of all comfort;
4 Who comforteth us in all our tribulation, that we may be able to comfort them which are in any trouble, by

the comfort wherewith we ourselves are comforted of God.

5 **For as the sufferings of Christ abound in us, so our consolation also aboundeth by Christ.**

6 **And whether we be afflicted,** *it is* **for your consolation and salvation,** which is effectual in the enduring of the same sufferings which we also suffer: or **whether we be comforted,** *it is* **for your consolation and salvation.**

7 **And our hope of you** *is* **stedfast, knowing, that as ye are partakers of the sufferings, so** *shall ye be* **also of the consolation.**

The consolation mentioned in these passages is the Blessed Hope itself. Our change upon the arrival of the return of our Bridegroom Jesus Christ. But afflictions in this life which are accompanied by and coupled to tribulations are the byproducts of separating ourselves from the world. Paul reaffirms this teaching several times in his letters, but here in 2ndCorinthians he does so twice. Once in the opening of the letter of chapter one shown above, and again in chapter six in even more dramatic detail.

2ndCorinthians 6:14-18

14 **Be ye not unequally yoked together with unbelievers:** for what fellowship hath righteousness with unrighteousness? and what communion hath light with darkness?

15 And what concord hath Christ with Belial? or what part hath he that believeth with an infidel?

16 And what agreement hath the temple of God with idols? for ye are the temple of the living God; as God hath said, I will dwell in them, and walk in *them*; and I will be their God, and they shall be my people.

17 **Wherefore come out from among them, and be ye separate**, saith the Lord, and **touch not the unclean** *thing*; and I will receive you,

18 And will be a Father unto you, and ye shall be my sons and daughters, saith the Lord Almighty.

In these passages, Paul asks a series of questions to the believer, then gives directives of living in this physical life that are based on the sole answer to each of these questions.

1. What fellowship does righteousness have with unrighteousness?
2. What communion or partnership has light with darkness?
3. What concord or commonality does Christ have with Belial?
4. What part has he that believes with one who does not believe?
5. What does the temple of God have in agreement with idols?

The answer to each one of these questions is none of the above. Absolutely nothing. They have no commonality, fellowship, communion, agreement, or otherwise part in each other whatsoever. Each of these models demonstrate a direct polar opposite of the other. Therefore, we are to refrain from being associated (or yoked) with unbelievers as exampled by each of these illustrations. That is not to say we should have no contact with unbelievers whatsoever, for it is our duty to witness and spread the good news of the gospel throughout the world community, but we are not to join ourselves to them in fellowship.

These passages command us to come out from among them (a phrase which denotes part of the Church has joined itself to them in violation) and we are to be noticeably separate from the world which would include all the events and activities it participates in to amuse or otherwise pacify itself in the physical. We are instructed by God, through Paul, that we are forbidden to have contact with anything that is considered to be unclean in comparison to a life of righteousness. Otherwise, association with the impure habits of the world, by their very nature, would lead us into disobedient behavior.

It will surprise the majority of the Church why, which is explained in verses sixteen through eighteen of this same passage.

God further reminds us that we are the temple of the living God. God has said, "I will dwell in them, and walk in them, and I will be their God, and they shall be my people". This is a condition that exists in every single believer through the salvation experience. It is a done deal. We are all, as believers possessors of the Holy Spirit of God through the indwelling. But, we are instructed as believers to come out from among them (the world), and be ye separate, saith the Lord, and touch not the unclean thing, and he will receive us. This is an additional reception beyond that of joining oneself to the family of God and becoming a participant of the indwelling.

It is a direct reference to what is referred to by the Church as the Blessed Hope (the Rapture), for if the people of God (believers) do not conform to the directives of separation (from the world), we will not be received by Jesus upon his return. This is confirmed in the final phrase by him informing us what we are to receive upon obedience to these directives.

If we conform and obey in compliance to the separation as per God's command, he will be a Father unto us (the Father of the Bridegroom, not just a God) and we shall be his sons and daughters (not just a people), says the Lord Almighty. But the nonconformists, although they remain a people of God, were disobedient and will be forced to endure the Great Tribulation along with the world. They are guilty of indulging in all the various available lusts of the world, however innocent the noncompliant have convinced themselves such practices to be. This can be verified from the phrase "come out from among them" which confirms their participation in the disobedient activities.

Another "yoke" mentioned by the scripture in connection to awaiting our hope, is the yoke of bondage. The New Testament uses this term to describe the relationship believers lived in while under the Old Covenant. While in effect the people of God were in bondage to the law. They were bound to the "letter" of the law, to perform the do's, and abstain from the don'ts prescribed by God. When found in violation it was by disobedience to the ordinances written into the law.

Galatians 3:10
10 For as many as are of the works of the law **are under the curse**: for it is written, Cursed *is* every one that continueth not in all things which are written in the book of the law to do them.

Transgression of the law "slew" the transgressor in that their fellowship was hindered by separating them from their heavenly Father until sacrifice according to the law was performed and compliance brought them back into fellowship. The Old Covenant was the physical representation of the spiritual New Covenant we as believers live under today. Paul, who lived under the Old Covenant as a Pharisee or doctor of the law, explained the fellowship inside the relationship established by God with the people of God.

Romans 7:10-11

10 And the commandment, which *was ordained* to life, **I found** *to be* **unto death**.

11 For sin, taking occasion by the commandment, deceived me, and **by it slew** *me*.

The New Covenant was established through the death and resurrection of Christ to initiated a spiritual relationship with God that could not and would not be severed in any way by this physical world. The only influence the physical could have on the New Covenant relationship would be in the hindrance of fellowship between the Father and the child of God, if the child were neglecting to walk in the Spirit.

Romans 8:1-3

1 *There is* therefore now no condemnation to them which are in Christ Jesus, **who walk not after the flesh, but after the Spirit**.

2 For the **law of the Spirit** of life in Christ Jesus hath made me **free from the law of sin and death**. (sin, which brings separation).

3 For what the law could not do, in that it was weak through the flesh, God sending his own Son in the likeness of sinful flesh, and for sin, **condemned sin in the flesh**:

The Christians of the church of Galatia made the same mistake many Christians today have fallen prey to. The New Covenant is spiritual. It contains no physical compliance required to keep us in relationship with our heavenly Father, only fellowship with him. The Galatians had attempted to reach back to the physical law, and began an integration of physical requirements into the law of the spirit of the New Covenant, circumcision being their first effort. This put them in violation of its purist principles, and at odds with their Heavenly Father through their Bridegroom Jesus Christ.

Galatians 5:1-5

1 **Stand fast** therefore in the liberty wherewith **Christ hath made us free**, and **be not entangled again with the yoke of bondage**.

2 Behold, I Paul say unto you, that if ye be circumcised, Christ shall profit you nothing.

3 For I testify again to every man that is circumcised, that he is a debtor to do the whole law.

4 Christ is become of no effect unto you, whosoever of you are justified by the law; **ye are fallen from grace**. (Not fallen from salvation, but fallen from God's good favor, grace).

5 For **we through the Spirit wait for the hope of righteousness** by faith.

Paul begins this teaching with the proclamation that the Galatians needed to stand fast in that which had made them free. This decree establishes that a believer can fall out of fellowship with God if one does not remain faithful. He warns them that what they are attempting to do will entangle them in the yoke of bondage within the old law which is unnecessary and has been replaced by the New Covenant.

The Galatians had reached back into the law and were trying to integrate circumcision into the law of the spirit. They were attempting to establish a physical ritual as a necessity of compliance under the New Covenant. No act of physicality is or can be applicable under the New Covenant to make any individual a child of God, or to keep any person a child of God. The New Law of the Spirit of Life in Jesus Christ is just that. Spiritual. It has literally made us free from the law of sin (disobedience) and death (separation) which Jesus conquered and triumphant over himself.

Nothing in the physical is required for entrance into the family of God, and no physical act can expel an individual from the family of God. Physical morality, and compliance to the will of God is only applicable inside the family for the purpose of maintaining fellowship with the Father. Any one individual, or any organized religious institution that claims any physical ritual act a necessary part of the initiating or maintaining of salvation, is in direct violation of the Law of the Spirit itself, and therefore out of fellowship with their Heavenly Father.

The Galatians had crossed that line during Paul's ministry, just as many Christian denominations have done so today. Any physical compliance required by the doctrine of any denomination being applied to becoming or remaining a Christian, a believer, or otherwise considered a child of God is in direct violation to the very "spirit" and intent of the Law of the Spirit of Life. If anyone attempts to justify themselves by any part of the old law, which is physical, they submit themselves to compliance with the ordinances of that law in its entirety (which can not be kept) and will suffer the same fate as the Galatians of which Paul was attempting to correct. He informed them, "You have fallen from grace" (Galatians 5:4). They had fallen out of God's good favor and were no longer in fellowship with the Father. Many Christian denominations stand in violation of the same and similar offences today.

Galatians 5:5

5 For **we through the Spirit wait for the hope of righteousness** by faith.

Confirming the spiritual nature of the New Covenant, Paul states it is through the Spirit we await our hope of righteousness, which is our resurrection from the dead in which includes our change. This event is promised in the future of every child of God which will initiate their new life in the "hereafter" and can be achieved only through the Holy Spirit of God. Period. No exceptions. In these next passages there appears no hint of an "if" connected to the final state of the subject matter in any way but a statement of fact pointing back in time in the life of every believer. In essence it teaches, "if" we have accomplished step 1, we will be a recipient of step 2.

Romans 6:3-5
3 **Know ye not, that so many of us as were baptized into Jesus Christ were baptized into his death?**
4 Therefore **we are buried with him by baptism into death**: that like as Christ was raised up from the dead by the glory of the Father, even so we also should walk in newness of life.
5 For **if** we have been **planted together in the likeness of his death, we shall be also** *in the likeness* **of** *his* **resurrection**:

If you have been baptized in the Spirit of God, you are kept by that presence in promise of the resurrection. Whether that resurrection takes place at the time of the "caught up" event or Rapture is the only concern that should be of interest to the current members of the Church. There will be several resurrections from the end of the Church Age, till the beginning of the kingdom of God when Jesus hands over his millennia kingdom (that exists throughout the one thousand year reign of Christ) to the Father himself of which Jesus will also rule. This kingdom will have no end throughout eternity. Other incredible references to the hope in which we are to be looking forward to and waiting on are as follows.

Ephesians 1:15-18

15 Wherefore I also, after I heard of your faith in the Lord Jesus, and love unto all the saints,

16 Cease not to give thanks for you, making mention of you in my prayers;

17 **That** the God of our Lord Jesus Christ, **the Father of glory, may give unto you the <u>spirit of wisdom</u> and <u>revelation</u> in the <u>knowledge of him</u>:**

18 **The eyes of your understanding being enlightened; <u>that ye may know</u>** what is the **<u>hope of his calling</u>,** and what the **riches of the glory of his inheritance** in the saints,

God not only wants all of his children to be recipients of our change at the time of the Rapture, but wishes for us to be knowledgeable in all aspects of his plan of which our change to immortality is the greatest of all the contained blessings. Through his Word and the Holy Spirit he wishes us to gain wisdom and knowledge which will lead us to revelations of understanding that we may know what is the hope of his calling and be enlightened in regards to all the riches involved in the glory of his inheritance reserved for all the saints.

Ephesians 4:4-6

4 *There is* one body, and one Spirit, even as ye are called in **one hope of your calling**;

5 One Lord, one faith, one baptism,

6 One God and Father of all, who *is* above all, and through all, and in you all.

Philippians 1:20

20 **According to my earnest expectation and** *my* **hope**, that in nothing I shall be ashamed, but *that* with all boldness, as always, *so* now also Christ shall

be magnified in my body, whether *it be* by life, or by death.

Paul was absolute in his assurance concerning the reception of God's promise of his resurrection. There was no doubt in him whatsoever that he had attained within the parameters set by the Almighty and had been transformed by spiritual baptism and was reborn a child of God. He was confident in his expectation of the change from mortal to immortality whenever that change was scheduled by God to occur. (We will also look at his teachings concerning the things which accompany salvation, which includes the possibility of not being included in the Blessed Hope of which he uses himself as example).

Colossians 1:4-6
  4 Since we heard of your faith in Christ Jesus, and of the love *which ye have* to all the saints,
  5 **For the hope which is laid up for you in heaven**, whereof ye heard before in the word of the truth of the gospel;
  6 Which is come unto you, as *it is* in all the world; and bringeth forth fruit, as *it doth* also in you, since the day ye heard *of it*, and knew the grace of God in truth:

Colossians 1:21-23
21 And you, that were sometime alienated and enemies in *your* mind by wicked works, yet now hath he reconciled
22 In the body of his flesh through death, to present you holy and unblameable and unreproveable in his sight:
23 **"If" ye continue** in the faith grounded and settled, and *be* <u>**not moved away**</u> from the <u>**hope of the gospel**</u>, which ye have heard, *and* which was preached to

every creature which is under heaven; whereof I Paul am made a minister;

24 Who now rejoice in my sufferings for you, and fill up that which is behind of the afflictions of Christ in my flesh for his body's sake, which is the church:

25 Whereof I am made a minister, according to the dispensation of God which is given to me for you, to fulfil the word of God;

26 *Even* **the mystery** which hath been hid from ages and from generations, **but now is made manifest to his saints:**

27 To whom God would **make known what** *is* **the riches of the glory of this mystery** among the Gentiles; which is Christ in you, **the hope of glory:**

28 Whom we preach, **warning every man**, and teaching every man in all wisdom; that we **may present every man perfect in Christ Jesus:**

29 Whereunto I also labour, striving according to his working, which worketh in me mightily.

1ˢᵗThessalonians 1:2-5

2 We give thanks to God always for you all, making mention of you in our prayers;

3 Remembering without ceasing your work of faith, and labour of love, and **patience of hope in our Lord Jesus Christ**, in the sight of God and our Father;

4 Knowing, brethren beloved, your election of God.

5 **For our gospel came** not unto you in word only, but also **in power, and in the Holy Ghost, and in much assurance**; as ye know what manner of men we were among you for your sake.

1ˢᵗThessalonians 4:13-18

13 But I would not have you to be ignorant, brethren, concerning them which are asleep, **that ye sorrow not,** even as **others which have no hope.**

14 For if we believe that Jesus died and rose again, even so **them also which sleep in Jesus will God bring with him.**

15 For this we say unto you by the word of the Lord, that we which are alive *and* remain unto the coming of the Lord **shall not prevent them which are asleep.**

16 For the Lord himself shall descend from heaven with a shout, with the voice of the archangel, and with the trump of God: and the **dead in Christ shall rise first:**

17 Then we which are alive *and* remain **shall be caught up together with them** in the clouds, to meet the Lord in the air: and **so shall we ever be with the Lord.**

18 **Wherefore comfort one another with these words.**

1ˢᵗThessalonians 5:8-9

8 But let us, who are of the day, be sober, putting on the breastplate of faith and love; and **for an helmet, the hope of salvation.**

9 For God hath not appointed us to wrath, but to obtain salvation by our Lord Jesus Christ,

2ⁿᵈThessalonians 2:16-17

16 Now our Lord Jesus Christ himself, and God, even our Father, which hath loved us, and hath given *us* **everlasting consolation and good hope through grace,**

17 Comfort your hearts, and stablish you in every good word and work.

Everlasting consolation is our assurance of the reception of the promise made to us by God. When I was a teenager, (and usually dumb as dirt) inside my denomination in our immediate church community the topic and discussion of eternal security (once saved always saved) was a frequent conversation piece and an occasional point of study. During one class room session a thought occurred to me that I shared with the group. Most of my peers agreed with me that it was almost to simple a concept to be overlooked by the Church for so long throughout the Church Age. But, it was also in such ideal agreement with eternal security.

The scripture refers to salvation repetitively as eternal life and everlasting life. Setting aside all the studies and evaluations that could be done with all the accumulative data provided on the subject by the Word of God, eternal and everlasting are the names given that life by the scripture. Based solely on that information and considering it evidence for analysis, I theorized if an individual could loose their salvation in any shape, form or fashion, what is everlasting or eternal about it. Made perfect sense to me as a youth. Today it remains a valid consideration.

1ˢᵗTimothy 1:1
1 Paul, an apostle of Jesus Christ by the commandment of God our Saviour, and **Lord Jesus Christ,** *which is* **our hope;**

Titus 1:1-2
1 Paul, a servant of God, and an apostle of Jesus Christ, according to the faith of God's elect, and the acknowledging of the truth which is after godliness;
2 **In hope of eternal life,** which God, that cannot lie, **promised before the world began;**

Titus 3:4-7

4 But after that the kindness and love of God our Saviour toward man appeared,

5 Not by works of righteousness which we have done, <u>but according to his mercy he saved us, by the washing of regeneration, and renewing of the Holy Ghost</u>;

6 Which he shed on us abundantly through Jesus Christ our Saviour;

7 <u>That being justified by his grace, we should be made heirs</u> **according to the hope of eternal life.**

Hebrews 3:6

6 But Christ as a son over his own house; <u>whose house are we</u>, **"if" we hold fast the confidence and the rejoicing of the hope firm unto the end.**

Hebrews 6:11-12

11 And we desire that every one of you do shew the same diligence **to the full assurance of hope unto the end**:

12 That ye be not slothful, but followers of them <u>who through faith and patience inherit the promises</u>.

Hebrews 6:16-20

16 For men verily swear by the greater: and an oath for confirmation *is* to them an end of all strife.

17 Wherein God, willing more abundantly to shew unto the heirs of promise the immutability of his counsel, confirmed *it* by an oath:

18 That by two immutable things, in which *it was* impossible for God to lie, we might have a strong consolation, who have fled for refuge **to lay hold upon the hope set before us:**

19 **Which** *hope* **we have as an anchor of the soul, both sure and stedfast**, and which entereth into that within the veil;

20 Whither the forerunner is for us entered, *even* Jesus, made an high priest for ever after the order of Melchisedec.

Hebrews 7:19-21

19 For the law made nothing perfect, **but the bringing in of a better hope** *did*; by the which we draw nigh unto God.

1ˢᵗPeter 1:3-5

3 Blessed *be* the God and Father of our Lord Jesus Christ, which according to his abundant mercy hath **begotten us again unto a lively hope** by the resurrection of Jesus Christ from the dead,

4 To an inheritance incorruptible, and undefiled, and that fadeth not away, reserved in heaven for you,

5 Who are kept by the power of God through faith unto salvation ready to be revealed in the last time.

1ˢᵗPeter 1:13-16

13 Wherefore gird up the loins of your mind, be sober, **and hope to the end** for the grace that is to be brought unto you at the revelation of Jesus Christ;

14 As obedient children, not fashioning yourselves according to the former lusts in your ignorance:

15 But as he which hath called you is holy, so be ye holy in all manner of conversation;

16 Because it is written, Be ye holy; for I am holy.

1 Peter 1:20-21

20 Who verily was foreordained before the foundation of the world, but was manifest in these last times for you,

21 Who by him do believe in God, that raised him up from the dead, and gave him glory; **that your faith and hope might be in God.**

1ˢᵗPeter 3:15

15 But sanctify the Lord God in your hearts: <u>and be ready always to *give* an answer to every man that asketh you a reason</u> **of the hope that is in you** with meekness and fear:

1ˢᵗJohn 3:1-3

1 Behold, what manner of love the Father hath bestowed upon us, that we should be called the sons of God: therefore the world knoweth us not, because it knew him not.

2 Beloved, now are we the sons of God, and it doth not yet appear what we shall be: but we know that, **when he shall appear, we shall be like him**; for we shall see him as he is.

3 And every man **that hath this hope in him purifieth himself,** even as he is pure.

I have saved the meat of our feast on the teaching of hope for last. In concluding this study we will look at the two primary Greek words that are translated into the King James English as hope in comparison with the Hebrew definition of the word used in Psalm 16:9. The definitions themselves set the stage for the teachings which the scripture conveys.

KJV - hope / Greek: elpis from elpo - To anticipate, usually with pleasure. Expectation, confidence, faith, hope.

Elpis is the most common Greek word used in the New Testament when referring to the hope of the resurrection. The Church as a whole is unaware that within the definition there is no insinuation in the Greek understanding of failure to receive that which is in question of being hoped for, as is present with its English counterpart. In the English, the meaning is implied by the context. In the Greek the context is defined by the use of the word itself.

The same is even more true and dramatic in the use of the Hebrew word betach.

KJV - hope / Hebrew - betach - a place of refuge or safety, both the fact (security) and the felling or emotion (trust). Assurance, boldly, careless (care free), without care, confidence, safe, safely, safety, secure, surely, hope.

If, in the Greek, one wishes to express the hope of something that has any chance of not being received, the word elpizo is substituted for elpis.

KJV - hope, hoped / Greek - elpizo from elpis - to expect or confide, have hope or have hoped for, trust.

It expresses the idea of a given thing literally "hoped" for, as we understand it in our modern English. Or in some cases, an illustration of us looking into the past to something we had hoped to have received, or would have preferred to have happened. This is quite easily seen by tracing out in scripture the usage of each in the passages in which they appear.

In all previous passages the use of the word "elpis" is conveying the expectancy of the arrival or reception of what is being waited on. In other words, it will arrive or will be received. The same can not be said of the word "elpizo".

Luke 6:34
34 And if ye lend *to them* of whom **ye hope** (elpizo) to receive, what thank have ye? for sinners also lend to sinners, to receive as much again.

Luke 23:8
8 And when Herod saw Jesus, he was exceeding glad: for he was desirous to see him of a long *season*, because he had heard many things of him; and **he hoped** (elpizo) to have seen some miracle done by him.

Acts 24:24-26
24 And after certain days, when Felix came with his wife Drusilla, which was a Jewess, he sent for Paul, and heard him concerning the faith in Christ.
25 And as he reasoned of righteousness, temperance, and judgment to come, Felix trembled, and answered, Go thy way for this time; when I have a convenient season, I will call for thee.
26 **He hoped** (elpizo) also that money should have been given him of Paul, that he might loose him: wherefore he sent for him the oftener, and communed with him.

2ndCorinthians 8:5
5 And *this they did*, not as **we hoped** (elpizo), but first gave their own selves to the Lord, and unto us by the will of God.

All of these passages display an event that is wished for or in hope of by an individual, but may or may not be forthcoming. It is clear that in some of these instances they were even denied "by providence" what they were hoping for. The same can not be said of elpis in the Greek and betach in the Hebrew. Both are declaring the assurance, confidence and security of the promises of God. And as the scripture confirms,

Titus 1:2
2 In hope (elpis) of eternal life, which God, that cannot lie, promised before the world began;

Grace and peace be multiplied to you all.

Chapter Twelve

The "If's" of the Scripture

As we documented in a previous chapter, the "if's" of the scripture are the most overlooked indicator of truth there exists in the Bible. They are not the most informative, they are not the most plentiful, but they are the most overlooked. Several passages of scripture falling into this category can not be accepted at face value by various denominations due to the fact they must be reinterpreted in order to fit into their preconceived teachings handed down over time from teacher to pupil which make possible their doctrine. As a consequence of the appearance of the "if" contained in various passages, phrases must be read in a manner so as to fit into each denominations accepted belief, thereby, not rocking their particular denominational boat.

Well, >◇ S P L A S H ◇<, start bailing, here we go.

The use of the word "if" is such a very simple concept even a child can understand it. And in truth, at a Bible conference I once held on the subject of the Rapture, it just so happened that a child did, perfectly. To illustrate the concept, I deliberately and completely unrehearsed, engaged a seven year old boy into my presentation out of the congregation. (That still small voice assured me I had nothing to fear and was taking no chances in not accomplishing my goal). I invited him to the front before the rest of the audience with the following proposition.

I said, "Jaylen, if you will come to the front, I will give you this dollar." I'll give you three guesses as to his reaction and response and the first two do not count.

He was going to receive a dollar. That was a fact. He could see it, as I had lifted it into the air for him to do just that. But, there was a catch, albeit in this particular circumstance, not much of one.

Because of the "if" contained inside the proposition, there was a condition laid down to be performed before acquisition of the afore mentioned currency could be obtained. Simply put, he would have to come get the dollar in order for it to become his. He understood the proposal perfectly, and without any further explanation or prompting, did just that.

This particular event took place some several years ago, and it is my belief that a child of seven would think a dollar a pretty meager sum today. I am sure the next time I use this illustration it would be prudent to raise my ante to at least a five dollar bill.

My point, however, was made and well taken. We had a wonderful time that Saturday at Damascus Baptist Church. I had known Jaylen's father, Philip Love for many years, and the church with which he served as deacon had asked me for a presentation on the Conditional Rapture teachings. It was a blessing to share my understandings with them. Never before had a congregation been so attentive and patience regarding my program. Not every member of the assembly was in total agreement with "my" teachings, but the majority that were present were very interested, and the remainder were intrigued.

I was very well received by everyone who attended. After each session they engaged me in conversation with questions they had concerning the obvious subject matter. There were skeptics present, of course, but they were quite respectful in their attitudes. There was a lot of love in that church. (No pun intended). I still get a happy tear in my eye when reminded of them and that day.

Because of the nature and frequent use of the word "if", it appears well over 1300 times in the scripture. Not surprisingly, the overwhelming majority of these appearances have nothing to do with the teachings of The Rapture in general or The Conditional Rapture specifically, but several are quite fascinating and a few have shown themselves to be tied directly to these teachings.

The first passage we will look at falls under the first category (has nothing to do with) as it is not related to our study. I only wish to establish that the writer (me) and the reader (you) are on the same train of thought.

Matthew 4:1-2
1 Then was Jesus led up of the Spirit into the wilderness to be tempted of the devil.
2 And when he had fasted forty days and forty nights, he was afterward an hungred.

This information is quite straight forward and direct. You know the story well. After the baptism of Jesus, he was driven (Mark 1:12) or led by the Spirit of God into the wilderness. The scripture says "to" (for the purpose of) be tempted of the devil or Satan, depending on which gospel one is reading from. (See also Luke 4:2-3). Then the tempter engages Jesus in a conversation concerning his hunger, disguising his suggested course of action as a solution to the supposed problem.

Matthew 4:3
3 And when the tempter came to him, he said, If thou be the Son of God, command that these stones be made bread.

Satan never mentions the power of God or that Jesus had access to that power. He makes no statements declaring God's nature of creativity nor Jesus' ability as the Son of God to be included in that act. All of this is implied inside the command he challenges Jesus to perform.

But, by the manner in which Satan's words are recorded by the writers of the gospels, and our knowledge of God's power over all creation, we know Jesus has the ability over this physical world (since his was the voice that spoke it into existence) to change stones into bread just as easily as he will soon turn water into wine. But the focal point of this illustration is the technique used by scripture to accomplish the implied lesson, which contains the truth. The technique in question is the ability of God's Word to teach through the omission of information. This ability declares the magnificence of its complexity in its divine style, and as I have clearly stated in previous chapters, never ceases to amaze me.

"If" you are the Son of God, command.

First, this statement implies that Satan knew (or more accurately, knows) the Son of God is capable of accomplishing such a feat. It is not stated directly in that manner, but it is easily understood by the context. If this were not true it could not be legitimately recognized in and gleaned from the text.

Second, Satan is actually questioning Jesus' divinity, attempting to persuade him to prove his heavenly origin through the accomplishment of a supernatural task. The operation of a miracle by Jesus through divine means in and of itself is not the temptation to be avoided. Jesus will perform multiple hundreds of them (if not thousands) during his terrestrial physical life.

However, each of them will be (or was) provoked by need, love or compassion. It is a different matter all together for him to respond at the request or prompting of the great deceiver and the father of lies. Proving himself to be the only begotten of the Father under the described circumstances would constitute an act of pride. For Jesus to perform such at the provocation of Satan, would be the equivalent of disobedience to the Father, an act he is quite incapable of carrying out.

If you, the reader, are saying to yourself, "Yea, well DUUH. So? Anyone can see that." Then we are both on the same page. The lessons learned from these passages are not stated by the text but they are easily understood after an individual has acquired even a rudimental knowledge of the Holy Spirits style in documenting the truth contained in God's Word.

Many other passages (I believe all passages) which contain the word "if" are just as simple to understand. They do however, become increasingly difficult to be accepted by those who's current beliefs differ from the suggested teachings.

Hebrews 3:1-14
1 Wherefore, holy brethren, partakers of the heavenly calling, consider the Apostle and High Priest of our profession, Christ Jesus;

Jesus is acknowledged as the ultimate apostle and our High Priest inside our faith. As the scripture says, he is the author and finisher of it (Hebrews 12:2). But before verse one makes this statement of fact, it first identifies whom the writer is speaking to.

I always make a point to clarify that the book of Hebrews was not written to the Church as a whole. All the lessons contained in it are of course applicable to all believers throughout the Church Age in the spiritual (as is the entire Bible), but in the physical, the letter itself was written to Christian Jews who had been converted from Judaism. This is the reason the book of Hebrews is laden with references of the Law and imagery of the Old Covenant. Its content can be difficult to understand and its full intent can not be grasped unless studied within that parameter.

The writer, presumably Hebrew himself due to his knowledge of law and Old Testament imagery, addresses his reader as Holy Brethren, partakers of the heavenly calling. This confirms the fact he is not only writing to his fellow brethren Jews but Hebrew believers in Christ. Most Christians think this point to be a trivial one, but when not taken into account and the lesson is misconstrued to include the unbelievers in the midst of an assembly or congregation, incorrect doctrine is the common result. The book of Revelation is the prime example of such an assumption.

Here it can be clearly understood that no unbeliever is being addressed. One can not be a partaker of the heavenly calling or be referred to as a member of the Holy Brethren without first being a believer.

Hebrews 3:2-5
2 Who was faithful to him that appointed him, as also Moses *was faithful* in all his house.
3 For this *man* was counted worthy of more glory than Moses, inasmuch as he who hath builded the house hath more honour than the house.
4 For every house is builded by some *man*; but he that built all things *is* God.
5 And Moses verily *was* faithful in all his house, as a servant, for a testimony of those things which were to be spoken after;

Verses 2 through 5 states Jesus was faithful in all the work that the Father had appointed him to accomplish. It then compares the mission of Jesus to the work of Moses, and makes mention of the building of a house (or household) in which both were faithful, confirming the success of each.

The household that Jesus has established is the family of God that is one in Christ and has been adopted into that family "legally" through his blood sacrifice on the cross (and his subsequent death/separation). This household of which the Church is a part under the grace (or good favor of God) of the New Covenant is espoused or engaged directly to Christ throughout the Church Age confirmed by 2ndCorinthians 11:1-2.

   2 Corinthians 11:1-2
   1 Would to God ye could bear with me a little in *my* folly: and indeed bear with me.
   2 For I am jealous over you with godly jealousy: for I have espoused you to one husband, that I may present *you as* a chaste virgin to Christ

The Church as the espoused Bride awaits the return of her Bridegroom that he might gather her and take her back to the Fathers house. This gathering will result in the presentation of her to the Father by the Son mentioned in verse two, which Paul examples himself for illustration.

The house itself that is "under construction" is the "many mansions" (dwelling places) he is preparing for us within New Jerusalem. As the Bride of Christ, the Holy City of God is our final destination as we await our Bridegrooms return. This represents the transition that takes place at the time the Son of the household makes his espoused Bride his wife through the completion of the marriage ceremony. (Rev. 19:7). Revelation 19:7 is a very important passage in relation to our next verse in Hebrews chapter three.

Hebrews 3:6

6 But Christ as a son over his own house; whose house are we, **"if" we hold fast the confidence** and the **rejoicing of the hope** firm unto the end.

As the son of a household takes a wife and begins his own which he himself resides as husband, it is done within the interior of his fathers house of which he is still a member and his bride is an addition. He retains his original status inside his fathers house but with the incorporation of he and his wife constituting a nucleus of their own, of which he is head.

Taking this into consideration in relation to verse six,

Hebrews 3:6

6 But Christ as a son over his own house; **whose house are we, "if"** we hold fast the confidence and the rejoicing of the **hope firm unto the end**.

That is what it says. This passage is speaking of course, to the entire Church. But the majority of the modern Church is forced to ignore the plain text reading of this verse due to the inability to fit its message into their current doctrine. The clarity of the passage is easy to grasp if read in the manner with which it is written.

"But Christ (Jesus) as a Son over his own house (his own contained inside the Father's household), whose house are we (who's household we are included in) **_"IF"_** we hold fast the confidence (holding firm to the belief and teachings of) the **rejoicing of the HOPE** (looking forward to the Blessed Hope) firm (with determination) unto the end. (end of the Church Age).

The comments accompanying this clarification are of course what I sincerely believe the Lord has impressed upon me to understand. There are critics that adamantly argue I am incorrect in "my" interpretation. I will say again, that we, mere mortal man, can not interpret what is of heavenly origin. It is the Holy Spirits function to interpret to us the truth.

Interpretation set aside however, I simply can not ignore the clear reading of the scripture upon its mention and inclusion of "If". This stipulation sets forth a condition to be met to be included as a member of the Son's household. All believers remain a member of the Father's house as a child of God, but according to this passage (and another in this same chapter) we have to "hold fast the confidence and the rejoicing of the hope firm unto the end" in order to be included in the Son's household which is the nucleus of the whole.

Any individual disagreeing with my "interpretation" is also charging themselves to explain the correct meaning of the passage if I am mistaken. Unfortunately, for each of my opponents, any response is itself interpretation as any teaching can be reinterpreted by their understanding of the procedure. Correct interpretation, however, is taught by God's word itself through the Spirit and corroborated by corresponding scripture through the same. (By two or three witnesses).

Verses seven through eleven refer back to a period in Israel's history during the time in the wilderness that God tried and tested their faith and obedience. He uses that situation as illustration to make point of a future rest we are all called to enter into (in the spiritual) as was Israel called in the desert to do so (in the physical), but only if we again meet the requirements to do so as was Israel's task.

Hebrews 3:7-11

7 Wherefore (as the Holy Ghost saith, To day **"if"** ye will hear his voice,

8 Harden not your hearts, as in the provocation, in the day of temptation in the wilderness:

9 When your fathers tempted me, proved me, and saw my works forty years.

10 Wherefore I was grieved with that generation, and said, They do alway err in *their* heart; and they have not known my ways.

11 So I sware in my wrath, **They shall not enter into my rest.**)

Israel failed in that endeavor, and was denied access into the rest God had prepared for them at that time in their history. Their first mistake was refusing to listen to the voice of God (Jehovah) and submit to the truth contained inside the commandments of God. In short, they refused to apply the truth of God and the Truth that is God to their lives. Then the scripture turns to the Christian Jew of the 1ˢᵗ Century (in the physical) and the modern Church of today (in the spiritual) and states,

Hebrews 3:12-13

12 Take heed, brethren, lest there be in any of you an **evil heart of unbelief, in departing from the living God.**

13 But exhort one another daily, while it is called To day; lest any of you be **hardened through the deceitfulness of sin.**

These verses confirm for us that it is possible for a believer to be guilty of turning away from God, or more accurately turning from God's will. This action is caused by an unbelief in us due to a disobedient heart. Since we are incapable of unbelief of the truth in Christ once enlightened of that truth, unbelief in the subject at hand is the only other possible option, namely, the entrance into the rest which is the subject matter. Coupled with the teachings here of the Father's and Son's individual households being the focal point of our lesson, verse fourteen goes on to confirm,

> Hebrews 3:14
> 14 For we are made partakers of Christ, **"if"** we hold the beginning of our confidence stedfast unto the end;

That is what it says. God's word again informs us that we are intended to be direct partakers of Christ, but only if we hold the beginning of our confidence in him steadfast till the end. Since all believers, baring no individual, are partakers of the Spirit of God upon our conversion, and Jesus promised upon his indwelling of himself in us he would never leave us nor forsake us, salvation itself can not be the issue here. In truth, all that is necessary is to believe the Word as written.

In this passage we are called to be partakers of Christ specifically. In other references in the scripture we are invited or commanded to participate in the plan of God through the Spirit of God, or salvation, or patiently await the kingdom to come among many other invitations of God. Here, however, we are charged to be partakers directly of Christ himself, the Son of the Father. The Bridegroom. He is pleading with the specific entity that is called by his name (the Christian Church) to hold to the faith and beliefs that were originally establish in her until the appointed time. When it arrives she is to be ready to be gathered to the Fathers house. Unfortunately, she does not yet appear to be prepared.

The modern Church resembles most closely the church of the scripture that needs constant correcting and reprimand at the hand of the men who penned the New Testament by way of the inspiration of the Holy Spirit of God. Akin to the book of Revelation, the greatest majority of teachings contain in the pages of the New Testament are corrective in nature. In layman's terms, something was wrong in the structure of the Church. The apostles, most notably Paul, identified problems that were brought to his attention through the tutorship of the Holy Spirit. He then promptly informed each assembly accordingly, so that the appropriate corrections could be applied. It is no different today.

1ˢᵗCorinthians 3:3

3 For ye are yet carnal: for whereas *there is* among you **envying**, and **strife**, and **divisions**, are <u>ye not carnal</u>, and <u>walk as men</u>?

Galatians 1:6

6 I marvel that **ye are so soon removed from him** that called you into the grace of Christ unto another gospel:

7 Which is not another; but there be some that trouble you, and would pervert the gospel of Christ.

Romans 6:12-13

12 **Let not sin therefore reign** in your mortal body, **that ye should obey it in the lusts thereof**.

13 **Neither yield** <u>ye your members *as* instruments of unrighteousness</u> **unto sin**: but yield yourselves unto God, as those that are alive from the dead, and your members *as* instruments of righteousness unto God.

Romans 8:12-13

12 Therefore, brethren, we are debtors, not to the flesh, to live after the flesh.

13 **For if ye live after the flesh, ye shall die**: but if ye through the Spirit do mortify the deeds of the body, ye shall live.

Galatians chapters five and six are most enlightening. When Paul is compelled to remind the recipient of an apparent short coming, the fault is not only possible by the believer, it was present.

Galatians 5:1
1 Stand fast therefore in the liberty wherewith Christ hath made us free, and **be not entangled again** with the yoke of bondage.

Galatians 5:13-16
13 For, brethren, ye have been called unto liberty; only *use* **not liberty for an occasion to the flesh**, but by love serve one another.
14 For all the law is fulfilled in one word, *even* in this; Thou shalt love thy neighbour as thyself.
15 But if ye **bite and devour one another**, take heed that ye be not consumed one of another.
16 *This* I say then, <u>Walk in the Spirit</u>, and **ye shall not fulfil the lust of the flesh.**

Galatians chapter six verse one is especially illuminating in regards to the opponents of the Conditional Rapture. I have found the following remark worded in a number of ways in the works of several authors. The following is the jest of all of these views accumulated in one illustration. The statement itself is contradictory to the teachings of the scripture.

There is a final view concerning the rapture of the church which has recently been brought to the attention of the church. It does not yet have a large following, since it stands in substantial disagreement with the scripture. There are even some differences of opinion among its small number of supporters, but it is usually depicted as follows: When the Lord Jesus comes to remove the church, only the "<u>spiritual believers</u>" will be taken. The carnal, or "backslidden" believers will be left behind to go through the Great Tribulation Period.

This statement hinges on the assumed belief that we are at fault in our concept that most of the Church is not "spiritual" or walking in the spirit. Our opposition maintains that the entire Church is spiritual because it houses the Holy Spirit within each believer.

Each believer does in fact possess the "indwelling" of the Holy Ghost. It is our opinion however, based on the scriptural evidence of qualification, that the majority of the Church fails to "walk in that presence". Failure to do so makes us vulnerable to the lust of the world. (See the afore mentioned Galatians 5:16) Indulgence in the lust of the flesh, supplied in sufficient doses by the world, when falling prey to such constitutes the sin of adultery against our Bridegroom Jesus Christ. The majority of the Church is in denial of the scriptural facts.

Galatians 6:1

1 Brethren, if a man be overtaken in a fault, **ye which are spiritual**, restore such an one in the spirit of meekness; considering thyself, lest thou also be tempted.

I shared this with a brother once who quickly pointed out that the passage does not state that the man over taken in the fault was a brother himself, suggesting that the individual in question was not a true believer, but simply associated with the church by numerical membership. This is a reasonable assumption at first glance, but, as I continually remind all believers, we need to leave no stone unturned. In truth, the directive itself possesses the response to this flawed assumption.

First, the brethren being addressed are directed to restore the individual that has been discovered in a fault. This directive is conditional on the assumption the person being dealt with is in a genuine state of repentance concerning the error he is guilty of. Therefore, the context of the passage suggests him to be sincere.

Second, whatever previous fellowship the man in question is to be restored to, the directive to reinstate him to that position or status, and the process of restoration itself defines that he had once achieved it. At some point in the passed he had been in possession of it. An individual can not be restored to something that was never theirs.

Third, whatever fault the man was guilty of, the passage warns the brethren to be cautious in their treatment of him, lest they themselves ever be found in the same situation as he. This not only suggests that all individuals mentioned in the passage are of the same spiritual blood, and capable of the same faults, it demands it.

See how the Spirit never ceases to supply us with information concerning a given subject, even through the absence of such information.

The following passages all define the fact that believers are capable of actions that are unbecoming a child of God. Every circumstance exampled constitutes unacceptable behavior, thereby rendering the offender a disobedient child. This in turn hinders their fellowship with their heavenly Father imposing a distancing (not a discontinuation) in their relationship to him.

Ephesians 5:1-8
1 Be ye therefore followers of God, as dear children;
2 And walk in love, as Christ also hath loved us, and hath given himself for us an offering and a sacrifice to God for a sweetsmelling savour.
3 But **fornication**, and all **uncleanness**, or **covetousness, let it not be once named among you**, as becometh saints;

4 Neither **filthiness**, nor **foolish talking**, nor **jesting**, which are not convenient: but rather giving of thanks.

5 For this ye know, that no whoremonger, nor unclean person, nor covetous man, who is an idolater, hath any inheritance in the kingdom of Christ and of God.

6 Let no man deceive you with vain words: for because of these things cometh the wrath of God **upon the children of disobedience**.

7 **Be not ye therefore partakers with them**.

8 For ye were sometimes darkness, but now *are ye* light in the Lord: walk as children of light:

Colossians 2:6-10

6 As ye have therefore received Christ Jesus the Lord, *so* walk ye in him:

7 Rooted and built up in him, and stablished in the faith, as ye have been taught, abounding therein with thanksgiving.

8 **Beware lest any man spoil you** through philosophy and vain deceit, **after the tradition of men, after the rudiments of the world, and not after Christ**.

9 For in him dwelleth all the fulness of the Godhead bodily.

10 And ye are complete in him, which is the head of all principality and power:

Getting back to the "If's" of the scripture,

Colossians 1:21-29

21 And you, that were sometime alienated and enemies in *your* mind by wicked works, yet now hath he reconciled

22 In the body of his flesh through death, **to present you holy and unblameable and unreproveable in his sight:**

23 **"If" ye continue in the faith grounded and settled, and** *be* **not moved away from the hope of the gospel**, which ye have heard, *and* which was preached to every creature which is under heaven; whereof I Paul am made a minister;

Colossians 3:1-4

1 **"If"** ye then be risen with Christ, seek those things which are above, where Christ sitteth on the right hand of God.

2 Set your affection on things above, **not on things on the earth.**

3 For ye are dead, and your life is hid with Christ in God.

4 <u>When Christ, *who is* our life, shall appear, **then** shall ye also appear with him in glory</u>.

2 Timothy 2:10-13

10 Therefore I endure all things for the elect's sakes, that they may also obtain the salvation which is in Christ Jesus with eternal glory.

11 *It is* a faithful saying: For **if** we be dead with *him*, we shall also live with *him*:

12 **If** we suffer, we shall also reign with *him*: **if** we deny *him*, he also will deny us:

13 **If** we believe not, *yet* he abideth faithful: he cannot deny himself.

This passage is significant given that Paul the apostle is writing to Timothy. Many scholars over look the importance of that acknowledgment. Most of Paul's letters were written to churches, and there are those that like to maintain the churches in the physical have within them members who are not yet saved. Therefore, the portion of those letters they wish not to be attributed to the Church are directed by them to the unbelievers in attendance in the church body.

Through this concept they further assert Paul's letters were written to the physical Church as a whole. Therefore, passages and phrases that we understand to be confirming The Conditional Rapture teachings, from their perspective, are directed to those imbedded inside the membership of the physical church that have not yet come to a knowledge of salvation.

Using this technique I call "selective acceptance" a denomination can pick and choose passages and phrases to be attributed to believers or unbelievers as their doctrine demands, as opposed to the correct procedure of the passages and the phrases of the scripture to establish doctrine.

In the case of Paul writing to Timothy, that can no longer be considered an issue. Both Paul and Timothy are not only believers, they are both active ministering evangelists. Although the Holy Spirit speaks by way of Paul's pen through Timothy to the entire Church throughout the whole of the Church Age in the spiritual, in the physical Paul the teacher is writing to Timothy the pupil.

2ndTimothy 2:10-13

10 Therefore I endure all things for the elect's sakes, that they may also obtain the salvation which is in Christ Jesus with eternal glory.

In verse ten, Paul is stating his will and desire for Israel as a nation to respond to the calling of the Holy Spirit and accept salvation that resides only in Jesus Christ. Verse eleven confirms the salvation that is found only in Christ is available to anyone who accepts the free gift.

2ndTimothy 2:11
11 *It is* a faithful saying: For **"if"** we be dead with *him*, we shall also live with *him*:

This verse is also one more proof passage in favor of the doctrine of eternal security of the believer. Anyone who is baptized into Jesus' death, (immersed in the Holy Spirit of God, who tasted death for every man) will live eternally in his presence. However,

2ndTimothy 2:12
12 **"If"** we suffer, we shall also reign with *him*: **"if"** we deny *him*, he also will deny us:

If we endure faithfully, looking forward to the fulfill-ments of all his promises, we will in turn reign with him. But, if we are not faithful in this life, as every believer is expected to be, he will deny us at the time he comes for his Bride. The unfaithful will be divorced, and denied transfor-mation of the body at that time and translation to the Father's house as Bride to Jesus the Son.

2ndTimothy 2:13
13 **If** we believe not, *yet* he abideth faithful: he cannot deny himself.

The unfaithful will miss the Rapture due to unbelief in the specifics of God's promises due primarily to willful ignorance (lack of understanding) of the details inside his plan which quite naturally leads to disobedience in relation to those particular factors. (Similar to adherence to the ordi-nance of the laws under the Old Covenant. Shadow of things to come? Hebrews 10:1.) But, the individuals of the Church that remain after the Rapture are still children of God, even though they have been disobedient to the teachings in his

Word in relation to the hope of the gospel in Christ. (Just as a Hebrew, even when in full violation of the Old Covenant Law could not change the fact he was still "born" Hebrew or Israelite, and would always be so.)

They still have in their possession through their spiritual birth, the Spirit that Jesus promised would never leave nor forsake them. Because of the presence of Jesus himself contained in all of Gods children, he cannot deny the presence of himself in them. This passage is indeed a confirmation of eternal security of the believer. Once a child of God always a child of God, but the unfaithful at the point of the Rapture will pay for their disobedience with the sacrifice of their physical life during the Great Tribulation Period.

Hebrews 2:1-4

1 Therefore we ought to give the more earnest heed to the things which we have heard, lest at any time we should let *them* slip.
2 For **"if"** the word spoken by angels was stedfast, and **every transgression and disobedience received a just recompence of reward**;
3 **How shall we escape, if we neglect so great salvation**; which at the first began to be **spoken by the Lord**, and was confirmed unto us by them that heard *him*;
4 God also bearing *them* witness, both with signs and wonders, and with divers miracles, and gifts of the Holy Ghost, according to his own will?

If every transgression and disobedience received a just "recompense" (compensation, or reimbursement) of reward, how shall we (ourselves) escape (the Great Tribulation), if we neglect (ignore all warnings of) so great a salvation (the teachings concerning that escape). This explanation is confirmed by the remainder of the verse in the mention that what is being discussed was first taught by the Lord himself, then confirmed by the teachings of the apostles.

Jesus, of course, was the first to disclose information regarding the mystery of the escape that was then expounded on and confirmed by the apostles which heard and shared those teachings with the early Church.

Sadly, the largest majority of the Church throughout the Church Age, has not heeded those warnings. She was constantly being corrected by the apostles of the early Church as confirmed by the corrective nature of the scripture. I pray the modern Church will awaken to the truth before it is too late. According to the teachings of the Conditional Rapture, it will fail to do so, but that is my prayer and the reason for the publication of this manuscript.

All true believers will spend eternity in the presence of God after the end of their physical life, but the Bride of Christ has even greater in store through the resurrection of The Blessed Hope at the time of our being "caught up". Among other things, Paul called it "The Prize of the High Calling of God".

Philippians 3:7-14
> 7 But what things were gain to me, those I counted loss for Christ.
> 8 Yea doubtless, and I count all things *but* loss for the excellency of the knowledge of Christ Jesus my Lord: for whom I have suffered the loss of all things, and do count them *but* dung, **that I may win Christ,**

In verses three through six Paul mentions a list of things which, from the Jewish perspective, are counted as accomplishments in the flesh. Some are by birth, others are attained by striving for them. But all are counted by him for naught (nothing, nada, zilch, zero, zip) in comparison to the excellency of just the knowledge of Christ. He puts them on the scale of waste, in order (for the sole purpose) to win Christ.

Question: If Paul is a Christian (and he has been since his conversion on the road to Damascus), what is this that he is striving (working) forward toward Christ to win of him?

It would appear to be related to the things the scripture says accompany salvation. Something that is possessed by salvation and only obtained through it after conversion has taken place in a persons life.

Hebrews 6:9
9 But, beloved, we are persuaded better things of you, and **things that accompany salvation**, though we thus speak.

(Our passage that confirms there are things that accompany salvation).

Philippians 3:9-14
9 And **be found in him**, not having mine own righteousness, which is of the law, but that which is through the faith of Christ, the righteousness which is of God by faith:

In verse nine Paul makes the statement he desires to be found "in Christ", not having his own righteousness. Not Christ in him, but he in Christ. This is a reference to walking in the Spirit, as all Christians are in possession of the indwelling but not all Christians live their lives under the influence of the Spirit, listening to the still small voice of God allowing him to lead, guide and direct them inside their life.

Philippians 3:10-14

10 That I may know him, and the power of his resurrection, and the fellowship of his sufferings, being made conformable unto his death;

11 **If** by any means I might attain unto the resurrection of the dead.

"**If**" I might attain (manage to achieve the accomplishment of) the resurrection of the dead. Paul states quite clearly that this is in fact what the actions and duties in his life were prayed to result in. To be included in the resurrection of the dead at the time of the Blessed Hope. He knows beyond the shadow of any doubt he is a child of God by God's grace which will ultimately result in "a" resurrection from the dead, but accompanying salvation is the promise of an even greater treasure. "The" resurrection of the dead at the time of the Blessed Hope. He goes on to state,

Philippians 3:12-14

12 Not as though I had already attained, either were already perfect: but I follow after, **if that I may apprehend that for which also I am apprehended of Christ Jesus**.

Jesus has apprehended each and every person who is a believer in him as the Son of God as a child of God themselves, making them a part of the family of God and a member of the Father's household. But Paul is placing himself in example of what all believers should be striving yet further for, which is the apprehending of Christ himself by us as our Bridegroom. This is what accompanies salvation. This is the purpose for which we are granted salvation in the first place "**if**" that we may apprehend that for which we are apprehended for by Christ.

Philippians 3:13-14

13 Brethren, **I count not myself to have apprehended**:
but *this* one thing *I do*, forgetting those things which
are behind, and reaching forth unto those things
which are before,

14 **I press toward the mark for the prize of the high
calling of God in Christ Jesus.**

Paul, the greatest documented evangelist that has ever
lived, who is responsible for almost half of the New Testament
Spirit inspired scripture, says "I press toward the mark for
the prize of the high calling of God". By his own admission,
under inspiration of the Holy Spirit by and through which he
can not lie or be mistaken, Paul informs us he is in continual
pursuit of this greatest prize contained inside the free gift
of salvation. It appears that this "prize" is attainable only
through a dedicated life of faithful service, of which Paul is
the perfect example.

Each and every child of God should be living our lives
in a fashion that is drawing us ever closer to our heavenly
Father. In that relationship the only goal on our part is the
reward of an ever closer fellowship with him through the
Spirit. Fellowship in itself is reward enough. Ironically
however, the fellowship we should be striving to achieve,
when realized, brings a host of benefits and advantages with
it that most Christians are barely aware are available to all
believers.

Inside that fellowship we find Jesus informing us that he
will return to the physical for the purpose of gathering the
faithful unto himself to transport them back to the Father's
house from whence he will come. In addition, he gives
warning to the entire Church concerning this gathering that
they might be ready at the time of its occurrence and that
they should not be found asleep at the time of his return.

Romans 13:10-11

10 Love worketh no ill to his neighbour: therefore love *is* the fulfilling of the law.

11 And that, knowing the time, that now *it is* high time to awake out of sleep: for now *is* our salvation nearer than when we believed.

1ˢᵗThessalonians 5:5-6

5 Ye are all the children of light, and the children of the day: we are not of the night, nor of darkness.

6 Therefore let us not sleep, as *do* others; but let us watch and be sober.

Mark 13:35-37

35 Watch ye therefore: for ye know not when the master of the house cometh, at even, or at midnight, or at the cockcrowing, or in the morning:

36 Lest coming suddenly he find you sleeping.

37 And what I say unto you I say unto all, Watch.

Are you watching? Are you ready? Grace and peace be multiplied unto you all.

Chapter Thirteen

The Evil and Wicked Servant

B efore we close our study, I wish to present additional
scripture which contains teachings that support the
Conditional Rapture view. These passages are easily overlooked by opponents of our position due to the fact when
studied, they only suggest support when examined with
the Conditional Rapture in mind. Outside of this view they
still possess a moral lesson or spiritual teachings and stand
on their own within the obvious subjects contained in the
surface text, hence the reason they have been overlooked by
the Church for what they are. But they take on a whole new
dimension when studied within the perimeters set forth by
the teachings of the Conditional Rapture.

We will quickly review what we consider to be our definitive passages. Through this reexamination we will give you
the opportunity to recognize them for at least what we believe
them to be, whether you have been convinced of these teachings or not. But, with the conclusion of this study, the individual who has familiarized themselves with our beliefs can
at least identify what we believe the scripture is teaching.

You may still be unconvinced of our position and possibly
remain so, but I believe once an individual is made aware of
the teachings of the true Rapture awaiting the Bride of Christ

within the Church, your spirit led by the Holy Spirit through the scripture will be persistent in making you aware of those teachings inside the phrasing of the text.

We believe the inclusions and exclusions contained in related passages will be pointed out to you repeatedly, regardless of whether you choose to accept or reject them. Through this study my prayer is for the reader to be able to easily identify the implications of the Conditional Rapture in the text. That is exactly what happened to me. I myself was in denial for some time until the evidence became overwhelming.

Always keep in mind, the truth is always the truth, no matter what we want or convince ourselves to believe. You will no doubt from now on as you study the scripture point to phrases in your own Bible and say to yourself, "Bro. Chip (that's my nick name) would say this verse points to a condition connected to the Rapture", whether you believe it to suggest such yourself or not. At the very least, we and what we believe will be on your mind.

I Love You. God's grace, mercy and peace be multiplied to you all.

Hebrews 9:27-28

27 **And as it is appointed** unto men once to die, but after this the judgment:

28 So Christ was once offered to bear the sins of many; and **unto them that look for him** shall he appear **the second time** without sin unto salvation.

Revelation 2:22

22 Behold, I will cast her into a bed, **and them that commit adultery** with her into great tribulation, **except they repent of their deeds.**

Hebrews 10:38
38 Now the just shall live by faith: but if *any man* **draw back**, my soul shall have no pleasure in him.

1ˢᵗ Corinthians 3:3
3 **For ye are yet carnal**: for whereas *there is* among you envying, and strife, and divisions, **are ye not carnal**, and walk as men?

Galatians 5:13-16
13 For, brethren, ye have been called unto liberty; only *use* **not liberty for an occasion to the flesh**, but by love serve one another.
14 For all the law is fulfilled in one word, *even* in this; Thou shalt love thy neighbour as thyself.
15 But if ye **bite and devour one another**, take heed that ye be not consumed one of another.
16 *This* I say then, **Walk in the Spirit, and ye shall not fulfil the lust of the flesh.**

Colossians 2:6-10
6 As ye have therefore received Christ Jesus the Lord, *so* **walk ye in him**:
7 Rooted and built up in him, and stablished in the faith, as ye have been taught, abounding therein with thanksgiving.
8 **Beware lest any man spoil you** through philosophy and vain deceit, **after the tradition of men, after the rudiments of the world, and not after Christ.**
9 For in him dwelleth all the fulness of the Godhead bodily.
10 **And ye are complete in him**, which is the head of all principality and power:

Ephesians 5:6-8

6 Let no man deceive you with vain words: for because of these things cometh the wrath of God upon the children of disobedience.

7 **Be not ye therefore partakers with them**.

8 For ye were sometimes darkness, but now *are ye* light in the Lord: <u>**walk as children of light**</u>:

Luke 21:34-36

34 And **take heed to yourselves**, lest at any time your hearts be overcharged with surfeiting, and drunkenness, **and cares of this life**, and *so* **that day come upon you unawares.**

35 For as a snare shall it come on all them that dwell on the face of the whole earth.

36 **Watch ye therefore, and pray always**, that ye may be **accounted worthy to escape all these things** that shall come to pass, and to stand before the Son of man.

2ndCorinthians 11:1-3

1 Would to God ye could bear with me a little in *my* folly: and indeed bear with me.

2 For I am jealous over you with godly jealousy: for I have espoused you to one husband, <u>**that I "may" present *you* as a chaste virgin to Christ**</u>.

3 **But I fear**, lest by any means, as the serpent beguiled Eve through his subtilty, **so your minds should be corrupted from the simplicity that is in Christ.**

1stCorinthians 15:1-2

1 Moreover, brethren, I declare unto you the gospel which I preached unto you, which also ye have received, and wherein ye stand;

2 **By which also ye are saved, "if" ye keep in memory what I preached unto you,** unless ye have believed in vain.

Titus 2:11-13

11 For the grace of God that bringeth salvation hath appeared to all men,

12 Teaching us that, **denying ungodliness and worldly lusts,** we should live soberly, righteously, and godly, **in this present world;**

13 **Looking for that blessed hope,** and the glorious appearing of the great God and our Saviour Jesus Christ;

Revelation 3:4

4 Thou hast a **few names** even in Sardis which **have not defiled their garments;** and they shall walk with me in white: **for they are worthy.**

2 Thessalonians 1:4-5

4 So that we ourselves glory in you in the churches of God for your **patience and faith** in all your **persecutions and tribulations that ye endure:**

5 *Which is* a **manifest token** of the righteous judgment of God, **that ye may be counted worthy of the kingdom of God,** for which ye also suffer:

Colossians 1:21-23

21 And you, that were sometime alienated and enemies in *your* mind by wicked works, yet now hath he reconciled

22 In the body of his flesh through death, **to present you holy and unblameable and unreproveable in his sight;**

23 "**If**" **ye continue in the faith** grounded and settled, **and** *be* **not moved away from the hope of the gospel**, which ye have heard, *and* which was preached to every creature which is under heaven; whereof I Paul am made a minister;

Hebrews 3:6

6 But Christ as a son over his own house; **whose house are we, "if" we hold fast the confidence and the rejoicing of the hope firm unto the end**.

Hebrews 3:12-13

12 Take heed, brethren, lest there be in any of you an **evil heart of unbelief, in departing from the living God**.

13 But exhort one another daily, while it is called To day; lest any of you be hardened through the deceitfulness of sin.

14 **For we are made partakers of Christ, "if" we hold the beginning of our confidence** stedfast unto the end;

These passages speak for themselves and confirm the teachings we have presented in this study. Some independently, others collectively. We are not trying to convince anyone that "we are right". Only God is correct, of which he instructs us through his Word. We have merely presented to you what we feel God and his Word has imparted to us. Our sole desire is to be in agreement with the truth which is found only in the Word of God. Only out of a sincere love for the entire body of Christ are these lessons made available to the Church at this time in this manner.

If you were made aware of a catastrophic event a loved one were in danger to endure that could be avoided by a simple warning from you, would you not voice that warning?

That premise is the sole intent behind the publishing of this manuscript. So on that note,

Matthew 24:37-38

37 But as the days of Noe *were*, so shall also the coming of the Son of man be.

38 For as in the days that were before the flood they were eating and drinking, marrying and giving in marriage, until the day that Noe entered into the ark,

39 And knew not until the flood came, and took them all away; so shall also the coming of the Son of man be.

This is our passage from Matthew when Jesus informed his disciples that the coming of the Lord would occur abruptly, similar in fashion as Noah and his family experienced the arrival of the global flood. (This also verifies the occurrence of the flood itself, as it is the Son of God confirming it as an actual event). He goes on to describe in what manner society will experience the coming of the Lord.

Matthew 24:40-42

40 Then shall two be in the field; the one shall be taken, and the other left.

41 Two *women shall be* grinding at the mill; the one shall be taken, and the other left.

He continues to tell his disciples (who he knows will not be physically alive to witness the event),

42 Watch therefore: for ye know not what hour your Lord doth come.

He is of course speaking to the Church as a whole, through his disciples. The last generation of the Church Age that is physically alive at the time of its occurrence is the only portion of the Church which will actually witness the events described. And I might add he is not speaking to the unbelieving world as a whole. In all of these passages he refers to himself as "your Lord".

The portion of the Church today that believes in the Pre-Tribulation Rapture, points to these verses and others like them to teach that believers will be taken by the Lord, and unbelievers will be "left behind" to go through the Great Tribulation. One shall be taken, and the other shall be left.

But, there are no indications in these verses that unbelievers are being made referenced to. Jesus is speaking to his disciples (in the physical), and through his disciples to the Church (in the spiritual). The group being addressed through the disciples are all believers, and the teachings of Jesus commanding them to be watchful and ready imply the lack of participation of unprepared believers from the event. Unbelievers have been excluded from the entire teaching, not merely from the event itself. This would of course agree with the teachings of the Conditional Rapture. This view is actually confirmed in the following verses.

Matthew 24:43-51

43 But know this, that if the goodman of the house had known in what watch the thief would come, he would have watched, and would not have suffered his house to be broken up.

44 **Therefore be ye also ready**: for in such an hour as ye think not the Son of man cometh.

45 Who then is a faithful and wise servant, whom **his lord** hath made ruler over his household, to give them meat in due season?

46 **Blessed** *is* **that servant**, whom **his lord** when he cometh shall find so doing.

47 Verily I say unto you, That he shall make him ruler over all his goods.

Jesus confirms here the rewards connected to faithful service to those who are in service to him. Again this neglects to mention anyone who is not in actual service to the Lord. Then he changes the premise of the storyline to depict an unfaithful, or evil servant. But inside the new illustration the individual in question is still in service to the Lord. And in point of fact, the evil servant not only still calls him Lord, but is even aware of his return although he is not in preparation for it.

48 But and if that **evil servant** shall say in his heart, **My lord delayeth his coming**;
49 And shall begin to smite *his* **fellowservants**, and to eat and drink with the drunken;
50 The **lord of that servant** shall come in a day when he looketh not for *him*, and in an hour that he is not aware of,

Verse forty-nine resembles perfectly the modern Christian world of today. There is a large amount of combative actions by believers toward fellow believers, inside and outside the physical church.

1stCorinthians 3:3
3 For ye are yet carnal: **for whereas** *there is* **among you envying, and strife, and divisions**, **are ye not carnal**, and walk as men?

And many believers who "forsake the assembling" of themselves to a body of believers, do not forsake the assembling of themselves to the activities of the world. They do in fact embrace them. Again, God has given warning to the Church against such practices.

Luke 21:34-36

34 And **take heed to yourselves**, lest at any time your hearts be overcharged with surfeiting, and drunkenness, **and cares of this life**, and *so* **that day come upon you unawares**.

Jesus informs us that the Lord of that servant (Jesus himself) will come in a day when the evil servant is not looking for him. In turn, he will arrive at a time that the evil servant will be oblivious of, due to the actions he has taken that have left him unprepared.

51 And shall cut him asunder, **and appoint** *him* **his portion with the hypocrites**: there shall be weeping and gnashing of teeth.

He will be appointed the portion of time that he has earned for himself with the hypocrites or unbelievers. This is a depiction of the unprepared believers at the end of the Church Age, that will have earned their place inside the Great Tribulation Period with the unbelieving world. If there is any doubt of these teachings as illustrated, let me point out Jesus repeated the same warning by having Luke record the same information but in even greater detail.

Luke 12:40-47

40 Be ye therefore ready also: for the Son of man cometh at an hour when ye think not.
41 Then Peter said unto him, Lord, speakest thou this parable unto us, or even to all?
42 And the Lord said, Who then is that faithful and wise steward, **whom** *his* **lord** shall make ruler over his

household, to give *them their* portion of meat in due season?

43 Blessed *is* that servant, **whom his lord** when he cometh shall find so doing.

44 Of a truth I say unto you, that he will make him ruler over all that he hath.

Again Jesus gives us the good news first by making us aware of the rewards awaiting those who are faithful in our service to him. But, then he makes clear the other side of that coin,

45 But and if **that servant** say in his heart, **My lord** delayeth his coming; and shall begin to beat the menservants and maidens, and to eat and drink, and to be drunken;

46 **The lord of that servant** will come in a day when he looketh not for *him*, and at an hour when he is not aware, and will cut him in sunder, and **will appoint him his portion with the unbelievers**.

In verse forty-six he states the Lord of that servant will come in a day when he is not looking for his return, at a time in which he will be unprepared therefore unaware of his Lord's actions. His Lord will then appoint him his portion (appointed time) with the unbelievers (the unbelieving world).

Then he adds what will take place inside this appointed time that the evil servant has earned himself a place and allotted time in. The reason for this punishment is clearly stated. This lesson and this one verse should be pointed out to and read by every single child of God.

47 <u>And that servant,</u> **which knew his lord's will, and prepared not** *himself*, <u>neither did according to his will,</u> **shall be beaten with many** *stripes*.

The evil servant was fully aware of the will of his Lord. He was fully aware of his duty, and did not perform it. He was fully aware of the preparations within that duty that were expected of him, and took no action for their completion.

Let me again point out the unbelieving world is not in service to the Lord. It has no ties to him in relationship and therefore has no duty to perform due to a lack of any fellowship. Simply put, neither exists. The world is unaware of his return because they are willfully ignorant of it, and in reality is in complete denial of its future occurrence.

But, the evil servant, although disobedient to the will of his Lord, is none the less identified as a servant repeatedly. There are many such individuals numbered as members, making up the current population of the modern Church today. They go through all the correct motions expected by their fellow believers in the eyes of the Church as a whole, but fail to apply the truth of their faith to and in active service to the Lord before the world. This will result in serious consequences when the Lord returns unannounced, just prior to the Great Tribulation.

I had a conversation with a friend of mine over one of the passages we have formerly discussed in an earlier chapter. It matters not which one, you have surely gotten the jest of these teachings ten times over. He argued with me that a particular verse and related passage did not mean what I proposed it did. I countered that I did not personally propose what it meant other than what it plainly appeared to say.

First he accused me of reading to much into the scripture, and that the passages I continually site did not say what I said they say. I offered him a chance at reinterpreting the passage for me. That particular proposal resulted in the all to familiar response of, "I don't know what they mean, but they don't mean that. Then we argued some "silly notion of mine" that the Word informs us of truths that the Church is incapable of accepting because that particular information (interpretation) conflicts with their individual wants or wishes. The conversation bartered back and forth in that manner for a short time when all at once a certain fact and thought occurred to me (thank you Spirit/spirit).

Monday through Friday and roughly one Saturday a month, I work a full time job, like any other regular Joe to pay life's bills, besides being the pastor of a small church. I do have the advantage of my own office as I am the supervisor over my department. My department is shipping where I am responsible for the count and tally of out going product. Except for my office, our shipping department is all but outdoors. It is an industrial mill type setting where what is called PPE (personal protective equipment) is required to be worn.

Vehicles that transport our product are in and out all day long. Every one of these vehicles requires at least one occupant for the purpose of its operation in and out of our mill. The operator (or driver) upon his entrance into the mill is directed by personnel to the shipping department of which my office borders. Upon the facing wall to the driver of my office there is a four foot by eight foot sign that sports a white background upon which a sequence of black and red letters spell out the following.

SHIPPING. PARK HERE. Hard Hats and Safety Glasses Required At All Times.

Several times a day (everyday) drivers exit their vehicles after parking them (usually correctly), and walk passed the sign into my office without any regard for the information that is posted on it.

Once upon a time a driver walked into my office (no hard hat no safety glasses) gave me the information for the load he was to pick up,
and asked, "Can I ask you a question"?
I replied, "You can ask me anything".
He continued, "I came by the front gate with a sign on it about safety equipment. I came through the front office and the secretary mentioned hard hat and safety glasses to me. I get down here to shipping, and your sign on your office reads hard hats and safety glasses required at all times. I don't really have to wear a hard hat and safety glasses, do I"?

I related this experience of mine to the friend whom I was discussing the scripture passages with. With the utilization of a little sarcasm (that I very seldom make use of), I replied to my friend in regards to the passages we were "discussing",

"Yes, maybe you are right. Just like the sign on my office reads, Hard hats and safety glasses required at all times. It doesn't literally mean that "everyone" is really "required" to actually "wear" a hard hat "and" safety glasses "at all times" while on the mill yard. Its really just a recommendation to do so if you wish to". **What's wrong with this picture** ?

Please keep this illustration in mind as we study our final passage. The last verse is significant.

In example I proposed that the Christian world looks at the scripture in the same manner. By taking such a position, the Church can accept what it wishes to believe, and reject as misinterpretation what it wishes not to believe. Hence, remaining comfortable and content inside its established comfort zone of recognized and accepted conventional doctrine. Actually, using a technique as this or one like it, one can prove whatever one wishes with and through the scripture, and come to any conclusion you like. By that, I mean, you can dream up or imagine whatever you wish to be true, then manipulate the scripture in a manner to success-fully make the appearance of your "beliefs" to be correct. By these means you can literally believe anything you wish.

Our final passage was very interesting to me upon discloser of it in the Word. I studied it intensely for some time. Over and over again I discovered a new piece of infor-mation that could be related either to salvation or the Great Tribulation. It was a most fascinating study.

Again, this is a passage that only examples the Conditional Rapture, and only if one wishes to interpret it as such. However, there is no question that the final verse gives a commandment by the Lord that must be adhered to by the entire Church, regardless of the teachings of the Conditional Rapture. It involves a transgression we have all been guilty of, and most of us remain in violation. This will not go unno-ticed by the Lord. Remember, we will all stand before the judgment seat of Christ and give account.

If not related to the Rapture, someone must present me with a legitimate reinterpretation and clear line of connection to the content of the verse. That is a tall order, considering the same must be accomplished with all the other passages presented in previous chapters in order to prove "me" wrong. I still, and will probably always, maintain that I am neither right nor wrong. The scripture is correct. I only wish to be in agreement with God's Word. I also refuse to accept, "I don't know what it means, but it don't mean that". This response is unacceptable, and old news to me.

Now pay very close attention to what is described to us by Jesus through his disciples, for he states this is what the kingdom of heaven is like unto. The perimeters he speaks within are the ones we are expected to abide by in this life as believers. The final verse dictates to us the offence involved by the violators, and the verse just prior to it contains the penalty for the offence. This is serious stuff folks. For real. Lt. Dennis Martin would say, "There it is"!

Matthew 18:23-35
23 Therefore is the kingdom of heaven likened unto a certain king, which would take account of his servants.
24 And when he had begun to reckon, one was brought unto him, which owed him ten thousand talents.
25 But **forasmuch as he had not to pay**, his lord commanded him to be sold, and his wife, and children, and all that he had, and **payment to be made**.

Every single person that draws breath in the physical owes God his life in exchange for the sin of unbelief. Verse twenty-five states the servant in question had not the resources to pay the debt that he owed. So his Lord was going to take in exchange everything he did have, which not only included himself and all his material possessions, but also his wife and children were to be sold into servitude. One could say his lord not only took everything he did have, but by confiscation of everything he owned, he in turn took away everything he could ever hope to have. The proceeds from all such transactions were to be used as a partial payment toward the debt he could not pay in full.

26 The servant therefore fell down, and worshipped him, saying, Lord, have patience with me, and I will pay thee all.

The servant, however, threw himself on the mercy of his Lord and begged him to have patience. Given the opportunity, from his perspective, he would make restitution and pay the debt in full.

27 Then the lord of that servant was moved with compassion, and loosed him, and forgave him the debt.

The Lord of the servant recognized him to be sincere, but also knows there is no possible means by which he himself can make good on his intentions however genuine his will and proposal to be. The debt is too great and can never be repaid by the servant. Moved with compassion by the servants request, he releases him and forgives him the debt in full. The Lord of the servant will bare and absorbed the debt that is owed him, himself.

This is a perfect illustration of the salvation offered by God to the world. Each of us owes a debt we are unable to pay even through the sacrifice of everything including eternal separation from the creator himself. The result of which would put us in the position of continually and perpetually making payment on the debt that will never be paid in full throughout all eternity.

28 But the same servant went out, and found one of his fellowservants, which owed him an hundred pence: and he laid hands on him, and took *him* by the throat, saying, Pay me that thou owest.

29 And his fellowservant fell down at his feet, and besought him, saying, Have patience with me, and I will pay thee all.

30 And he would not: but went and cast him into prison, till he should pay the debt.

However, the same servant, now forgiven of the original debt, seeks out a fellow servant which owed him a debt of a much lesser amount. Refusing to give him the same opportunity he was given by his Lord, he has him thrown into prison until he can, in some way, eventually make payment in full.

31 So when his fellowservants saw what was done, they were very sorry, and came and told unto their lord all that was done.

32 Then his lord, after that he had called him, said unto him, O thou wicked servant, I forgave thee all that debt, because thou desiredst me:

The original debt has been forgiven. But, before that had occurred, the price for repayment was beyond all that the servant had or could ever hope to have, ever. This ultimate price was forgiven in full by the Lord. Now, because of his error concerning his fellow servant, the scripture informs us he has a new problem.

33 Shouldest not thou also have had compassion on thy fellowservant, even as I had pity on thee?

34 And his lord was wroth, and delivered him to the tormentors, till he should pay all that was due unto him.

This represents a new debt. One that will be paid by the disobedient or wicked servant. The mention of him being sold is omitted from this passage. His wife and children are not mentioned in this verse in stark contrast to the preceding passages as they were to be sold as partial payment for the original debt. His property (all that he had) is also excluded in reference to the new debt.

This verse clearly states, because of the debt he now owes to his Lord, the wicked servant will be handed over to the tormentors until this debt is repaid. The new debt (or second debt) was incurred through the un-forgiving behavior of the wicked servant toward his fellow servant after the original debt was forgiven.

The most crucial portion of these passages appears in the last verse. It is written and recorded for the benefit of the entire Church. We are told directly by Jesus himself that this example or parable is given to us for the express purpose of us avoiding in our future what the wicked servant became subject to in illustration. He was handed over to tormentors, for the offense of not forgiving his fellow servant as was he forgiven himself by his Lord.

35 So likewise shall my heavenly Father do also unto you, if ye from your hearts forgive not every one his brother their trespasses.

After the salvation experience, each and every believer is responsible for his or her own behavior inside their service to the Lord. Many believers today are unforgiving of their fellow brothers and sisters in Christ for trespasses committed against us by them. God expects each member of the family of God to be forgiving of one another, but genuinely from the heart.

It is a simple matter to see examples of unforgiving behavior in our day and age. When this subject is brought to my attention in conversation, my first thoughts are to the members of the Church that have split congregations and have taken separate paths to form their own church bodies under new names. These groups tend to hold grudges toward one another due to the differences that led them to part ways. This is merely one example, and all similar behavior can not be in good favor with the Lord, and certainly resembles the offense the Lord is warning the Church of in these verses.

Matthew 18:34-35

34 And his lord was wroth, and delivered him to the tormentors, till he should pay all that was due unto him.

35 So likewise shall my heavenly Father do also unto
you, if ye from your hearts forgive not every one his
brother their trespasses.

The disobedient members of the Church today who refuse
from their heart to forgive each and every other member who
happens to trespass against them, will be handed over by
God to a tormentor of some type, at some time in the future
in accordance with this passage. That is the penalty incurred
for the offense committed. **That is what is says.**

If the torment in verse thirty-four is not a representation
of the Great Tribulation, someone needs to explain to me
what it does characterize, because we have all been guilty of
this offense, and most of the Church still stands in violation
today. I see nothing it can correspond to during the Church
Age, since all believers of all types (obedient and disobedient alike) can both be seen to experience any and all types
of misfortune or tribulation that anyone can imagine.

The offense of verse thirty-five literally exists today
inside the body of the Church. No matter how few, some
members have failed to forgive others of some trespasses.
Both parties are out of fellowship with the Lord. One stands
in fault of trespass and the other is guilty of not forgiving
the trespasser. This premise is even confirmed in the Lord's
prayer that was given to us by Jesus himself per his instructions concerning how we are to be in a continual state of
forgiveness toward one another.

Matthew 6:9-15
9 After this manner therefore pray ye: Our Father which
art in heaven, Hallowed be thy name.
10 Thy kingdom come. Thy will be done in earth, as *it
is* in heaven.
11 Give us this day our daily bread.

12 **And forgive us our debts, as we forgive our debtors.**

13 And lead us not into temptation, but deliver us from evil: For thine is the kingdom, and the power, and the glory, for ever. Amen.

14 For if ye forgive men their trespasses, your heavenly Father will also forgive you:

15 **But if ye forgive not men their trespasses, neither will your Father forgive your trespasses.**

Such conditions existing inside believers lives today would place them into the category resembling what we teach concerning the Conditional Rapture. Therefore, although we admit freely that some of the information presented here has been interpreted from the perspective of these teachings, the conclusions reached agree completely with the "theory" of the Conditional Rapture and are in agreement with the Word of God when studied within these perimeters.

In closing, throughout the complete body of this manuscript I have continued to remove statements that I felt were unnecessary for the reader to be exposed to repeatedly, therefore I will express those comments here with these final thoughts.

It is my profound wish and prayer that no part of the body of Christ be subject to endure The Great Tribulation Period. I have a large family, many of which are not particularly "religious" although virtually all profess to be Christians (and in my opinion, as I understand the conversion process, I have no reason to believe they are not). Every member of my family, and all but one of my friends believe these teachings to be (and I quote) "a bunch of hooey". But, what I had learned of the Great Tribulation Period before I became aware of the Conditional Rapture was horrifying enough knowing what Israel and the tribulation saints were going to be forced to endure. Augmenting the largest majority of the Church into that mix by way of the teachings of the Conditional Rapture was the single most bitter pill I have ever had to swallow.

For all of you who have persevered and completed the reading of this manuscript, and still side with the majority that believes I am in error, I have two final responses.

1 Thank you for finishing the reading of this book. It was a long time coming but I enjoyed every moment. I hope my writing style was not excessively cumbersome to you. May God richly bless you.

2 For the sake of my friends, family, children, grandchildren and every other brother and sister in Christ who's actions and habits in this physical life make them appear to be uncommitted in their service to the Lord and seemingly unprepared for his imminent return, I earnestly and genuinely "hope" and pray **you are correct**.

It will not hurt my pride in the least for "me" to be wrong. I hope I am.

I Love You. God's grace, mercy and peace be multiplied to you all.

Until our next encounter, may you keep yourself safe, in God's will. God Bless.

Rev. J. W. (Bro. Chip) White, Jr.
Post Office Box 550
Queen City, Texas 75572-0550